OVERCOMING CHURCH
PROBLEMS

THE CHURCH
CURE

What Is the Greatest Problem Facing the Church Today?

EDWARD D. ANDREWS

THE CHURCH CURE

Overcoming Church Problems

Edward D. Andrews

Christian Publishing House

Cambridge, Ohio

CHRISTIAN
PUBLISHING
HOUSE

FOUNDED 2005

THE CHURCH CURE: Overcoming Church Problems by Edward D. Andrews

ISBN-10: 1949586022

ISBN-13: 978-1949586022

Table of Contents

Preface 9

   The Urgent Need for Unity in Christianity 9

   Recognizing the Fulfillment of Prophecy 12

Introduction 16

Chapter 1: The Foundation of True Christianity 19

   The Establishment of the Early Church 19

   The Growth from Pentecost to 150 C.E. 22

   Core Teachings and Practices of the Apostolic Church 26

Chapter 2: Prophetic Warnings and Early Divisions 31

   Prophecies by Jesus, Paul, and Peter 31

   Early Schisms and Their Causes 35

   Historical Accounts of Early Christian Factions 38

Chapter 3: The Influence of Catholicism and the Reformation 43

   The Rise and Domination of Catholicism 43

   Atrocities and Abuses During the Middle Ages 46

   The Reformation: A Pendulum Swing 50

Chapter 4: The Modern Landscape of Christianity 55

   The Proliferation of Denominations 55

   Current State of Christian Unity 60

   The Impact of Diverse Doctrinal Views 65

Chapter 5: Analyzing the Roots of Division 69

   Eisegesis and Its Consequences 69

   The Quest for Church Power and Control 73

   The Misuse of the Term "Church" vs. "Congregation" 79

Going Beyond Scriptural Positions of Pastor, Elder, and Overseer with Religious Titles for Power and Prestige 82

Chapter 6: The Poison of Higher Criticism 87

The Emergence and Impact of Biblical Criticism 87

Turning God's Word into Man's Word 92

Interpretive Translations and Their Detrimental Effects 96

Chapter 7: Textual Criticism and the Search for Original Words 101

The Importance of Textual Integrity 101

Abandoning Core Principles 105

Strategies for Restoring Biblical Accuracy 109

Chapter 8: The Failure to Evangelize 114

The Early Church's Evangelism Model 114

Modern Failures and Their Causes 119

Solutions for Effective Evangelism Today 124

Chapter 9: The Independent Spirit and Its Consequences 129

The Rise of Independent Churches 129

Balancing Denominational Control and Individual Freedom 132

Biblical Principles for Unity and Cooperation 137

Chapter 10: The Role of Human Nature in Church Division 141

Understanding Genesis 6:5; 8:21; Jeremiah 17:9; and Romans 7:18 141

The Sinful Nature and Its Impact on Unity 144

Overcoming Human Flaws Through Biblical Teachings 149

Chapter 11: A Balanced Approach to Church Governance 154

Avoiding the Extremes of Authoritarianism and Anarchy ... 154

Establishing Effective Denominational Control..................... 158

Mechanisms for Doctrinal Accountability and Correction .. 162

Chapter 12: Developing a Unified Evangelism Program .168

Implementing a Comprehensive Evangelism Strategy.......... 168

Ensuring Consistent Doctrinal Teaching Across Congregations
.... 171

Implementing the Strategy... 175

Developing a Unified Evangelism Program: Training and
Equipping All Members for Evangelism 177

Practical Training Components.. 179

Table of Contents 182

Chapter 13: Restoring Doctrinal Purity............................188

Identifying Core Doctrines Based on Biblical Teaching....... 188

Addressing and Correcting False Doctrines 193

Encouraging Theological Education and Biblical Literacy .. 198

**Chapter 14: Creating a New Denomination for True
Christians 204**

Defining the Mission and Vision of the New Denomination
.... 204

Establishing Foundational Beliefs and Practices.................... 208

Strategies for Attracting True Christians from Divided
Denominations.. 212

**Chapter 15: Maintaining Unity and Addressing
Disagreements 216**

Principles for Maintaining Unity in the Congregation 216

Procedures for Addressing Doctrinal Disagreements........... 219

Ensuring a Humble and Teachable Spirit Among Leaders and
Members... 223

Chapter 16: The Role of Church Leadership....................228

Biblical Qualifications for Church Leaders 228

Responsibilities of Pastors, Elders, and Deacons 232

Accountability and Transparency in Leadership 237

Chapter 17: Effective Church Discipline 243

Biblical Principles of Church Discipline 243

Procedures for Handling Disobedience and Division........... 248

The Importance of Restoration and Reconciliation 255

Chapter 18: Skillful Counselors Are a Blessing to Their Churches 262

The Essence and Importance of Pastoral Counseling........... 262

Scriptural Approaches to Common Counseling Issues......... 265

Implementing the Strategic Pastoral Counseling Model 271

Appendix Recommended Reading List for Church Members and Church Leaders...278

Christian Publishing House Bookstore 278

Bibliography...279

Preface

The Urgent Need for Unity in Christianity

The Christian church today stands divided across a landscape populated by countless denominations, sects, and independent congregations. This fragmentation contrasts sharply with the unity that characterized the early Christian community and hinders the collective mission to spread the Gospel effectively. To address this urgent need for unity, it is essential to first understand the biblical mandate for oneness, the historical development of divisions, and the practical steps required to restore harmony among believers.

Biblical Mandate for Unity

The New Testament emphasizes the importance of unity among believers. In his letter to the Corinthians, the apostle Paul implored, "I appeal to you, brothers, by the name of our Lord Jesus Christ, that all of you agree, and that there be no divisions among you, but that you be united in the same mind and the same judgment" (1 Corinthians 1:10). This call to unity was not merely a suggestion but a command rooted in the teachings of Jesus Christ. In John 17:21, Jesus prayed for His disciples, "that they may all be one, just as you, Father, are in me, and I in you, that they also may be in us, so that the world may believe that you have sent me."

Unity is not simply an ideal but a necessary condition for the credibility and effectiveness of the Christian witness. When believers are united, they reflect the character of God and demonstrate the transformative power of the Gospel. Conversely, division and discord within the church undermine the message of reconciliation and love that lies at the heart of Christianity.

Historical Development of Divisions

The unity of the early Christian church was soon challenged by various internal and external pressures. Within a few decades of the apostles' deaths, schisms began to appear. Early church leaders such as Irenaeus and Epiphanius documented numerous factions and heresies that emerged, indicating that the seeds of division were sown early on. The second-century opponent of Christianity, Celsus, observed, "Christians were 'split up into ever so many factions, each individual desiring to have his own party.'" By the fourth century, Epiphanius counted eighty varieties of Christianity.

The rise of the Roman Catholic Church and its subsequent dominance over Christendom brought about a different kind of unity, one maintained through hierarchical control and often enforced through persecution. The Reformation in the sixteenth century, while necessary to address significant theological and moral corruption, led to further fragmentation. Protestant reformers, in their bid to return to biblical truth, often found themselves at odds with one another, resulting in the formation of numerous denominations.

Today, the landscape of Christianity is more fragmented than ever, with estimates suggesting over 41,000 different denominations worldwide. This division has diluted the church's collective voice and weakened its ability to present a unified message to the world.

Practical Steps to Restore Unity

Restoring unity in Christianity is a daunting but necessary task. It requires a return to the biblical principles that emphasize the importance of oneness in the body of Christ. Practical steps towards achieving this unity include:

1. **Commitment to Biblical Truth**: Unity must be grounded in the truth of Scripture. All believers must commit to a sound understanding of biblical doctrines and reject the subjective interpretations that have led to division. This requires adherence to the Historical-Grammatical method of

interpretation, ensuring that the Bible is understood as its authors intended.

2. **Humility and Repentance**: Both leaders and congregants must exhibit humility and a willingness to repent of attitudes and actions that have contributed to division. This includes acknowledging historical wrongs and seeking reconciliation with other believers.

3. **Open Dialogue and Cooperation**: Churches and denominations must engage in open dialogue, focusing on common beliefs and goals rather than differences. Cooperation in evangelism, community service, and other ministry efforts can foster a spirit of unity and shared purpose.

4. **Strong Leadership**: Church leaders play a crucial role in promoting unity. They must model humility, teach sound doctrine, and encourage their congregations to prioritize unity. Leaders should also establish mechanisms for resolving doctrinal disagreements and maintaining accountability within the church.

5. **Comprehensive Evangelism Programs**: A unified approach to evangelism can help bridge divides within the church. By working together to fulfill the Great Commission, Christians can demonstrate their shared commitment to spreading the Gospel and building God's kingdom.

6. **Education and Discipleship**: Ongoing education and discipleship programs can help believers understand the importance of unity and equip them to contribute to the church's mission. This includes teaching the biblical basis for unity and practical ways to foster it within their communities.

The need for unity in Christianity is urgent. Divisions within the church not only weaken its witness but also hinder its mission. By returning to biblical principles, exhibiting humility, engaging in open dialogue, providing strong leadership, implementing comprehensive evangelism programs, and prioritizing education and discipleship, Christians can work towards restoring the unity that characterized the early church. This journey will require effort and commitment, but the result will be a stronger, more effective witness for the Gospel in a divided world.

Recognizing the Fulfillment of Prophecy

Understanding the current state of the Christian church requires a recognition of the prophetic warnings given by Jesus, Paul, and Peter about the rise of false teachers and the subsequent divisions within the body of Christ. These prophecies not only provide insight into why the church finds itself fractured but also offer a framework for addressing and overcoming these issues.

Jesus' Prophecies

Jesus Christ, in His teachings, foresaw the emergence of false prophets and divisions within the church. In Matthew 7:15, He warned, "Beware of false prophets, who come to you in sheep's clothing but inwardly are ravenous wolves." This vivid imagery emphasizes the deceptive nature of these false teachers who would appear harmless but would lead many astray. Moreover, in Matthew 24:11, Jesus foretold, "And many false prophets will arise and lead many astray." This prophecy indicates that the presence of false teachers is not an anomaly but a predicted occurrence that believers must be vigilant against.

Jesus also spoke about the division within the church. In Luke 12:51-53, He said, "Do you think that I have come to give peace on earth? No, I tell you, but rather division. For from now on in one house there will be five divided, three against two and two against three. They will be divided, father against son and son against father, mother against daughter and daughter against mother, mother-in-law against her daughter-in-law and daughter-in-law against mother-in-law." This prophecy highlights that even within close familial relationships, the truth of the Gospel would cause division, reflecting the broader schisms within the church.

Paul's Warnings

The Apostle Paul also provided prophetic warnings about the infiltration of false teachers and the resulting discord. In his farewell address to the Ephesian elders, Paul stated, "I know that after my departure fierce wolves will come in among you, not sparing the flock; and from among your own selves will arise men speaking twisted things, to draw away the disciples after them" (Acts 20:29-30). Paul's foresight into the rise of internal threats underscores the seriousness of the issue, indicating that false teachings would originate from within the Christian community itself.

Furthermore, in 2 Timothy 4:3-4, Paul warned, "For the time is coming when people will not endure sound teaching, but having itching ears they will accumulate for themselves teachers to suit their own passions, and will turn away from listening to the truth and wander off into myths." This prophecy highlights the proclivity of people to seek out teachings that cater to their desires rather than adhering to the sound doctrine of the Scriptures.

Peter's Prophecies

The Apostle Peter echoed similar warnings about false teachers and the resulting divisions. In 2 Peter 2:1-2, he wrote, "But false prophets also arose among the people, just as there will be false teachers among you, who will secretly bring in destructive heresies, even denying the Master who bought them, bringing upon themselves swift destruction. And many will follow their sensuality, and because of them the way of truth will be blasphemed." Peter's prophecy emphasizes that false teachings would lead many astray and cause the truth to be maligned.

Additionally, Peter admonished believers to be vigilant and steadfast in their faith. In 1 Peter 5:8-9, he urged, "Be sober-minded; be watchful. Your adversary the devil prowls around like a roaring lion, seeking someone to devour. Resist him, firm in your faith, knowing that the same kinds of suffering are being experienced by your brotherhood throughout the world." This exhortation underscores the constant threat posed by false teachings and the need for believers to remain alert and grounded in their faith.

Historical Fulfillment

Within a few decades of the apostles' deaths, the Christian church began to experience significant divisions. Early church historians such as Irenaeus and Epiphanius documented numerous sects and heresies, indicating that the prophecies of Jesus, Paul, and Peter were being fulfilled. For example, Irenaeus, writing in the late second century, listed twenty varieties of Christianity, while Epiphanius, in the fourth century, counted eighty. This proliferation of differing beliefs and practices among those who professed to follow Christ demonstrated the early fulfillment of the apostolic warnings.

The rise of the Roman Catholic Church and its subsequent consolidation of power introduced another dimension to the fulfillment of prophecy. While the church achieved a form of unity through hierarchical control, it often did so at the expense of biblical truth and through methods of coercion and persecution. The Reformation, while addressing many of the doctrinal errors and moral corruptions of the Catholic Church, led to further fragmentation as reformers, driven by a desire to return to biblical fidelity, often found themselves at odds with one another.

Modern Implications

Today, the Christian church is more fragmented than ever, with an estimated 41,000 denominations worldwide. This division, while lamentable, should not lead to despair but rather to a sober recognition that it is a fulfillment of biblical prophecy. Understanding this helps believers to approach the problem with both a sense of urgency and a measure of hope.

Recognizing the fulfillment of these prophecies should also compel believers to return to the foundational truths of Scripture. The way forward involves a recommitment to sound doctrine, a rejection of false teachings, and a collective effort to restore the unity that Jesus prayed for in John 17:21, "that they may all be one, just as you, Father, are in me, and I in you, that they also may be in us, so that the world may believe that you have sent me."

By understanding the prophetic foundations laid by Jesus, Paul, and Peter, Christians can better comprehend the reasons behind the current divisions and be motivated to work towards the restoration of unity within the church. This unity is not merely an ideal but a biblical mandate, essential for the effective witness of the Gospel in a divided world. Recognizing the fulfillment of prophecy is the first step towards addressing and overcoming the problems that plague the modern church.

Edward D. Andrews

Author of 220+ books

Introduction

The church today is facing an unprecedented crisis of division, disunity, and doctrinal confusion. The proliferation of denominations, the rise of independent churches, and the increasing acceptance of unbiblical teachings have led to a fragmented and weakened body of Christ. This book, "The Church Cure: Overcoming Church Problems," aims to address these issues head-on, offering a path toward restoration, unity, and doctrinal purity based on the unwavering truth of God's Word.

In the New Testament, Jesus and the apostles frequently warned about the dangers of false teachings and divisions within the church. Matthew 7:21-23 serves as a sobering reminder of the importance of adhering to true doctrine and living out our faith in accordance with God's will. As we navigate the complexities of modern Christianity, these warnings are more relevant than ever.

The early church, established on the foundation of the apostles' teachings, exemplified unity, doctrinal soundness, and a fervent commitment to evangelism. However, as history progressed, deviations from this foundation led to significant theological and organizational shifts. The rise of Catholicism and the subsequent Reformation marked pivotal moments in church history, each bringing its own set of challenges and changes. Today, the landscape of Christianity is marked by a multitude of denominations and doctrinal disputes, often leaving believers confused and disillusioned.

The purpose of this book is not merely to highlight the problems but to provide biblically grounded solutions. Through an in-depth examination of church history, doctrinal development, and contemporary issues, we seek to identify the root causes of division and offer practical steps for achieving unity and doctrinal integrity. This journey involves a return to the foundational teachings of the early church, a rejection of human-centered interpretations, and a recommitment to the authority of Scripture.

Each chapter of this book addresses a specific aspect of the church's current challenges, from the impact of higher criticism and textual corruption to the failures in evangelism and the rise of the independent spirit. By analyzing these issues through the lens of the Historical-Grammatical method of interpretation, we aim to uncover the true meaning of Scripture and apply its timeless principles to today's church.

The journey to overcoming church problems begins with understanding the establishment of the early church and its growth from Pentecost to 150 C.E. (Chapter 1). We then delve into the prophetic warnings and early divisions that set the stage for future conflicts (Chapter 2). The influence of Catholicism and the Reformation are examined to understand their long-lasting impact on the church (Chapter 3), followed by an analysis of the modern landscape of Christianity (Chapter 4).

Subsequent chapters address the roots of division, the dangers of higher criticism, and the importance of textual integrity. We also explore the church's failures in evangelism, the consequences of the independent spirit, and the role of human nature in church division. Practical solutions for these issues are offered, including a balanced approach to church governance, the development of a unified evangelism program, and strategies for restoring doctrinal purity.

Creating a new denomination for true Christians (Chapter 14) involves defining the mission and vision, establishing foundational beliefs, and attracting believers from divided denominations. Maintaining unity and addressing disagreements require clear principles, procedures, and a humble, teachable spirit among leaders and members.

The role of church leadership is crucial in this endeavor. Biblical qualifications for leaders, their responsibilities, and the need for accountability and transparency are thoroughly discussed. Effective church discipline, based on biblical principles and procedures, is essential for handling disobedience and division, as well as promoting restoration and reconciliation.

Finally, the importance of pastoral counseling is highlighted. Skillful counselors are a blessing to their churches, providing scriptural approaches to common counseling issues and implementing the Strategic Pastoral Counseling Model to support and guide congregants through their challenges.

As we embark on this journey together, let us remember that the ultimate goal is to glorify God by building a church that reflects His truth, love, and unity. By addressing and overcoming the problems that plague the church today, we can become a stronger, more faithful body of believers, committed to fulfilling the Great Commission and living out our faith in a way that honors our Lord and Savior, Jesus Christ.

This book is a call to action for all believers to engage in the hard work of church restoration. It is a reminder that true unity and doctrinal purity are not optional but essential for the health and witness of the church. May we approach this task with humility, diligence, and an unwavering commitment to the truth of God's Word.

Chapter 1: The Foundation of True Christianity

The Establishment of the Early Church

The establishment of the early Christian church is a pivotal event in human history, marking the inception of a faith that would grow from a small group of dedicated followers to a movement that spans the globe. This period, from Pentecost 33 C.E. to approximately 150 C.E., is characterized by rapid growth, doctrinal purity, and a strong sense of community among believers. Understanding the foundation of the early church is essential for addressing the challenges and divisions that plague modern Christianity.

The Birth of the Church at Pentecost

The early church was born on the day of Pentecost, fifty days after the resurrection of Jesus Christ. This event is recorded in Acts 2, where the apostles, filled with the Holy Spirit, began to speak in different languages, proclaiming the mighty works of God. Peter, standing with the eleven, delivered a powerful sermon, explaining that what the people witnessed was the fulfillment of the prophecy spoken by the prophet Joel. He declared, "And it shall come to pass that everyone who calls upon the name of Jehovah shall be saved" (Acts 2:21, UASV). Peter's message culminated in a call to repentance and baptism in the name of Jesus Christ for the forgiveness of sins, resulting in about three thousand souls being added to the church that day (Acts 2:41).

The Apostles' Teaching and Fellowship

The early church was characterized by its devotion to the apostles' teaching, fellowship, the breaking of bread, and prayers (Acts 2:42).

The apostles, who had been taught directly by Jesus, were the primary sources of doctrinal instruction. They conveyed the teachings of Jesus with clarity and authority, ensuring that the new believers understood the core principles of the faith. The communal aspect of the early church is also noteworthy. Believers were united, sharing their possessions and meeting daily in the temple and in their homes. This sense of community fostered a supportive environment where the faith could flourish.

Rapid Growth and Expansion

The early church experienced remarkable growth despite facing persecution. From the initial 120 believers gathered in the upper room (Acts 1:15) to over a million Christians by 150 C.E., the expansion of the church was extraordinary. This growth was driven by the evangelistic zeal of the apostles and early Christians who took seriously the Great Commission given by Jesus: "Go therefore and make disciples of all nations, baptizing them in the name of the Father and of the Son and of the Holy Spirit, teaching them to observe all that I have commanded you" (Matthew 28:19-20, UASV).

The geographical spread of Christianity during this period was significant. The faith reached beyond Jerusalem to Judea, Samaria, and to the ends of the earth (Acts 1:8). Key figures such as Paul, Barnabas, and others undertook missionary journeys, establishing churches in major cities across the Roman Empire. These new communities were often formed in the face of opposition, yet they thrived, reflecting the divine power behind the mission.

Doctrinal Purity and Challenges

Maintaining doctrinal purity was a central concern for the early church. The apostles were vigilant in correcting false teachings and ensuring that the Gospel message remained unaltered. Paul's letters to various churches often addressed doctrinal errors and provided guidance on maintaining sound teaching. For example, in his letter to the Galatians, Paul sternly warned against turning to a different gospel, saying, "But even if we or an angel from heaven should preach to you a gospel contrary to the one we preached to you, let him be accursed" (Galatians 1:8, UASV).

Despite these efforts, the early church faced significant challenges. False teachers and heresies began to emerge, necessitating the development of creeds and statements of faith to safeguard the truth. The Council of Jerusalem (Acts 15) is an early example of the church addressing doctrinal disputes, particularly regarding the requirements for Gentile converts. The council's decision, guided by the Holy Spirit, affirmed the inclusion of Gentiles without the necessity of adhering to the full Mosaic Law, marking a significant moment in the church's history.

The Role of Persecution

Persecution played a paradoxical role in the growth of the early church. While it posed a constant threat to believers, it also served to strengthen their faith and resolve. The martyrdom of Stephen (Acts 7) marked the beginning of severe persecution, yet it also scattered believers, spreading the Gospel to new regions (Acts 8:1-4). The Roman Empire, initially indifferent, became increasingly hostile towards Christians, culminating in state-sponsored persecutions under emperors such as Nero and Domitian.

The steadfastness of early Christians in the face of persecution had a profound impact. Their willingness to suffer and even die for their faith served as a powerful testimony to the authenticity of the Gospel. Tertullian, an early Christian apologist, famously remarked, "The blood of the martyrs is the seed of the church." This period of suffering and resilience laid a foundation of courage and conviction that would inspire future generations.

Apostolic Succession and the Formation of the Canon

As the original apostles began to pass away, the early church faced the challenge of preserving their teachings and maintaining doctrinal continuity. Apostolic succession, the practice of appointing new leaders to carry on the work of the apostles, helped ensure the transmission of authentic teachings. Figures such as Timothy and Titus, mentored by Paul, played crucial roles in this process.

The formation of the New Testament canon was another significant development. While the apostles' writings were already held in high regard, the need to establish a definitive collection of inspired texts became more pressing as heresies proliferated. By the end of the second century, the core books of the New Testament were widely recognized and accepted within the church. This canon provided a reliable standard for teaching and refuted false doctrines.

The Enduring Legacy

The foundation laid by the early church has had an enduring impact on Christianity. Their commitment to sound doctrine, the emphasis on community, and the willingness to suffer for the faith are hallmarks that continued to inspire true believers throughout the history of Christianity. Understanding the establishment of the early church is not merely an academic exercise but a call to return to the principles that underpinned its growth and strength.

The Growth from Pentecost to 150 C.E.

The growth of the early Christian church from Pentecost to 150 C.E. is a remarkable testament to the power of the Holy Spirit and the unwavering commitment of the early Christians to spread the Gospel. This period witnessed an extraordinary expansion of the church, both in terms of geographical reach and the number of adherents, despite facing significant challenges and persecution.

The Day of Pentecost and Initial Expansion

The day of Pentecost, 33 C.E., marks a significant turning point in the history of Christianity. Recorded in Acts 2, this event saw the apostles filled with the Holy Spirit, enabling them to speak in various tongues. This miraculous occurrence attracted a large crowd in Jerusalem, comprising Jews from different regions who had come for the feast. Peter stood up and addressed the crowd, explaining that what they were witnessing was the fulfillment of Joel's prophecy and that Jesus, whom they had crucified, was the promised Messiah. His powerful sermon led to the conversion of about three thousand people that day (Acts 2:41).

Following Pentecost, the early church continued to grow rapidly. Acts 2:47 records that "Jehovah added to their number day by day those who were being saved." This period of initial expansion was characterized by a strong sense of community among the believers, who devoted themselves to the apostles' teaching, fellowship, the breaking of bread, and prayer (Acts 2:42). They shared their possessions and met daily in the temple courts and from house to house, fostering a supportive and unified community.

Apostolic Missions and the Spread of the Gospel

The growth of the early church was significantly propelled by the missionary efforts of the apostles and early disciples. One of the most prominent figures in this regard was the Apostle Paul, whose missionary journeys are detailed in the Book of Acts. Paul, formerly known as Saul, was a zealous persecutor of Christians until his dramatic conversion on the road to Damascus (Acts 9). Following his conversion, Paul dedicated his life to spreading the Gospel, undertaking three major missionary journeys that took him across the Roman Empire.

Paul's missionary strategy involved preaching in synagogues and public places, engaging both Jews and Gentiles. His efforts led to the establishment of numerous churches in key cities such as Philippi, Thessalonica, Corinth, and Ephesus. Paul's letters to these churches, many of which are included in the New Testament, provided doctrinal instruction, encouragement, and correction, playing a crucial role in maintaining the unity and doctrinal purity of the early church.

Other apostles and early Christians also played significant roles in spreading the Gospel. Peter, for instance, is credited with opening the door of faith to the Gentiles through his encounter with Cornelius, a Roman centurion (Acts 10). This event marked a pivotal moment in the history of the church, signifying the inclusion of Gentiles into the body of Christ without the need for adherence to the full Mosaic Law.

Persecution and Its Role in Church Growth

Despite the remarkable growth, the early church faced severe persecution from both Jewish religious leaders and Roman authorities. The martyrdom of Stephen, recorded in Acts 7, marked the beginning of intense persecution in Jerusalem, leading to the scattering of believers. However, this dispersion played a crucial role in the spread of Christianity, as those who were scattered preached the word wherever they went (Acts 8:4).

The Roman Empire initially viewed Christianity as a sect of Judaism, but as the distinctiveness of the Christian faith became apparent, the Roman authorities began to see it as a threat. Emperor Nero's reign (54-68 C.E.) saw one of the first major state-sponsored persecutions of Christians, following the Great Fire of Rome in 64 C.E., for which Christians were scapegoated. Despite the brutality of these persecutions, the faith continued to spread, often growing stronger in the face of adversity. The courage and steadfastness of the martyrs served as a powerful testimony, inspiring others to embrace the faith.

Geographical Spread and the Formation of Early Churches

By 150 C.E., Christianity had spread far beyond its Jewish roots in Jerusalem to major urban centers across the Roman Empire. Cities such as Antioch, Alexandria, and Rome became significant centers of Christian activity. Antioch, in particular, is noteworthy as the place where the followers of Jesus were first called Christians (Acts 11:26). It also served as a base for Paul's missionary journeys and was a hub for early Christian teaching and community life.

The spread of Christianity was facilitated by the extensive network of Roman roads and the relative peace (Pax Romana) that allowed for safer travel. Early Christians, both leaders and laypersons, utilized these advantages to disseminate the Gospel widely. Commerce and trade routes also played a role, as Christian merchants and travelers brought the message of Christ to new regions.

Challenges and Responses

The rapid growth of the church brought about various challenges, particularly in maintaining doctrinal purity and unity. False teachings and heresies began to emerge, necessitating a robust response from church leaders. The Apostle Paul's letters often addressed these issues, providing clear doctrinal guidelines and correcting errors. For example, in his letter to the Galatians, Paul rebuked those who were distorting the Gospel by insisting on adherence to the Mosaic Law for salvation, emphasizing that justification comes through faith in Jesus Christ alone (Galatians 1:6-9).

The Council of Jerusalem, held around 49 C.E., was a significant event in addressing doctrinal disputes. This council, recorded in Acts 15, dealt with the issue of whether Gentile converts needed to observe the Mosaic Law, particularly circumcision. The decision, guided by the Holy Spirit, was that Gentiles were not required to follow the Law of Moses, except for abstaining from certain practices associated with idolatry and immorality. This ruling helped to maintain unity between Jewish and Gentile believers and facilitated the continued spread of the Gospel.

The period from Pentecost to 150 C.E. was marked by remarkable growth and expansion of the early Christian church. This growth was driven by the empowerment of the Holy Spirit, the dedicated efforts of apostles and early Christians, and the resilient faith of believers in the face of persecution. Understanding this foundational period is crucial for addressing the divisions and challenges facing modern Christianity. By returning to the principles and zeal of the early church, contemporary Christians can find guidance and inspiration for fostering unity and spreading the Gospel in today's world.

Core Teachings and Practices of the Apostolic Church

The apostolic church, rooted in the teachings of Jesus Christ and the guidance of the Holy Spirit, established a foundation of core doctrines and practices that have significantly influenced Christianity. Understanding these foundational elements is crucial for addressing contemporary church problems and fostering unity.

The Centrality of Jesus Christ

At the heart of the apostolic church's teaching was the centrality of Jesus Christ. The apostles emphasized His role as the Messiah, the Son of God, and the Savior of humanity. Peter's sermon on the day of Pentecost, as recorded in Acts 2, underscores this focus. He declared, "Let all the house of Israel therefore know for certain that God has made him both Lord and Christ, this Jesus whom you crucified" (Acts 2:36, UASV). The early Christians believed and taught that salvation could be found only through Jesus Christ, as Peter later affirmed, "And there is salvation in no one else, for there is no other name under heaven given among men by which we must be saved" (Acts 4:12, UASV).

The apostolic church also proclaimed the death, resurrection, and ascension of Jesus as the cornerstone of the Gospel message. Paul encapsulated this in his first letter to the Corinthians, stating, "For I delivered to you as of first importance what I also received: that Christ died for our sins in accordance with the Scriptures, that he was buried, that he was raised on the third day in accordance with the Scriptures" (1 Corinthians 15:3-4, UASV). This message of Christ's sacrificial death and victorious resurrection was central to the apostles' preaching and teaching.

The Doctrine of the Trinity

Although the term "Trinity" is not found in the New Testament, the doctrine of the Trinity was implicitly taught by the apostles. They affirmed the existence of one God in three persons: Father, Son, and

Holy Spirit. This understanding is evident in the Great Commission given by Jesus, "Go therefore and make disciples of all nations, baptizing them in the name of the Father and of the Son and of the Holy Spirit" (Matthew 28:19, UASV). The apostolic writings reflect this triune understanding of God, as seen in Paul's benediction, "The grace of the Lord Jesus Christ and the love of God and the fellowship of the Holy Spirit be with you all" (2 Corinthians 13:14, UASV).

The Authority of Scripture

The early church held the Scriptures in the highest regard, viewing them as the authoritative Word of God. The Old Testament was the foundational text, and the apostles' teachings and writings, which would later form the New Testament, were considered divinely inspired. Paul emphasized the inspiration and usefulness of Scripture, writing to Timothy, "All Scripture is breathed out by God and profitable for teaching, for reproof, for correction, and for training in righteousness" (2 Timothy 3:16, UASV). The Bereans were commended for their diligence in examining the Scriptures daily to verify Paul's teachings (Acts 17:11).

Salvation by Grace through Faith

A fundamental doctrine of the apostolic church was salvation by grace through faith. The apostles taught that salvation was a gift from God, not something that could be earned by human effort. Paul articulated this clearly in his letter to the Ephesians, "For by grace you have been saved through faith. And this is not your own doing; it is the gift of God, not a result of works, so that no one may boast" (Ephesians 2:8-9, UASV). This doctrine was crucial in distinguishing the Christian faith from other religious systems that emphasized works-based righteousness.

The Role of Baptism

Baptism was a central practice in the apostolic church, symbolizing the believer's identification with the death, burial, and resurrection of Jesus Christ. It was an outward expression of an inward faith and commitment to follow Christ. Peter's exhortation on the day of Pentecost included a call to baptism, "Repent and be baptized every one of you in the name of Jesus Christ for the forgiveness of your sins, and you will receive the gift of the Holy Spirit" (Acts 2:38, UASV). Baptism was seen as an essential step in the believer's journey of faith and entry into the Christian community.

The Lord's Supper

The Lord's Supper, also known as Communion, was instituted by Jesus and faithfully observed by the early church. This practice commemorated Jesus' sacrificial death and anticipated His return. Paul provided instructions for its observance in his first letter to the Corinthians, emphasizing the significance of this memorial meal: "For I received from the Lord what I also delivered to you, that the Lord Jesus on the night when he was betrayed took bread, and when he had given thanks, he broke it, and said, 'This is my body, which is for you. Do this in remembrance of me.' In the same way also he took the cup, after supper, saying, 'This cup is the new covenant in my blood. Do this, as often as you drink it, in remembrance of me'" (1 Corinthians 11:23-25, UASV).

The Practice of Prayer

Prayer was a vital aspect of the apostolic church's life. The early Christians devoted themselves to prayer, both individually and corporately. The Book of Acts records numerous instances of prayer, reflecting its centrality in their community. The apostles prayed for guidance, boldness, healing, and the outpouring of the Holy Spirit. One significant example is found in Acts 4:31, where after the believers prayed, "the place in which they were gathered together was shaken, and they were all filled with the Holy Spirit and continued to speak the word of God with boldness" (UASV).

The Importance of Fellowship

The apostolic church placed a high value on fellowship, recognizing the importance of mutual support and encouragement among believers. This fellowship was not merely social but deeply spiritual, involving the sharing of lives, resources, and spiritual gifts. Acts 2:44-47 describes the early Christian community: "And all who believed were together and had all things in common. And they were selling their possessions and belongings and distributing the proceeds to all, as any had need. And day by day, attending the temple together and breaking bread in their homes, they received their food with glad and generous hearts, praising God and having favor with all the people" (UASV).

The Great Commission

The mission to evangelize and make disciples of all nations was a core mandate given by Jesus to His followers, encapsulated in the Great Commission (Matthew 28:18-20). The early church took this commission seriously, spreading the Gospel far and wide through preaching, teaching, and personal witness. The Book of Acts documents the fulfillment of this mandate, with the apostles and early Christians carrying the message of Christ from Jerusalem to Judea, Samaria, and the ends of the earth (Acts 1:8).

Apostolic Authority and Church Discipline

The apostles exercised a unique authority given to them by Jesus to establish and guide the early church. This authority included teaching, performing miracles, and exercising church discipline. For example, Peter's confrontation of Ananias and Sapphira for lying to the Holy Spirit (Acts 5:1-11) demonstrates the seriousness with which the apostles upheld the integrity and holiness of the church. Paul also addressed issues of discipline in his letters, urging the Corinthian church to deal decisively with immorality in their midst (1 Corinthians 5:1-13).

The core teachings and practices of the apostolic church laid a solid foundation for the faith that has endured through the centuries. By adhering to the centrality of Jesus Christ, the authority of Scripture, salvation by grace through faith, the ordinances of baptism and the Lord's Supper, the practice of prayer, the importance of fellowship, the Great Commission, and apostolic authority and discipline, the early Christians established a robust and dynamic community of believers. These foundational elements continue to guide and inspire the church today as it seeks to overcome division and faithfully proclaim the Gospel.

Chapter 2: Prophetic Warnings and Early Divisions

Prophecies by Jesus, Paul, and Peter

The warnings given by Jesus, Paul, and Peter regarding false teachers and divisions within the church are crucial for understanding the current state of Christianity. These prophecies were not mere predictions; they were divine revelations intended to prepare believers for the challenges that would arise. Recognizing and responding to these warnings is essential for restoring the unity and purity of the church.

Jesus' Prophecies

Jesus Christ, during His earthly ministry, provided clear warnings about the rise of false prophets and the resulting divisions within His followers. In Matthew 7:15, Jesus cautioned, "Beware of false prophets, who come to you in sheep's clothing but inwardly are ravenous wolves." This vivid imagery underscores the deceptive nature of these false teachers, who would appear harmless but would cause significant harm to the flock. Jesus' warning highlights the importance of discernment and vigilance among believers.

In Matthew 24:11, Jesus expanded on this warning, stating, "And many false prophets will arise and lead many astray." This prophecy indicates that the presence of false teachers would be widespread and impactful, leading many away from the truth. Jesus further emphasized the destructive nature of these influences in Matthew 24:24: "For false christs and false prophets will arise and perform great signs and wonders, so as to lead astray, if possible, even the elect." This forewarning underscores the severity of the threat posed by false teachers and the need for believers to be firmly grounded in the truth.

31

Jesus also predicted internal divisions among His followers. In Luke 12:51-53, He stated, "Do you think that I have come to give peace on earth? No, I tell you, but rather division. For from now on in one house there will be five divided, three against two and two against three. They will be divided, father against son and son against father, mother against daughter and daughter against mother, mother-in-law against her daughter-in-law and daughter-in-law against mother-in-law." This prophecy reveals that the Gospel would bring not only unity but also division, as individuals respond differently to the message of Christ.

Paul's Warnings

The Apostle Paul provided extensive warnings about the infiltration of false teachers and the resulting discord within the church. In his farewell address to the Ephesian elders, Paul issued a solemn warning: "I know that after my departure fierce wolves will come in among you, not sparing the flock; and from among your own selves will arise men speaking twisted things, to draw away the disciples after them" (Acts 20:29-30, UASV). Paul's foresight into the rise of internal threats underscores the seriousness of the issue, indicating that false teachings would originate from within the Christian community itself.

Paul's letters are replete with warnings and instructions regarding false teachings. In 1 Timothy 4:1, he wrote, "Now the Spirit expressly says that in later times some will depart from the faith by devoting themselves to deceitful spirits and teachings of demons." This prophecy highlights the spiritual dimension of false teachings, emphasizing their demonic origin and the grave danger they pose to believers.

In 2 Timothy 4:3-4, Paul further elaborated on the issue: "For the time is coming when people will not endure sound teaching, but having itching ears they will accumulate for themselves teachers to suit their own passions, and will turn away from listening to the truth and wander off into myths." This prophecy underscores the proclivity of people to seek out teachings that cater to their desires rather than adhering to the sound doctrine of the Scriptures. Paul's warnings serve as a call to vigilance and fidelity to the truth.

Peter's Prophecies

The Apostle Peter echoed similar warnings about false teachers and the resulting divisions within the church. In 2 Peter 2:1-2, he wrote, "But false prophets also arose among the people, just as there will be false teachers among you, who will secretly bring in destructive heresies, even denying the Master who bought them, bringing upon themselves swift destruction. And many will follow their sensuality, and because of them the way of truth will be blasphemed." Peter's prophecy emphasizes that false teachings would lead many astray and cause the truth to be maligned.

Peter also stressed the importance of vigilance and steadfastness in the faith. In 1 Peter 5:8-9, he urged, "Be sober-minded; be watchful. Your adversary the devil prowls around like a roaring lion, seeking someone to devour. Resist him, firm in your faith, knowing that the same kinds of suffering are being experienced by your brotherhood throughout the world." This exhortation underscores the constant threat posed by false teachings and the need for believers to remain alert and grounded in their faith.

Early Fulfillment and Continued Relevance

Within a few decades of the apostles' deaths, the Christian church began to experience significant divisions, fulfilling the prophecies of Jesus, Paul, and Peter. Early church historians such as Irenaeus and Epiphanius documented numerous sects and heresies, indicating that the warnings of the apostles were becoming a reality. Irenaeus, writing in the late second century, listed twenty varieties of Christianity, while Epiphanius, in the fourth century, counted eighty. This proliferation of differing beliefs and practices among those who professed to follow Christ demonstrated the early fulfillment of the apostolic warnings.

The rise of the Roman Catholic Church and its consolidation of power introduced another dimension to the fulfillment of prophecy. While the church achieved a form of unity through hierarchical control, it often did so at the expense of biblical truth and through methods of coercion and persecution. The Reformation, while addressing many of the doctrinal errors and moral corruptions of the Catholic Church, led to further fragmentation as reformers, driven by a desire to return to biblical fidelity, often found themselves at odds with one another.

Today, the Christian church is more fragmented than ever, with an estimated 41,000 denominations worldwide. This division, while lamentable, should not lead to despair but rather to a sober recognition that it is a fulfillment of biblical prophecy. Understanding this helps believers to approach the problem with both a sense of urgency and a measure of hope.

Responding to the Prophecies

Recognizing the fulfillment of these prophecies should compel believers to return to the foundational truths of Scripture. The way forward involves a recommitment to sound doctrine, a rejection of false teachings, and a collective effort to restore the unity that Jesus prayed for in John 17:21, "that they may all be one, just as you, Father, are in me, and I in you, that they also may be in us, so that the world may believe that you have sent me."

To combat the influence of false teachers and heal divisions, the church must prioritize biblical literacy and sound teaching. Believers need to be equipped with a thorough understanding of Scripture to discern truth from error. Church leaders must be vigilant in upholding doctrinal purity and addressing false teachings decisively.

Additionally, fostering a culture of humility and repentance within the church is crucial. Both leaders and congregants must be willing to acknowledge and correct doctrinal errors and sinful behaviors that contribute to division. This humility extends to seeking reconciliation with those who have been led astray by false teachings, gently guiding them back to the truth.

The prophetic warnings of Jesus, Paul, and Peter regarding false teachers and divisions within the church are as relevant today as they were in the first century. Recognizing and responding to these warnings is essential for addressing the current fragmentation of Christianity. By returning to the foundational truths of Scripture, prioritizing sound teaching, and fostering a culture of humility and repentance, the church can work towards the unity and purity that Jesus desired for His followers.

Early Schisms and Their Causes

The early church, despite its remarkable growth and initial unity, began to experience significant schisms and doctrinal disputes shortly after the apostles' deaths. These divisions, prophesied by Jesus, Paul, and Peter, were driven by various factors, including the rise of false teachers, cultural differences, and the inherent challenges of maintaining doctrinal purity in a rapidly expanding faith community.

The Role of False Teachers

One of the primary causes of early schisms was the rise of false teachers who introduced heretical doctrines into the church. These individuals, often motivated by personal gain or a desire for power, led many believers astray. The apostles consistently warned against such individuals. Paul, in his letter to the Galatians, expressed his astonishment that the Galatians were so quickly deserting the true Gospel for a different one, which he declared was no gospel at all (Galatians 1:6-7). He sternly warned, "But even if we or an angel from heaven should preach to you a gospel contrary to the one we preached to you, let him be accursed" (Galatians 1:8, UASV).

The influence of Gnosticism, a prevalent heretical movement, significantly contributed to early church divisions. Gnosticism espoused a dualistic worldview, positing a stark contrast between the material and spiritual worlds, and claimed that salvation was attainable through esoteric knowledge. This belief system directly contradicted the apostolic teaching of salvation through faith in Jesus Christ alone. John addressed this issue in his first epistle, combating the Gnostic denial of Jesus' incarnation: "By this you know the Spirit of God: every spirit that confesses that Jesus Christ has come in the flesh is from

God, and every spirit that does not confess Jesus is not from God" (1 John 4:2-3, UASV).

Cultural and Ethnic Differences

The early church was composed of a diverse group of individuals from various cultural and ethnic backgrounds. This diversity, while a testament to the universal appeal of the Gospel, also posed challenges. Tensions arose between Jewish and Gentile believers over the observance of the Mosaic Law. The Council of Jerusalem, recorded in Acts 15, addressed the issue of whether Gentile converts needed to be circumcised and observe the Law of Moses. The decision, guided by the Holy Spirit, was that Gentiles were not required to follow the full Mosaic Law, but should abstain from practices associated with idolatry and immorality. This ruling helped to maintain unity between Jewish and Gentile believers, but cultural tensions persisted.

Paul's letters frequently addressed these cultural conflicts. In his letter to the Galatians, Paul confronted Peter for his hypocritical behavior of withdrawing from Gentile believers out of fear of the circumcision party. Paul rebuked Peter, stating, "But when I saw that their conduct was not in step with the truth of the gospel, I said to Cephas before them all, 'If you, though a Jew, live like a Gentile and not like a Jew, how can you force the Gentiles to live like Jews?'" (Galatians 2:14, UASV). This incident underscores the ongoing struggle to integrate diverse cultural practices into a unified Christian faith.

Doctrinal Disputes

Doctrinal disputes were another significant cause of early schisms. The early church faced challenges in defining and defending orthodox Christian beliefs against heretical interpretations. One notable example is the Arian controversy, which arose in the early fourth century. Arius, a priest from Alexandria, taught that Jesus Christ was a created being and not co-eternal with the Father. This view was vehemently opposed by Athanasius and other church leaders who upheld the doctrine of the Trinity.

The Council of Nicaea in 325 C.E. addressed this controversy, resulting in the formulation of the Nicene Creed, which affirmed the consubstantiality of the Son with the Father. The creed declared that Jesus Christ was "begotten, not made, being of one substance with the Father." Despite this official resolution, Arianism continued to influence segments of the church for several centuries, demonstrating the persistent nature of doctrinal disputes.

The Influence of Personal Ambitions and Power Struggles

Personal ambitions and power struggles among church leaders also contributed to early schisms. The desire for authority and control over congregations led to rivalries and conflicts. Paul addressed this issue in his first letter to the Corinthians, rebuking the believers for their divisions based on allegiance to different leaders. He wrote, "For when one says, 'I follow Paul,' and another, 'I follow Apollos,' are you not being merely human?" (1 Corinthians 3:4, UASV). Paul emphasized that all believers are servants of Christ and that divisions based on personal loyalties were contrary to the unity that should characterize the church.

The early church also experienced conflicts between prominent leaders. For example, the disagreement between Paul and Barnabas over John Mark led to their separation and the formation of separate missionary teams (Acts 15:36-40). While this division was over a practical matter rather than doctrinal differences, it highlights the impact of personal disagreements on the unity of the church.

The Challenge of Maintaining Doctrinal Purity

The rapid expansion of Christianity brought with it the challenge of maintaining doctrinal purity across diverse and geographically dispersed communities. The apostles and early church leaders worked diligently to provide clear doctrinal instruction and to correct errors. Paul's epistles, for instance, addressed a wide range of theological and ethical issues, offering guidance to young churches on maintaining sound doctrine.

However, the absence of a complete New Testament canon in the early years of the church meant that many congregations relied heavily on oral tradition and the teachings of itinerant preachers. This situation left them vulnerable to the influence of false teachers. The eventual formation of the New Testament canon provided a more stable foundation for doctrinal instruction, but the process of canonization itself was marked by debates and disagreements over which books should be included.

The Impact of External Persecution

External persecution, while often strengthening the resolve and faith of believers, also played a role in early schisms. The pressure to conform to Roman religious practices led some Christians to apostatize, creating divisions within the church over how to deal with those who had denied their faith. The issue of the lapsed—those who had renounced Christianity under persecution but later sought to return to the church—was a contentious one. Some, like Novatian, argued for strict exclusion, while others advocated for more lenient measures. This debate led to the formation of schismatic groups and further fragmentation within the church.

The early schisms in the Christian church were the result of a complex interplay of factors, including the rise of false teachers, cultural and ethnic differences, doctrinal disputes, personal ambitions, and external persecution. These divisions, while prophesied by Jesus, Paul, and Peter, serve as a sobering reminder of the challenges inherent in maintaining doctrinal purity and unity. Addressing these issues with a commitment to biblical truth and a spirit of humility is essential for overcoming the divisions that continue to plague the church today.

Historical Accounts of Early Christian Factions

The early Christian church, despite its initial unity and rapid growth, soon encountered significant internal divisions. These schisms, foreseen in the prophecies of Jesus, Paul, and Peter, were driven by a variety of factors including doctrinal disagreements, cultural conflicts, and the rise of heretical movements. Historical accounts from the first few centuries of Christianity provide a detailed picture of these early factions and their impact on the church.

The Ebionites

One of the earliest known sects within Christianity was the Ebionites. This group emerged in the first century and is often associated with Jewish Christians who insisted on the necessity of following the Mosaic Law, including circumcision and dietary regulations. The Ebionites viewed Jesus as the Messiah but denied His divinity and virgin birth, seeing Him merely as a human prophet. They also rejected the writings of Paul, considering him an apostate from the Law. This insistence on maintaining Jewish customs created a significant rift between the Ebionites and the broader Christian community, which was moving towards a more inclusive understanding of the faith.

The Gnostics

Gnosticism was another major source of division in the early church. This movement, which gained prominence in the second century, espoused a dualistic worldview that sharply distinguished between the material and spiritual realms. Gnostics believed that salvation was attained through secret knowledge (gnosis) rather than through faith in Jesus Christ. They often viewed the material world as inherently evil, created by a lesser deity, and considered Jesus to be a spiritual being who imparted hidden knowledge to a select few.

Church fathers such as Irenaeus, in his work "Against Heresies," vigorously opposed Gnostic teachings. Irenaeus argued for the unity of the Old and New Testaments and emphasized the incarnation of Christ, asserting that Jesus was both fully divine and fully human. The Gnostic emphasis on secret knowledge and their denial of the material creation as good posed a significant theological challenge to the early church, leading to extensive efforts to refute these doctrines and preserve orthodox teaching.

The Marcionites

Marcion of Sinope, a prominent figure in the second century, founded a sect that posed another major challenge to early Christian unity. Marcion rejected the Old Testament and its God, whom he viewed as a lesser, wrathful deity distinct from the benevolent Father of Jesus Christ. Marcion created his own canon, excluding the Old Testament and including only a modified version of Luke's Gospel and ten of Paul's epistles, purged of what he considered Jewish interpolations.

The church vehemently opposed Marcion's teachings, as they undermined the continuity and integrity of the Christian faith. The response to Marcionism contributed significantly to the development of the New Testament canon, as church leaders sought to clearly define the authoritative texts that reflected the true teachings of Jesus and the apostles. Marcion's radical dichotomy between the Old and New Testaments highlighted the need for a coherent theological framework that affirmed the unity of Scripture.

The Montanists

Montanism, a movement that began in the late second century, was characterized by its emphasis on new prophetic revelations and a rigorous moral code. Montanus, along with two prophetesses, Priscilla and Maximilla, claimed to receive direct revelations from the Holy Spirit, which they believed were on par with, or even surpassed, the authority of the apostles' teachings. Montanists practiced extreme asceticism and held a belief in the imminent end of the world.

The church's response to Montanism was complex. While acknowledging the legitimate role of the Holy Spirit, church leaders rejected the Montanists' claims to new revelation that superseded the established apostolic tradition. The movement's emphasis on ecstatic prophecy and its stringent moral demands created a significant division, leading to the eventual condemnation of Montanism as heretical. This controversy highlighted the need for discernment in distinguishing genuine spiritual experiences from those that threatened the unity and doctrinal integrity of the church.

The Donatists

The Donatist schism, which emerged in the early fourth century, was primarily a dispute over the nature of the church and the validity of sacraments administered by bishops who had lapsed during persecution. The Donatists, named after Donatus Magnus, argued that the sanctity of the church was compromised by leaders who had betrayed the faith under duress. They maintained that sacraments performed by such bishops were invalid, insisting on the necessity of a pure and holy clergy.

The controversy centered in North Africa and persisted for several centuries. Augustine of Hippo was a key figure in opposing the Donatists, arguing that the validity of the sacraments did not depend on the moral purity of the minister but on the grace of Christ. Augustine's writings emphasized the unity and universality of the church, countering the Donatist emphasis on separation and purity. This schism underscored the challenges of maintaining ecclesiastical unity in the face of internal moral failures and differing theological perspectives.

The Arian Controversy

Arianism, a theological dispute that arose in the early fourth century, centered on the nature of Christ's divinity. Arius, a priest from Alexandria, taught that Jesus Christ was a created being, distinct from and subordinate to God the Father. This view directly contradicted the traditional understanding of the Trinity, which affirmed the co-eternity and co-equality of the Father, Son, and Holy Spirit.

The Arian controversy prompted the convening of the First Council of Nicaea in 325 C.E., which sought to address and resolve the theological dispute. The council condemned Arianism and formulated the Nicene Creed, which articulated the orthodox Christian belief in the consubstantiality of the Son with the Father. Despite the council's decisions, Arianism continued to influence segments of the church for centuries, illustrating the enduring nature of theological conflicts and the difficulty of achieving doctrinal consensus.

The Nestorian and Monophysite Controversies

In the fifth century, further Christological debates led to the Nestorian and Monophysite controversies. Nestorius, Patriarch of Constantinople, proposed a distinction between the human and divine natures of Christ, leading to accusations that he divided Christ into two separate persons. The Council of Ephesus in 431 C.E. condemned Nestorianism and affirmed the unity of Christ's two natures in one person.

Conversely, the Monophysite controversy arose from the teachings of Eutyches, who argued that Christ had only one nature, a fusion of divine and human elements. The Council of Chalcedon in 451 C.E. rejected Monophysitism and declared the doctrine of the two natures of Christ—fully divine and fully human, united without confusion or division.

These Christological debates and the resulting schisms highlight the early church's struggle to articulate a coherent and orthodox understanding of the nature of Christ. The councils' decisions played a crucial role in shaping Christian doctrine, but the controversies also demonstrated the challenges of maintaining unity in the face of complex theological questions.

The early Christian church experienced significant internal divisions, driven by doctrinal disputes, cultural differences, and the rise of heretical movements. Historical accounts of these early factions, such as the Ebionites, Gnostics, Marcionites, Montanists, Donatists, and the proponents of Arianism, Nestorianism, and Monophysitism, provide valuable insights into the challenges of maintaining doctrinal purity and unity. By understanding these early schisms, contemporary Christians can better appreciate the importance of sound teaching, discernment, and a commitment to the foundational truths of the faith.

Chapter 3: The Influence of Catholicism and the Reformation

The Rise and Domination of Catholicism

The development and domination of the Roman Catholic Church significantly impacted the course of Christian history. From its early beginnings in the aftermath of the apostolic era to its consolidation of power throughout the Middle Ages, the Catholic Church played a pivotal role in shaping the theological, political, and cultural landscape of Western Christianity. Analyzing this period requires a candid examination of both the church's contributions and its profound deviations from the teachings of early Christianity.

Early Beginnings and Consolidation

In the first few centuries following the death of the apostles, the Christian church faced numerous challenges, including persecution, doctrinal disputes, and internal divisions. During this period, the church in Rome gradually gained prominence. Rome's significance as the capital of the Roman Empire, combined with its large and influential Christian community, contributed to the rise of the Roman bishop's authority.

The concept of apostolic succession, the belief that church authority was derived from the apostles and passed down through an unbroken line of bishops, became a cornerstone of the Roman church's claim to primacy. This idea was rooted in the assertion that the Apostle Peter, whom Jesus called "the rock" upon which He would build His church (Matthew 16:18, UASV), was the first bishop of Rome. As a result, subsequent bishops of Rome viewed themselves as

43

Peter's successors and thus claimed a unique authority over the entire Christian church.

Establishment of Doctrinal Authority

As the church in Rome grew in influence, it sought to establish itself as the ultimate arbiter of Christian doctrine. This effort culminated in the development of a centralized ecclesiastical structure with the pope, the bishop of Rome, at its head. The first ecumenical councils, such as Nicaea (325 C.E.) and Chalcedon (451 C.E.), were convened to address critical theological issues and to define orthodox Christian beliefs. While these councils included bishops from across the Christian world, the Roman church played a significant role in shaping their outcomes and enforcing their decrees.

One of the most significant contributions of these early councils was the formulation of the Nicene Creed, which articulated the church's understanding of the Trinity and the nature of Christ. The Roman church's involvement in these councils helped to solidify its doctrinal authority and reinforce its claim to primacy.

The Political Power of the Papacy

The fall of the Western Roman Empire in 476 C.E. marked a turning point for the Roman church. As secular political structures crumbled, the church stepped in to fill the power vacuum. The papacy, through its network of bishops and clergy, became a stabilizing force in a time of chaos and uncertainty. This period saw the rise of powerful popes, such as Gregory the Great (590-604 C.E.), who not only provided spiritual leadership but also engaged in political and social governance.

The Donation of Constantine, a forged document from the eighth century, claimed that the Roman Emperor Constantine had transferred authority over Rome and the Western Empire to the pope. Although later proven to be a forgery, this document was used to justify the papacy's temporal power and its authority over secular rulers. The papal states, territories in Italy directly governed by the pope, further exemplified the blending of spiritual and temporal authority.

The Medieval Church and Its Abuses

The medieval period saw the Catholic Church reach the height of its power and influence, but it was also marked by significant corruption and abuses. The church's vast wealth, political power, and control over education and religious life led to widespread corruption among the clergy. Simony, the buying and selling of church offices, was rampant, and many church leaders lived opulent lifestyles, far removed from the ideals of Christian humility and service.

The practice of indulgences, which allowed individuals to purchase remission of sins, became a significant source of revenue for the church but also a major point of contention. The selling of indulgences, often under the pretext of funding church projects like the construction of St. Peter's Basilica, was seen by many as a blatant abuse of spiritual authority for financial gain.

The Inquisition, established to root out heresy, became notorious for its brutal methods and suppression of dissent. The church's heavy-handed approach to maintaining doctrinal purity often led to the persecution of those who sought to challenge its authority or promote alternative theological views.

Theological Deviations and Doctrinal Innovations

The dominance of the Catholic Church also led to significant theological deviations from early Christian teachings. The veneration of saints and the Virgin Mary, the belief in purgatory, and the doctrine of transubstantiation (the belief that the bread and wine of the Eucharist become the actual body and blood of Christ) are examples of doctrines and practices that developed over centuries and became central to Catholic theology. These innovations, often lacking clear biblical support, were seen by many as departures from the simplicity and purity of apostolic Christianity.

The doctrine of papal infallibility, formally defined in 1870 during the First Vatican Council, declared that the pope is preserved from the possibility of error when he solemnly proclaims a doctrine of faith or morals. This doctrine further entrenched the absolute authority of the pope and was a point of significant controversy, both within and outside the Catholic Church.

The Call for Reform and the Prelude to the Reformation

By the late medieval period, calls for reform within the Catholic Church were growing louder. Figures such as John Wycliffe in England and Jan Hus in Bohemia criticized the church's corruption and doctrinal deviations, advocating for a return to biblical Christianity. These early reformers faced severe persecution, with Hus being burned at the stake in 1415.

The invention of the printing press in the mid-15th century played a crucial role in disseminating reformist ideas and the Bible itself, challenging the church's control over religious knowledge. The groundwork was laid for the Reformation, a movement that would profoundly reshape the Christian world.

The rise and domination of the Roman Catholic Church significantly influenced the development of Western Christianity. While the church played a vital role in preserving Christian doctrine and providing stability during tumultuous times, its accumulation of power and wealth led to significant corruption and theological deviations. Understanding this period of church history is essential for recognizing the need for reform and the ongoing challenges of maintaining doctrinal purity and ecclesiastical integrity. By examining the rise of Catholicism and its impact, contemporary Christians can better appreciate the importance of adhering to the foundational truths of the faith and addressing the issues that continue to divide the church today.

Atrocities and Abuses During the Middle Ages

The Middle Ages, a period stretching roughly from the 5th to the late 15th century, was marked by significant influence and control exerted by the Roman Catholic Church. This era, while contributing to

46

the preservation and spread of Christianity, was also characterized by numerous atrocities and abuses that marred the church's history. These transgressions, stemming from the consolidation of power and the church's entanglement with secular authorities, reveal the dangers of deviating from the foundational principles of the early Christian faith.

The Crusades

One of the most notorious examples of the church's involvement in violence and coercion is the series of military campaigns known as the Crusades. Beginning in 1095 C.E. and spanning several centuries, the Crusades were initiated by Pope Urban II, who called upon Christian knights to reclaim the Holy Land from Muslim control. While ostensibly religious in nature, the Crusades were driven by a mix of piety, political ambition, and economic gain.

The First Crusade (1096-1099 C.E.) resulted in the capture of Jerusalem, but it also witnessed horrific acts of violence. The crusaders massacred thousands of Muslims and Jews, often in brutal and indiscriminate fashion. Subsequent Crusades continued this pattern of violence and destruction, including the infamous Fourth Crusade (1202-1204 C.E.), which saw the sacking of Constantinople, a Christian city, by fellow Christians. This betrayal deepened the schism between the Roman Catholic and Eastern Orthodox Churches and highlighted the moral and spiritual corruption that had infiltrated the church's leadership.

The Inquisition

Another dark chapter in the church's history is the Inquisition, a series of ecclesiastical tribunals established to root out heresy and enforce doctrinal conformity. The Medieval Inquisition began in the 12th century, targeting groups such as the Cathars and Waldensians, who were deemed heretical by the church. The most infamous phase, however, was the Spanish Inquisition, established in 1478 C.E. by King Ferdinand II and Queen Isabella of Spain with the approval of Pope Sixtus IV.

The Inquisition employed severe methods, including torture, to extract confessions from accused heretics. The auto-da-fé, or "act of faith," was a public ceremony during which condemned heretics were punished, often by burning at the stake. Thousands of individuals, including Jews and Muslims who had ostensibly converted to Christianity, were subjected to these brutal practices. The Inquisition's emphasis on coercion and fear starkly contrasted with the teachings of Jesus, who preached love, forgiveness, and repentance.

Corruption within the Clergy

The Middle Ages also saw rampant corruption within the clergy, further eroding the moral authority of the church. Simony, the practice of buying and selling church offices, was widespread. Wealthy individuals could purchase positions of power within the church hierarchy, leading to the appointment of bishops and abbots who were more interested in personal gain than spiritual leadership.

Nepotism, the favoritism shown to relatives by those in power, was another common abuse. Popes and bishops frequently appointed family members to lucrative and influential positions, regardless of their qualifications or piety. This practice not only undermined the church's credibility but also created powerful dynastic families who wielded significant influence over church affairs.

The sale of indulgences was perhaps the most egregious abuse. Indulgences were meant to reduce the temporal punishment for sins, but they became a means for the church to raise money. Johann Tetzel, a Dominican friar, famously sold indulgences with the slogan, "As soon as the coin in the coffer rings, the soul from purgatory springs." This commercialization of salvation was a blatant exploitation of the faithful and a significant factor leading to the Reformation.

Moral Decay and Immorality

The moral decay of the clergy during the Middle Ages was another significant issue. Many church leaders lived opulent and immoral lifestyles, far removed from the ascetic ideals of early Christianity. Monasteries, which were intended to be centers of spiritual discipline and learning, often became sites of excess and vice. Monks and nuns engaged in scandalous behavior, and the vows of celibacy were frequently ignored.

Papal decadence reached its zenith during the Renaissance. The papal court in Rome became notorious for its lavishness and moral laxity. Popes such as Alexander VI (Rodrigo Borgia) openly flaunted their wealth and engaged in blatant nepotism and immorality. Alexander VI fathered several children and used his position to advance the fortunes of the Borgia family, exemplifying the moral degradation that had permeated the highest levels of the church.

The Avignon Papacy and the Great Schism

The Avignon Papacy (1309-1377 C.E.) and the subsequent Great Schism (1378-1417 C.E.) further exemplified the church's internal corruption and its detrimental impact on Christian unity. During the Avignon Papacy, the popes resided in Avignon, France, rather than Rome, leading to accusations of French political influence over the church. This period was marked by lavish spending and the accumulation of wealth by the papal court.

The Great Schism occurred when two, and later three, rival claimants to the papacy emerged, each with their own following. This division severely undermined the church's authority and credibility, as competing popes excommunicated each other and their respective followers. The schism was not resolved until the Council of Constance (1414-1418 C.E.), which deposed the rival popes and elected Martin V as the sole pope. However, the damage to the church's reputation and unity was profound.

Persecution of Dissenters

The church's persecution of dissenters during the Middle Ages extended beyond heretics to include individuals and movements that sought to reform the church or promote alternative theological perspectives. Figures such as John Wycliffe and Jan Hus, who advocated for a return to biblical Christianity and criticized the church's corruption, were met with severe opposition. Wycliffe's writings were condemned, and Hus was burned at the stake in 1415 C.E. for his reformist views.

The suppression of dissent stifled theological and intellectual development within the church and created a climate of fear and conformity. This environment inhibited genuine reform and allowed the abuses and corruption to persist unchallenged until the Reformation.

The Need for Reformation

The cumulative effect of these atrocities and abuses created an urgent need for reform within the church. The moral and spiritual decay, coupled with the exploitation of the faithful, called for a return to the foundational principles of Christianity. The Reformation, which began in the early 16th century, was a response to these deep-seated issues. Reformers such as Martin Luther, John Calvin, and Huldrych Zwingli sought to restore the authority of Scripture, address the corruption of the clergy, and return to the core teachings of the apostolic church.

The atrocities and abuses during the Middle Ages highlight the dangers of the church's entanglement with political power and its departure from the teachings of early Christianity. The corruption, violence, and moral decay that characterized this period serve as a sobering reminder of the need for continual vigilance and reform within the church. By examining this dark chapter in church history, contemporary Christians can better understand the importance of adhering to biblical principles and maintaining the integrity and purity of the faith.

The Reformation: A Pendulum Swing

The Reformation represents one of the most significant upheavals in Christian history, fundamentally altering the landscape of Western Christianity. It was a reaction against the widespread corruption, doctrinal errors, and moral decay that had infiltrated the Roman

Catholic Church during the Middle Ages. The movement aimed to return to the foundational principles of Christianity, but it also resulted in significant fragmentation within the Christian community. Analyzing the Reformation through an objective lens reveals both the necessary reforms it achieved and the unintended consequences that followed.

The Catalysts of the Reformation

By the early 16th century, the Catholic Church had accumulated vast wealth and political power, but it was also plagued by corruption and abuse. The sale of indulgences, simony, and the moral laxity of the clergy were glaring issues that called for reform. Figures like John Wycliffe and Jan Hus had already laid the groundwork by challenging the church's authority and advocating for a return to biblical Christianity.

The immediate catalyst for the Reformation was Martin Luther, a German monk and theologian. In 1517 C.E., Luther nailed his Ninety-Five Theses to the door of the Wittenberg Castle Church, criticizing the sale of indulgences and other church practices. Luther's theses quickly spread across Europe, igniting a movement that sought to address the fundamental problems within the Catholic Church.

Key Figures and Their Contributions

Martin Luther was not alone in his efforts. Other reformers, such as John Calvin, Huldrych Zwingli, and John Knox, played crucial roles in shaping the Reformation. Each brought unique perspectives and emphases, contributing to the diversity of Reformation thought.

Luther's central teachings included the doctrine of justification by faith alone (sola fide), the authority of Scripture alone (sola scriptura), and the priesthood of all believers. He translated the Bible into German, making it accessible to ordinary people and encouraging them to read and interpret it for themselves.

John Calvin, a French theologian, emphasized the sovereignty of God and developed a systematic theology that came to be known as

Calvinism. His work, "Institutes of the Christian Religion," became a foundational text for Reformed churches. Calvin's influence extended to various aspects of church governance, including the establishment of a presbyterian polity that emphasized the role of elected elders.

Huldrych Zwingli, a Swiss reformer, led a parallel movement in Zurich. He shared many of Luther's views but differed on issues such as the nature of the Eucharist. Zwingli saw the Lord's Supper as a symbolic act rather than a literal transformation of the elements, a view that became a defining feature of Reformed theology.

John Knox, influenced by Calvin, brought Reformation ideas to Scotland, where he established the Presbyterian Church. Knox's efforts laid the groundwork for Presbyterianism, which would later spread to other parts of the world.

Theological Shifts and Innovations

The Reformation brought significant theological shifts that sought to realign Christian practice with biblical teachings. One of the most important shifts was the emphasis on sola scriptura, the belief that Scripture alone is the ultimate authority in matters of faith and practice. This principle challenged the Catholic Church's reliance on tradition and the authority of the pope.

The doctrine of justification by faith alone was another critical innovation. Reformers argued that salvation could not be earned through good works or purchased through indulgences but was a gift of God's grace received through faith in Jesus Christ. This doctrine was encapsulated in the phrase sola fide.

The priesthood of all believers democratized the Christian faith, asserting that every believer had direct access to God and could interpret Scripture. This principle undermined the hierarchical structure of the Catholic Church and empowered laypeople to take an active role in their faith communities.

Political and Social Impact

The Reformation was not merely a theological movement; it had profound political and social implications. The rise of nation-states and the decline of papal authority were closely intertwined with the Reformation. Many political leaders saw the movement as an opportunity to assert their independence from Rome and consolidate their power.

In Germany, the Reformation led to the fragmentation of the Holy Roman Empire as various princes adopted Lutheranism or other forms of Protestantism. The Peace of Augsburg in 1555 C.E. allowed for the coexistence of Catholicism and Lutheranism within the empire, but it also institutionalized religious division.

In England, the Reformation took a unique path with the establishment of the Church of England. King Henry VIII's desire for an annulment from his first wife, Catherine of Aragon, led to a break with Rome and the creation of a national church under the king's authority. Although initially motivated by personal and political reasons, the English Reformation eventually adopted many Protestant theological principles.

The social impact of the Reformation was equally significant. The emphasis on literacy and education, driven by the need for individuals to read and interpret the Bible, led to the establishment of schools and universities. The Protestant work ethic, with its focus on hard work, frugality, and discipline, had lasting effects on the economic and cultural development of Europe.

The Unintended Consequences

While the Reformation achieved necessary reforms, it also led to unintended consequences. The most significant was the fragmentation of Western Christianity into numerous denominations. The principle of sola scriptura, while empowering, also opened the door to diverse interpretations of Scripture. This diversity led to theological disputes and the formation of various Protestant traditions, each with its own distinct beliefs and practices.

The religious wars that followed the Reformation, including the Thirty Years' War (1618-1648 C.E.), were devastating. These conflicts, driven by both religious and political motives, caused immense suffering and loss of life. The wars ultimately led to a weariness of religious conflict and a push towards secularization in European politics.

The Counter-Reformation, launched by the Catholic Church in response to the Reformation, aimed to address some of the abuses highlighted by the reformers while reaffirming Catholic doctrine. The Council of Trent (1545-1563 C.E.) played a central role in this effort, implementing reforms in church discipline and clarifying Catholic teachings. The Counter-Reformation revitalized the Catholic Church but also intensified the division between Catholics and Protestants.

The Reformation's Lasting Legacy

The Reformation's impact on Christianity is profound and enduring. It restored the centrality of Scripture and the doctrine of justification by faith, principles that continue to shape Protestant theology. The movement also emphasized the importance of personal faith and direct access to God, empowering laypeople and fostering a sense of individual responsibility in matters of faith.

However, the fragmentation that resulted from the Reformation poses ongoing challenges for Christian unity. The proliferation of denominations reflects the complexity of interpreting Scripture and the diverse ways in which Christians understand their faith. While the Reformation addressed critical issues within the Catholic Church, it also revealed the difficulty of maintaining unity without compromising doctrinal integrity.

The Reformation was a necessary and transformative movement that addressed significant abuses within the Roman Catholic Church and sought to return Christianity to its biblical foundations. The theological innovations and reforms it introduced had a lasting impact on Western Christianity. However, the movement also led to unintended consequences, including the fragmentation of the church and religious conflicts. Understanding the Reformation as a pendulum swing helps to appreciate both its achievements and its challenges, offering insights for addressing the ongoing issues within contemporary Christianity.

Chapter 4: The Modern Landscape of Christianity

The Proliferation of Denominations

The modern landscape of Christianity is characterized by an astonishing diversity of denominations, each with its own distinct beliefs, practices, and organizational structures. This proliferation, while reflecting the freedom of religious expression, also underscores the deep divisions that have emerged within the body of Christ. Understanding the causes and implications of this fragmentation is essential for addressing the challenges it presents to achieving the unity that Jesus prayed for in John 17:21.

Historical Context and Root Causes

The proliferation of Christian denominations can be traced back to the Reformation, a movement that began in the 16th century as a response to the corruption and doctrinal deviations of the Roman Catholic Church. The Reformers sought to return to the foundational principles of Christianity, emphasizing the authority of Scripture, justification by faith alone, and the priesthood of all believers. However, the principle of sola scriptura, which empowered individuals to interpret the Bible independently, also led to diverse interpretations and the formation of new religious groups.

Key Factors in Denominational Fragmentation

Several key factors have contributed to the proliferation of denominations:

Theological Disputes: Theological disagreements have been a primary driver of denominational splits. Differences in the interpretation of key doctrines, such as the nature of the sacraments, predestination, and the authority of church tradition, have led to the formation of distinct denominational bodies. For example, the debate over the presence of Christ in the Eucharist resulted in the formation of Lutheran, Reformed, and Anabaptist traditions, each with its own theological stance.

Cultural and Social Differences: Cultural and social factors have also played a significant role in the development of denominations. As Christianity spread across different regions and cultures, local customs and traditions influenced the expression of faith. These cultural variations often led to the establishment of denominations that reflected the unique characteristics of their contexts. In the United States, for instance, the Methodist, Baptist, and Pentecostal movements each developed distinct identities shaped by the social and cultural milieu of American society.

Political and Historical Contexts: Political and historical events have frequently influenced denominational splits. The establishment of the Church of England under Henry VIII, motivated by political and personal reasons, created a distinct Anglican tradition. Similarly, the political turmoil and religious conflicts of the Thirty Years' War in Europe contributed to the establishment of state churches and further denominational fragmentation.

Revivalist Movements and New Theological Emphases: Periods of religious revival and the emergence of new theological emphases have often given rise to new denominations. The Great Awakening in the 18th century, for example, sparked the formation of evangelical and revivalist movements such as the Methodist and Baptist denominations. In the 19th and 20th centuries, the Pentecostal and Charismatic movements introduced new emphases on the gifts of the Holy Spirit, leading to the creation of numerous Pentecostal and independent charismatic churches.

Reactions to Perceived Doctrinal Errors: Throughout history, groups within the church have often separated themselves in response to perceived doctrinal errors or moral failures within existing denominations. The Puritans, for example, sought to purify the Church of England from what they saw as lingering Catholic influences, eventually leading to the formation of Congregationalist and Presbyterian denominations. Similarly, the Disciples of Christ movement in the 19th century aimed to restore the New Testament pattern of Christianity, resulting in the establishment of the Christian Church (Disciples of Christ).

Theological and Practical Implications

The proliferation of denominations has both theological and practical implications for contemporary Christianity:

Theological Diversity: On one hand, denominational diversity reflects the richness of Christian thought and the freedom to explore different theological perspectives. This diversity can foster a deeper understanding of the faith as believers engage with a variety of doctrinal viewpoints. However, it also poses the risk of relativizing truth and fostering an environment where essential doctrines are treated as mere opinions.

Challenges to Unity: The fragmentation of the church into numerous denominations poses significant challenges to achieving the unity that Jesus prayed for in John 17:21. Denominational divisions often lead to competition, misunderstanding, and even hostility between different Christian groups. This lack of unity can undermine the church's witness to the world and hinder efforts to address common social and moral issues.

Strengths and Weaknesses of Denominationalism: Denominationalism has both strengths and weaknesses. On the positive side, it allows for a diversity of worship styles, theological emphases, and organizational structures, accommodating the varied needs and preferences of believers. Denominationalism can also provide a check against authoritarianism by distributing power among multiple independent bodies. On the negative side, it can lead to duplication of efforts, inefficient use of resources, and a fragmented witness to the world.

The Role of Ecumenism: In response to the challenges posed by denominational fragmentation, the ecumenical movement has sought to promote greater unity and cooperation among different

Christian traditions. While recognizing the distinctives of each denomination, ecumenism emphasizes common beliefs and shared mission. Efforts such as the World Council of Churches and various bilateral dialogues have made significant strides in fostering mutual understanding and cooperation. However, ecumenism also faces significant obstacles, including deeply held theological differences and historical grievances.

Contemporary Examples and Trends

In the contemporary context, several trends illustrate the ongoing dynamics of denominational proliferation and convergence:

Non-Denominational Churches: One significant trend is the rise of non-denominational churches. These congregations seek to transcend traditional denominational boundaries, emphasizing a direct, personal relationship with Jesus Christ and often adopting contemporary worship styles. Non-denominational churches appeal to those who are disillusioned with institutional religion or who seek a more flexible and informal approach to faith.

Denominational Mergers and Alliances: Despite the trend toward fragmentation, there have also been efforts to bring together different denominations through mergers and alliances. For example, the United Church of Christ was formed in 1957 by the merger of the Congregational Christian Churches and the Evangelical and Reformed Church. Similarly, the Evangelical Lutheran Church in America was created in 1988 through the merger of three Lutheran bodies. These mergers reflect a desire for greater unity and cooperation while maintaining theological and organizational integrity.

Global South Christianity: The growth of Christianity in the Global South has introduced new dynamics into the denominational landscape. African, Asian, and Latin American churches often bring different cultural perspectives and theological emphases, challenging traditional Western denominational categories. The rapid growth of Pentecostalism and other charismatic movements in these regions illustrates the global and diverse nature of contemporary Christianity.

Digital and Online Churches: The rise of digital and online churches represents another trend in the modern denominational landscape. These virtual congregations leverage technology to reach people who may not attend traditional church services. While offering greater accessibility and flexibility, online churches also raise questions about the nature of community, accountability, and the sacraments in a digital age.

Addressing Denominational Fragmentation

Given the complexities and challenges posed by denominational fragmentation, what steps can be taken to promote greater unity within the body of Christ?

Reaffirming Core Doctrines: One approach is to reaffirm the core doctrines of the Christian faith that unite all believers. Focusing on essentials such as the divinity of Christ, the authority of Scripture, and the doctrine of salvation can help to bridge denominational divides and foster a sense of common purpose.

Promoting Mutual Understanding and Respect: Encouraging dialogue and cooperation between different denominations can promote mutual understanding and respect. By building relationships and working together on common goals, Christians from diverse traditions can learn from one another and find common ground.

Fostering a Spirit of Humility and Repentance: Addressing denominational fragmentation requires a spirit of humility and repentance. Recognizing the limitations and shortcomings of one's own tradition and being open to learning from others can pave the way for greater unity. This involves acknowledging historical grievances, seeking forgiveness, and working towards reconciliation.

Emphasizing Mission and Service: Focusing on the mission and service of the church can also promote unity. By working together to address social and moral issues, care for the needy, and spread the Gospel, Christians from different denominations can demonstrate the love of Christ and witness to the world the power of the Gospel to transform lives.

The proliferation of denominations within Christianity is a complex phenomenon with deep historical roots and significant theological and practical implications. While denominational diversity reflects the richness of Christian thought and practice, it also poses challenges to achieving the unity that Jesus prayed for. By reaffirming core doctrines, promoting mutual understanding, fostering humility, and emphasizing mission and service, the church can work towards greater unity and fulfill its calling to be one body in Christ.

Current State of Christian Unity

The current state of Christian unity, or rather disunity, presents a complex and multifaceted landscape. Despite Jesus' prayer for His followers to be one (John 17:21), the modern church is deeply fragmented, with over 41,000 denominations worldwide. This fragmentation undermines the witness of the church and presents significant challenges for achieving the unity that Christ intended. Analyzing the causes and manifestations of this disunity is crucial for understanding how to address and overcome these divisions.

Theological and Doctrinal Divisions

Theological and doctrinal differences remain one of the primary causes of disunity within Christianity. These differences often revolve around key issues such as the nature of the sacraments, the role of tradition, interpretations of Scripture, and views on salvation and eschatology.

For example, the interpretation of the Eucharist has historically divided Christians. The Roman Catholic Church teaches the doctrine of transubstantiation, believing that the bread and wine become the actual body and blood of Christ. In contrast, many Protestant denominations, such as Baptists and Pentecostals, view the Eucharist as a symbolic memorial. These doctrinal differences are not merely academic; they shape the core practices and beliefs of each denomination, making reconciliation challenging.

Similarly, the role of tradition versus sola scriptura (Scripture alone) creates significant divides. While the Catholic and Orthodox churches place a high value on sacred tradition alongside Scripture, most Protestant denominations adhere to sola scriptura, rejecting traditions that they believe are not grounded in the Bible. This fundamental difference in approaching religious authority perpetuates theological rifts.

Cultural and Societal Influences

Cultural and societal influences have also contributed to the fragmentation of the church. As Christianity spread across different regions and cultures, it naturally adapted to local customs and traditions. This adaptation, while beneficial in making the faith accessible to diverse populations, also led to the development of distinct denominational identities.

In the United States, for instance, denominationalism has been significantly influenced by cultural and social factors. The Great Awakenings, periods of religious revival in the 18th and 19th centuries, led to the formation of new denominations such as Methodists and Baptists, which reflected the revivalist spirit of the times. Similarly, the Civil Rights Movement and other social changes in the 20th century saw the emergence of denominations and church movements that aligned with specific social and political agendas.

Political and Historical Contexts

Political and historical contexts have played a significant role in shaping denominational identities and divisions. The establishment of state churches, such as the Church of England, and the intertwining of religious and national identities have often led to divisions based on political lines.

The Reformation itself was as much a political movement as it was a theological one. Martin Luther's challenge to the Catholic Church was supported by various German princes who saw an opportunity to assert their independence from the Holy Roman Empire. The subsequent religious wars and treaties, such as the Peace of Augsburg in 1555, which allowed for the coexistence of

Lutheranism and Catholicism within the empire, institutionalized religious division.

Organizational Structures and Governance

Different organizational structures and governance models also contribute to denominational fragmentation. The hierarchical structure of the Catholic Church, with the Pope as the ultimate authority, contrasts sharply with the congregational polity of many Protestant denominations, where each congregation governs itself independently.

The Presbyterian model, which emphasizes a representative form of church government with elected elders, differs from both the hierarchical and congregational models. These differences in governance are not just about organizational preferences; they reflect deep theological convictions about the nature of church authority and leadership.

Revivalist and Charismatic Movements

The rise of revivalist and charismatic movements in the 20th century introduced new dimensions of diversity within Christianity. Pentecostalism, with its emphasis on the gifts of the Holy Spirit such as speaking in tongues and healing, represents one of the fastest-growing segments of Christianity. While these movements have brought renewed vitality and growth, they have also introduced new theological and practical differences that contribute to the overall fragmentation.

Ecumenical Efforts and Their Limitations

Despite the profound disunity, there have been significant ecumenical efforts aimed at promoting Christian unity. The World Council of Churches, established in 1948, represents one of the most ambitious attempts to foster dialogue and cooperation among different Christian traditions. Various bilateral dialogues between Catholic,

Orthodox, and Protestant churches have also sought to address theological differences and promote mutual understanding.

However, these efforts often face significant limitations. Deep-seated theological differences, historical grievances, and institutional inertia can make meaningful progress difficult. While there have been notable successes, such as the Joint Declaration on the Doctrine of Justification between the Lutheran World Federation and the Catholic Church in 1999, these agreements often represent the beginning of a lengthy process rather than a final resolution.

The Role of Non-Denominational and Independent Churches

The rise of non-denominational and independent churches represents a significant trend in the contemporary Christian landscape. These churches often seek to transcend traditional denominational boundaries and focus on a more flexible and contemporary approach to worship and ministry. While this movement reflects a desire for greater unity and simplicity, it also contributes to the overall diversity and fragmentation by creating new, loosely affiliated networks of churches.

Non-denominational churches often appeal to those who are disillusioned with institutional religion or who seek a more personal and less formal expression of their faith. However, the lack of formal denominational ties can also lead to a lack of accountability and doctrinal consistency, further complicating efforts to achieve broader unity.

Challenges to Achieving Unity

The current state of Christian disunity poses significant challenges for achieving the unity that Jesus desired for His followers. Theological, cultural, political, and organizational differences create formidable barriers to reconciliation. Additionally, the sheer number of denominations and independent churches makes it difficult to find common ground.

One of the most significant challenges is the need for humility and repentance on the part of all Christian traditions. Achieving unity requires a willingness to acknowledge past mistakes, forgive historical grievances, and prioritize the common goal of glorifying God and advancing His kingdom.

Potential Pathways to Greater Unity

While the challenges are significant, there are potential pathways to greater unity within the body of Christ:

Reaffirming Core Beliefs: Focusing on the core doctrines of the Christian faith that unite all believers can provide a foundation for greater unity. Emphasizing the divinity of Christ, the authority of Scripture, and the doctrine of salvation through faith in Jesus Christ can help to bridge denominational divides.

Encouraging Mutual Respect and Dialogue: Promoting dialogue and mutual respect between different Christian traditions can foster greater understanding and cooperation. Building relationships and working together on common goals can help to break down barriers and promote a spirit of unity.

Fostering a Culture of Humility and Repentance: Encouraging a culture of humility and repentance within the church is essential for achieving unity. Recognizing the limitations and shortcomings of one's own tradition and being open to learning from others can pave the way for reconciliation and cooperation.

Emphasizing Shared Mission and Service: Focusing on the shared mission of the church to spread the Gospel and serve the needy can help to unite Christians from different traditions. Working together on common projects and initiatives can demonstrate the love of Christ to the world and show that unity is possible despite theological differences.

The current state of Christian disunity is a complex and multifaceted issue with deep historical and theological roots. While the proliferation of denominations reflects the richness of Christian thought and practice, it also poses significant challenges for achieving the unity that Christ intended. By reaffirming core beliefs, promoting mutual respect and dialogue, fostering humility and repentance, and emphasizing shared mission and service, the church can work towards greater unity and fulfill its calling to be one body in Christ.

The Impact of Diverse Doctrinal Views

The diverse doctrinal views within Christianity have created a complex and fragmented landscape. These differences, which encompass fundamental beliefs about salvation, inerrancy, creation, and other key aspects of the faith, have significant implications for the unity and witness of the church. Understanding these impacts is crucial for addressing the challenges they present and working towards greater cohesion within the body of Christ.

Theological Diversity and Its Origins

The theological diversity within Christianity stems from various historical, cultural, and interpretive factors. The Reformation in the 16th century played a pivotal role in this diversity, as it challenged the monolithic authority of the Roman Catholic Church and encouraged individual interpretation of Scripture. This emphasis on sola scriptura led to the development of numerous Protestant denominations, each with its own doctrinal distinctives.

Further contributing to this diversity are differences in biblical hermeneutics—the methods and principles used to interpret Scripture. Some traditions adhere strictly to a literal interpretation of the Bible, while others employ historical-critical methods or allegorical readings. These differing approaches to Scripture significantly influence doctrinal beliefs and practices.

Core Areas of Doctrinal Divergence

Views on Hell: There are four primary views on hell within Christianity: traditionalism, which holds to eternal conscious torment; annihilationism, which believes the wicked will be completely destroyed; universalism, which asserts that all will eventually be saved; and conditional immortality, which posits that only the saved receive eternal life. These views reflect differing interpretations of biblical texts and theological emphases on God's justice and mercy.

Creation: The debate over creation includes young earth creationism, which interprets the Genesis account as a literal six-day creation; old earth creationism, which allows for an ancient universe but sees God's hand in the process; theistic evolution, which integrates evolutionary theory with divine guidance; and intelligent design, which posits that certain features of the universe are best explained by an intelligent cause. These views highlight the intersection of science and faith and the varying degrees to which Christians engage with contemporary scientific theories.

Inerrancy: The doctrine of inerrancy, which asserts that the Bible is without error in all its teachings, is interpreted differently across denominations. Some hold to strict inerrancy, affirming that every detail in the Bible is accurate, while others adopt a more nuanced view, distinguishing between the Bible's theological truths and its historical or scientific descriptions.

Salvation: Views on salvation also vary widely. Some traditions emphasize predestination and the sovereignty of God in salvation (e.g., Calvinism), while others stress free will and human responsibility (e.g., Arminianism). Additionally, there are differences in understanding the role of sacraments, such as baptism and the Eucharist, in the process of salvation.

Christology: The nature of Christ has been a point of contention, with two primary views being the Chalcedonian definition, which affirms that Jesus is fully God and fully man in one person, and other perspectives that emphasize either his divinity or humanity more heavily. These differences influence how Christians understand the incarnation and the work of Christ.

Practical Implications of Doctrinal Diversity

Church Unity: The proliferation of doctrinal views has significant implications for church unity. Divergent beliefs can lead to schisms and the formation of new denominations, as groups seek to preserve what they perceive as true doctrine. This fragmentation often undermines the collective witness of the church, as Christians appear divided and contentious.

Ecumenical Efforts: Efforts to promote unity among different Christian traditions are often hampered by doctrinal differences. While ecumenical movements aim to find common ground and foster cooperation, deeply held theological convictions can create barriers to full communion. Successful ecumenical dialogues typically focus on shared beliefs and practical cooperation while respecting doctrinal distinctives.

Worship Practices: Doctrinal differences also influence worship practices. For instance, beliefs about the sacraments affect how and when they are administered, the structure of liturgy, and the overall worship experience. These variations can make it challenging for Christians from different traditions to worship together harmoniously.

Moral and Ethical Teachings: Divergent doctrinal views extend to moral and ethical teachings. Issues such as the role of women in ministry, the church's stance on social justice, and responses to contemporary cultural issues are often shaped by underlying theological beliefs. These differences can lead to varying approaches to ministry and social engagement.

Educational Approaches: Theological diversity impacts Christian education, as different denominations develop their own seminaries, Bible colleges, and curricula to train clergy and lay leaders. These institutions often emphasize their distinct doctrinal perspectives, reinforcing denominational identities and perpetuating theological differences.

Navigating Doctrinal Diversity

Promoting Dialogue: Encouraging open and respectful dialogue between different Christian traditions is essential for navigating doctrinal diversity. By engaging in honest conversations, Christians can better understand each other's perspectives and find common ground.

This dialogue should be rooted in a shared commitment to Scripture and the core tenets of the Christian faith.

Focusing on Essentials: One approach to fostering unity amidst diversity is to focus on the essential doctrines of the faith—those beliefs that are foundational to Christianity. By emphasizing what unites rather than what divides, Christians can work together more effectively and present a more cohesive witness to the world.

Respecting Differences: While striving for unity, it is also important to respect and appreciate the differences that exist within the body of Christ. These differences can enrich the church's understanding and practice of the faith, provided they are approached with humility and a spirit of mutual respect.

Collaborative Mission Work: Focusing on collaborative mission work and service can help bridge doctrinal divides. When Christians from different traditions join forces to address social issues, care for the needy, and spread the Gospel, they demonstrate the practical outworking of their faith and the unity that transcends theological differences.

Educating for Unity: Christian education should include a focus on unity and the importance of the whole body of Christ. Teaching about the history and reasons for doctrinal diversity, as well as the principles of respectful dialogue and cooperation, can prepare believers to engage constructively with those from different traditions.

The impact of diverse doctrinal views within Christianity is profound and multifaceted. While these differences reflect the richness of Christian thought and the freedom to interpret Scripture, they also pose significant challenges for unity and collective witness. By promoting dialogue, focusing on essential beliefs, respecting differences, engaging in collaborative mission work, and educating for unity, the church can navigate these challenges and work towards the unity that Christ prayed for.

Chapter 5: Analyzing the Roots of Division

Eisegesis and Its Consequences

Eisegesis, the process of interpreting a text by reading one's own ideas or biases into it, stands in stark contrast to exegesis, which seeks to draw out the text's original meaning. Within the realm of biblical interpretation, eisegesis has had profound and often detrimental consequences for the unity and doctrinal purity of the Christian church. By imposing personal or cultural perspectives onto the Scriptures, eisegesis distorts the intended message of the Bible and contributes significantly to the divisions within Christianity.

The Nature of Eisegesis

Eisegesis occurs when an interpreter projects their own presuppositions, desires, or cultural norms onto the biblical text, rather than allowing the text to speak for itself. This practice can stem from various motives, including the desire to validate pre-existing beliefs, the influence of contemporary cultural trends, or the aim to reconcile the Bible with modern scientific or philosophical viewpoints. Regardless of the motivation, eisegesis undermines the authority of Scripture by subjecting it to human interpretation rather than divine revelation.

Historical Examples of Eisegesis

Throughout church history, numerous examples of eisegesis can be identified, each illustrating the profound impact this practice has had on Christian doctrine and practice.

Allegorical Interpretation in the Early Church: One of the earliest forms of eisegesis can be seen in the allegorical interpretation of Scripture, which became popular in the Alexandrian school of

69

theology. Influenced by Greek philosophy, figures like Origen sought to uncover deeper, spiritual meanings behind the literal text. While this method aimed to highlight the spiritual significance of Scripture, it often led to speculative and subjective interpretations that diverged from the intended message of the biblical authors.

Medieval Scholasticism: During the medieval period, scholastic theologians such as Thomas Aquinas integrated Aristotelian philosophy with Christian doctrine. While Aquinas' work contributed significantly to Christian theology, his approach sometimes led to eisegetical readings that harmonized Scripture with philosophical concepts not originally present in the text. This blending of philosophy and theology introduced interpretations that were more reflective of human reasoning than divine revelation.

Liberal Theology and Higher Criticism: In the 19th and 20th centuries, the rise of liberal theology and higher criticism brought about new forms of eisegesis. The historical-critical method, which sought to analyze the Bible through the lens of historical and literary criticism, often approached the text with skepticism towards its supernatural elements. Scholars like Julius Wellhausen and Rudolf Bultmann reinterpreted biblical narratives in ways that downplayed or dismissed their divine inspiration. This approach frequently led to conclusions that were more aligned with modern secular thought than with traditional Christian doctrine.

The Consequences of Eisegesis

The practice of eisegesis has had far-reaching consequences for the Christian church, contributing to doctrinal confusion, fragmentation, and the erosion of biblical authority.

Doctrinal Confusion: Eisegesis introduces subjective interpretations that can lead to significant doctrinal confusion. When interpreters impose their own ideas onto the text, the clear and consistent message of Scripture becomes muddled. This confusion can result in contradictory teachings within the church, as different individuals or groups promote divergent interpretations based on their own eisegetical readings.

Fragmentation of the Church: The introduction of subjective interpretations has been a major factor in the fragmentation of the church. As individuals and groups adopt eisegetical methods to support their own doctrinal positions, they often break away from existing denominations to form new ones. This has led to the proliferation of denominations, each claiming to have the correct understanding of Scripture. The resulting divisions weaken the unity of the church and hinder its collective witness to the world.

Erosion of Biblical Authority: Eisegesis undermines the authority of the Bible by subjecting it to human interpretation. When interpreters impose their own views onto the text, they elevate their personal or cultural perspectives above the divinely inspired message of Scripture. This can lead to a diminished view of the Bible as the ultimate authority in matters of faith and practice. As the authority of Scripture erodes, the church becomes more susceptible to doctrinal error and moral compromise.

Contemporary Manifestations of Eisegesis

Eisegesis continues to manifest in various forms within contemporary Christianity, reflecting ongoing challenges in maintaining doctrinal purity and biblical fidelity.

Prosperity Gospel: One prominent example of modern eisegesis is the prosperity gospel, which teaches that faith in Christ will lead to financial success and physical well-being. Proponents of this doctrine often cherry-pick verses that seem to support their message, while ignoring the broader biblical context that emphasizes suffering, sacrifice, and the spiritual nature of true blessings. This eisegetical approach distorts the gospel and leads many believers to place their hope in material wealth rather than in Christ.

Cultural Accommodation: In an effort to remain relevant, some churches and theologians engage in eisegesis by accommodating contemporary cultural norms and values. This can be seen in debates over issues such as sexuality, gender roles, and social justice. While seeking to make the church more inclusive, this approach often results in interpretations that compromise biblical teachings. By imposing modern cultural perspectives onto the text, these interpreters risk distorting the timeless truths of Scripture.

Political Agendas: Eisegesis is also evident when Scripture is used to support specific political agendas. Individuals or groups may selectively interpret biblical passages to justify their political views, whether conservative or liberal. This politicization of the Bible can lead to a distorted understanding of its message and can alienate believers who hold different political perspectives. It also detracts from the church's primary mission of proclaiming the gospel and making disciples.

Addressing the Problem of Eisegesis

To overcome the divisions and distortions caused by eisegesis, the church must recommit to sound hermeneutical principles and prioritize exegetical methods that seek to uncover the original meaning of the biblical text.

Commitment to Exegesis: The church must prioritize exegesis, the careful and disciplined interpretation of Scripture that seeks to understand the text in its original historical and literary context. This involves using sound hermeneutical principles, such as considering the author's intent, the historical setting, and the genre of the text. By allowing the Bible to speak for itself, interpreters can avoid the pitfalls of eisegesis and uphold the authority of Scripture.

Hermeneutical Training: Providing training in hermeneutics and biblical interpretation is essential for equipping believers to engage in sound exegesis. This training should be incorporated into theological education for pastors and lay leaders, as well as within local church discipleship programs. By equipping believers with the tools to interpret Scripture accurately, the church can promote doctrinal unity and resist the influence of eisegetical interpretations.

Accountability and Peer Review: Encouraging accountability and peer review among theologians and pastors can help to guard against eisegesis. By fostering a culture of humility and openness to correction, interpreters can receive constructive feedback and ensure that their interpretations are aligned with sound exegesis. This collaborative approach can help to identify and address eisegetical tendencies before they take root.

Emphasis on Scriptural Authority: Reaffirming the authority of Scripture is crucial for countering the effects of eisegesis. The church must consistently emphasize that the Bible is the ultimate standard for faith and practice, and that personal or cultural perspectives must be subordinated to its teachings. This involves teaching believers to approach Scripture with reverence and a willingness to submit to its authority, even when its message challenges their preconceived notions.

Eisegesis, the practice of reading one's own ideas into the biblical text, has had significant and detrimental consequences for the unity and doctrinal purity of the Christian church. By introducing subjective interpretations, eisegesis has contributed to doctrinal confusion, the fragmentation of the church, and the erosion of biblical authority. Addressing this problem requires a recommitment to sound exegetical methods, hermeneutical training, accountability, and a steadfast emphasis on the authority of Scripture. By prioritizing these principles, the church can overcome the divisions caused by eisegesis and work towards greater unity and faithfulness to the teachings of Christ.

The Quest for Church Power and Control

The quest for power and control within the church has been a significant factor in the divisions and conflicts that have plagued Christianity throughout its history. From the early church's struggles with hierarchical authority to the medieval church's consolidation of power, and into the modern era's denominational conflicts, the desire for control has often overshadowed the church's mission and unity. This section will explore the historical and contemporary manifestations of this quest for power and its consequences for the church.

Early Church Struggles

The early Christian church, as depicted in the New Testament, began with a relatively simple and communal structure. Leadership was based on service, as exemplified by Jesus' washing of the disciples' feet (John 13:14-15) and His teachings about servant leadership (Matthew 20:25-28). The apostles and elders provided spiritual oversight, but the emphasis was on mutual submission and humility.

However, even in the early church, there were struggles for power and control. The apostle Paul frequently addressed issues of division and rivalry within the congregations. For example, in 1 Corinthians 1:10-13, Paul admonished the Corinthian church for their factions, each claiming allegiance to different leaders (Paul, Apollos, Cephas, or Christ). This early example illustrates how personal ambition and loyalty to human leaders can disrupt church unity.

The Rise of Hierarchical Structures

As Christianity spread and became more institutionalized, the church developed hierarchical structures to manage its growing complexity. Bishops emerged as key figures with authority over multiple congregations. This hierarchical model was seen as a way to maintain order and doctrinal purity, but it also created opportunities for power struggles.

By the fourth century, the consolidation of church authority became more pronounced with the conversion of Emperor Constantine and the subsequent establishment of Christianity as the state religion of the Roman Empire. The church's alignment with political power brought significant benefits, such as the end of persecution and the ability to influence societal norms. However, it also led to the church's increasing entanglement with political affairs and the pursuit of power.

The Council of Nicaea in 325 C.E., convened by Constantine, was a pivotal moment in this process. The council sought to address the Arian controversy and establish doctrinal unity, but it also reinforced the authority of the bishops and the emperor's role in church matters.

The development of creeds and the centralization of ecclesiastical authority marked the beginning of a more hierarchical and controlled church structure.

Medieval Church Power and Control

The medieval period saw the apex of the church's temporal power, particularly in the Western Roman Catholic Church. The papacy emerged as the central authority, with the Pope asserting supremacy over both spiritual and temporal matters. This period was characterized by significant power struggles, both within the church hierarchy and between the church and secular rulers.

The Investiture Controversy of the 11th and 12th centuries exemplifies the struggle for control between the papacy and European monarchs. This conflict centered on who had the authority to appoint bishops and abbots. The Concordat of Worms in 1122 eventually resolved the dispute by delineating the powers of the church and the state, but it underscored the church's desire to maintain control over its appointments and influence.

The Crusades, beginning in 1095 C.E., further illustrate the church's quest for power. Ostensibly launched to reclaim the Holy Land from Muslim control, the Crusades were also driven by the church's desire to expand its influence and consolidate its power. The violent and often politically motivated nature of the Crusades demonstrated the extent to which the church had departed from its original mission of spreading the Gospel and serving others.

The Reformation and the Response to Power Abuse

The abuses of power within the medieval church were a major catalyst for the Reformation in the 16th century. Reformers such as Martin Luther, John Calvin, and Huldrych Zwingli criticized the corruption and moral decay of the Catholic Church, particularly the sale of indulgences, simony, and the extravagant lifestyles of the clergy. They called for a return to the authority of Scripture and a rejection of the hierarchical and autocratic structures that had developed.

Luther's posting of the Ninety-Five Theses in 1517 C.E. marked the beginning of a movement that sought to dismantle the entrenched power structures of the church. The Reformation led to the establishment of various Protestant denominations, each with its own governance models that sought to avoid the centralization of power seen in the Catholic Church. However, the fragmentation of the church also introduced new challenges for unity and cooperation.

The Catholic Church's response to the Reformation, known as the Counter-Reformation, included efforts to reform internal abuses and reaffirm core doctrines. The Council of Trent (1545-1563 C.E.) played a significant role in addressing issues of corruption and standardizing church practices. While these reforms were necessary, they also reinforced the hierarchical structures and central authority of the papacy, maintaining the church's control over its followers.

Modern Denominational Conflicts

In the modern era, the quest for power and control continues to manifest in various ways within different Christian denominations. Denominational splits often arise from disagreements over doctrinal, moral, or governance issues. These conflicts can be exacerbated by the ambitions of leaders seeking to establish their own authority or doctrinal purity.

For example, the 20th century saw significant schisms within mainline Protestant denominations over issues such as biblical inerrancy, the role of women in ministry, and responses to social and ethical issues. The Southern Baptist Convention experienced a conservative resurgence in the late 20th century, driven by a desire to reassert traditional theological positions and gain control over denominational institutions.

Similarly, within the Anglican Communion, conflicts over issues such as the unbiblical ordination of women and LGBTQ+ inclusion have led to the formation of breakaway movements and new alignments. These disputes often reflect deeper struggles for control over the direction and identity of the church. In these cases, you have those who seek to separate themselves from an unbiblical denomination.

The Consequences of the Quest for Power

The quest for power and control within the church has several detrimental consequences:

Division and Fragmentation: The pursuit of power often leads to division and fragmentation within the church. As leaders and factions vie for control, they may prioritize their own agendas over the unity and well-being of the church. This results in the proliferation of denominations and independent movements, each claiming to represent the true faith.

Erosion of Witness: The church's witness to the world is weakened by internal power struggles and divisions. When non-believers see Christians fighting for control and influence, it undermines the credibility of the Gospel message. Jesus emphasized that unity among His followers would be a powerful testimony to the world (John 17:21), but the quest for power often works against this ideal.

Moral and Spiritual Corruption: The desire for control can lead to moral and spiritual corruption within the church. Leaders who prioritize power over service may engage in unethical or manipulative behavior to achieve their goals. This corruption can manifest in various forms, from financial misconduct to abuse of authority.

Distraction from Mission: The church's primary mission of spreading the Gospel and making disciples can be overshadowed by internal power struggles. When resources and energy are diverted towards maintaining or gaining control, less attention is given to evangelism, discipleship, and social justice.

Moving Towards Servant Leadership

To address the issues arising from the quest for power, the church must recommit to the principles of servant leadership exemplified by

Jesus and the apostles. This involves a shift from seeking control to prioritizing service, humility, and the well-being of the community.

Emphasizing Servant Leadership: Church leaders must model servant leadership, prioritizing the needs of their congregations and communities over personal ambition. This involves a commitment to humility, transparency, and accountability. Leaders should be willing to relinquish control and empower others to serve and lead.

Promoting Shared Governance: Developing shared governance structures can help to mitigate the concentration of power within the church. This includes fostering a collaborative approach to decision-making, where multiple voices and perspectives are considered. Congregational and presbyterian models of governance can provide a framework for shared leadership and accountability.

Fostering a Culture of Humility: Cultivating a culture of humility within the church is essential for addressing the quest for power. This involves teaching and practicing the biblical principles of humility, submission, and mutual respect. By prioritizing these values, the church can create an environment where power is seen as a means to serve rather than dominate.

Focusing on Mission: The church must remain focused on its primary mission of proclaiming the Gospel and making disciples. This involves aligning resources and efforts towards evangelism, discipleship, and social engagement, rather than internal power struggles. By keeping the mission at the forefront, the church can avoid the distractions and divisions that arise from the quest for control.

The quest for power and control has been a significant factor in the divisions and conflicts within Christianity throughout its history. From the early church to the modern era, the desire for control has often overshadowed the church's mission and unity. Addressing this issue requires a recommitment to servant leadership, shared governance, humility, and a focus on the church's primary mission. By prioritizing these principles, the church can overcome the divisions caused by the quest for power and work towards greater unity and faithfulness to the teachings of Christ.

The Misuse of the Term "Church" vs. "Congregation"

The terminology used to describe the body of believers in Christ plays a significant role in shaping both theological understanding and practical application of Christian principles. One of the fundamental issues contributing to division within Christianity is the misuse of the term "church" as opposed to "congregation." This distinction, seemingly subtle, carries profound implications for how believers perceive their identity, mission, and structure.

Historical and Biblical Context

In the New Testament, the Greek word "ekklesia" is commonly translated as "church" in most English Bibles. However, "ekklesia" more accurately means "assembly" or "congregation." This term was used to describe a gathering of people called out for a specific purpose. In the context of the New Testament, it referred to the community of believers in Jesus Christ, both at the local level (a specific assembly of believers) and at the universal level (all believers everywhere).

The translation of "ekklesia" as "church" has its roots in historical developments and linguistic choices that have shaped Christian thought and practice. The English word "church" is derived from the Greek "kuriakos," meaning "belonging to the Lord." While this term is not inherently incorrect, its usage over time has evolved to convey connotations that differ from the original intent of "ekklesia."

Theological Implications

The misuse of the term "church" can lead to several theological misunderstandings:

Institutional Focus: The term "church" has come to be associated with buildings, denominations, and institutional structures. This institutional focus can detract from the biblical emphasis on the community of believers. When believers think of the "church" primarily as a building or an organization, they may neglect the relational and communal aspects that are central to the New Testament concept of "ekklesia."

Hierarchical Structures: The institutional connotation of "church" often brings with it hierarchical structures of authority and control. While leadership and organization are necessary for any community, the New Testament model emphasizes servant leadership and mutual submission (Matthew 20:25-28; Ephesians 5:21). The misuse of "church" can lead to power dynamics that are contrary to the teachings of Jesus and the apostles.

Clericalism: Another consequence of this misuse is the rise of clericalism, where ordained ministers are seen as the primary or sole mediators between God and the congregation. This can create a divide between clergy and laity, undermining the priesthood of all believers (1 Peter 2:9) and the idea that all members of the congregation have important roles to play in the body of Christ (1 Corinthians 12:12-27).

Practical Consequences

The practical consequences of misusing the term "church" are evident in various aspects of Christian life and ministry:

Building-Centered Worship: Many Christians equate the "church" with a physical building, leading to an overemphasis on the location and structure of worship rather than the gathering of believers. This can result in significant resources being allocated to maintaining and building physical structures at the expense of mission and ministry.

Denominational Divisions: The term "church" is often used to distinguish between different denominations, reinforcing divisions rather than promoting unity. When believers identify more strongly with their denominational "church" than with the universal body of Christ, it can lead to sectarianism and a lack of cooperation among different Christian groups.

Disempowerment of Laity: The institutional and hierarchical connotations of "church" can disempower the laity, making them feel less responsible for the ministry and mission of the congregation. This can lead to a passive approach to faith, where members rely on the clergy to perform the work of the ministry rather than actively participating themselves.

Reclaiming "Congregation" and "Assembly"

To address these issues, it is important to reclaim the biblical understanding of "ekklesia" as "congregation" or "assembly." This involves a shift in language and mindset that emphasizes the community and mission of believers.

Emphasizing Community: Using the term "congregation" helps to highlight the relational aspect of the Christian community. It reminds believers that they are part of a family of faith, called to love, support, and encourage one another (Hebrews 10:24-25). This emphasis on community fosters a sense of belonging and mutual responsibility.

Focusing on Mission: The term "assembly" underscores the purpose for which believers are gathered. The congregation is called to be a light to the world, proclaiming the gospel and making disciples (Matthew 28:19-20). This mission-focused perspective encourages believers to engage actively in evangelism, social justice, and service.

Promoting Shared Leadership: Reclaiming the biblical terms can also promote shared leadership within the congregation. By recognizing that all believers are part of the priesthood, the congregation can foster a culture where everyone's gifts and contributions are valued (Romans 12:4-8; Ephesians 4:11-13). This shared leadership model aligns with the New Testament teachings on servant leadership and mutual edification.

Overcoming the Institutional Mindset

Shifting from an institutional mindset to a congregational mindset requires intentional effort and teaching:

Biblical Teaching: Pastors and leaders need to teach the biblical meaning of "ekklesia" and its implications for church life. This involves correcting misconceptions about the church as a building or an institution and emphasizing the relational and missional aspects of the congregation.

Language Shift: Encouraging the use of terms like "congregation" and "assembly" in place of "church" can help to change mindsets over time. This linguistic shift can reinforce the theological and practical emphasis on community and mission.

Structural Changes: Implementing structural changes that promote shared leadership and community involvement can help to overcome the institutional mindset. This may include creating opportunities for lay members to lead ministries, participate in decision-making, and use their gifts in service.

Cultural Transformation: Finally, fostering a culture of humility, service, and mutual respect within the congregation is essential. This cultural transformation involves modeling servant leadership, valuing each member's contribution, and prioritizing relationships over programs and structures.

The misuse of the term "church" versus "congregation" has significant theological and practical implications for the body of Christ. By reclaiming the biblical terms "congregation" and "assembly," Christians can foster a greater sense of community, mission, and shared leadership. This shift requires intentional teaching, language changes, structural adjustments, and cultural transformation. By aligning more closely with the New Testament vision of "ekklesia," the church can overcome divisions and fulfill its calling to be a unified and vibrant community of believers.

Going Beyond Scriptural Positions of Pastor, Elder, and Overseer with Religious Titles for Power and Prestige

One of the significant issues contributing to division and corruption within the Christian church is the misuse and expansion of religious titles beyond the scriptural positions of pastor, elder, and overseer. This practice often stems from a desire for power, prestige, and control, which contradicts the biblical model of humble, servant leadership. Understanding the scriptural basis for church leadership and the dangers of deviating from it is essential for addressing this root cause of division.

Scriptural Positions of Leadership

The New Testament outlines specific roles for church leadership, primarily using the terms pastor (shepherd), elder (presbyter), and overseer (bishop). These roles are not hierarchical but are meant to function collaboratively within the body of Christ.

Pastor (Shepherd): The term "pastor" comes from the Greek word "poimen," which means shepherd. This role emphasizes caring for and guiding the flock, as seen in passages such as Ephesians 4:11 and 1 Peter 5:2-3. Pastors are called to nurture and protect the spiritual well-being of the congregation, modeling their ministry after Jesus, the Good Shepherd (John 10:11).

Elder (Presbyter): The term "elder" is derived from the Greek word "presbyteros," which indicates a mature and respected leader within the church. Elders are responsible for teaching, governing, and providing spiritual oversight. Key passages include 1 Timothy 3:1-7 and Titus 1:5-9, which outline the qualifications and duties of elders.

Overseer (Bishop): The Greek word "episkopos," translated as overseer or bishop, conveys the idea of someone who watches over the congregation. This role is closely associated with that of an elder and often used interchangeably in the New Testament (Acts 20:28; 1 Peter 5:1-2). Overseers are tasked with ensuring doctrinal purity and the proper functioning of the church.

These roles emphasize servanthood, humility, and mutual accountability, aligning with Jesus' teachings on leadership (Matthew 20:25-28).

The Expansion of Religious Titles

Over time, the simplicity and humility of these scriptural roles have been overshadowed by the creation of numerous religious titles and positions. This expansion often reflects a desire for authority, recognition, and influence, rather than a commitment to biblical leadership principles.

Historical Development: The early church maintained a relatively simple structure, with local congregations led by a plurality of elders. However, as the church grew and became institutionalized, hierarchical structures emerged. The development of the papacy in the Roman Catholic Church, for instance, introduced titles such as pope, cardinal, and archbishop, which were not present in the New Testament.

Modern Examples: In contemporary Christianity, many denominations and independent churches have continued to introduce titles and positions that extend beyond the biblical framework. Titles such as reverend, doctor, apostle, and prophet are frequently used to confer status and authority. While some of these titles may reflect genuine ministry roles, they can also lead to an unhealthy focus on prestige and hierarchy.

Consequences of Misusing Titles

The expansion and misuse of religious titles have several negative consequences for the church:

Hierarchical Control: The creation of hierarchical structures can lead to centralized control and a top-down approach to ministry. This undermines the New Testament model of shared leadership and mutual submission. It can also create an environment where decisions are made by a few individuals, often disconnected from the needs and perspectives of the congregation.

Clericalism: Elevating certain titles and positions above others fosters clericalism, where ordained leaders are seen as spiritually superior to lay members. This division can discourage lay participation and create a passive congregation that relies excessively on clergy for spiritual guidance and ministry.

Division and Competition: The pursuit of titles and positions can lead to competition and division within the church. Leaders may seek to advance their careers or reputations rather than focusing on serving others. This ambition can result in factions and power struggles, detracting from the church's unity and mission.

Erosion of Servant Leadership: The focus on titles and prestige undermines the biblical principle of servant leadership. Jesus taught that true greatness comes from serving others, not from seeking status

(Mark 10:42-45). When leaders prioritize their titles and authority, they fail to model the humility and selflessness that Jesus exemplified.

Addressing the Issue

To overcome the problems associated with the misuse of religious titles, the church must return to the scriptural principles of leadership and foster a culture of humility and service.

Reaffirming Biblical Roles: Churches should emphasize the biblical roles of pastor, elder, and overseer, as outlined in the New Testament. This involves teaching and reinforcing the qualifications and responsibilities of these positions, as well as promoting a collaborative and non-hierarchical approach to leadership.

Eliminating Unnecessary Titles: Where possible, churches should eliminate titles that do not align with the New Testament model. This may involve reevaluating the use of honorifics such as reverend or doctor and focusing instead on the function and character of leadership. By simplifying titles, the church can reduce the emphasis on status and authority.

Promoting Servant Leadership: Leaders must model servant leadership, prioritizing the needs of the congregation over their own ambitions. This involves demonstrating humility, transparency, and a willingness to serve in practical ways. Training programs and mentorship can help develop these qualities in current and future leaders.

Encouraging Lay Participation: To combat clericalism, churches should encourage active participation and ministry by lay members. This includes recognizing and valuing the diverse gifts and contributions of all believers (1 Corinthians 12:4-7). By empowering lay members, the church can foster a more inclusive and dynamic community.

Cultivating a Culture of Humility: Teaching and practicing humility is essential for addressing the quest for titles and prestige. This involves creating a church culture that values character over credentials and service over status. Regularly highlighting examples of humble and selfless leadership can inspire others to follow suit.

The misuse of religious titles beyond the scriptural positions of pastor, elder, and overseer has led to significant issues within the church, including hierarchical control, clericalism, division, and the erosion of servant leadership. Addressing these problems requires a return to the biblical principles of leadership, the elimination of unnecessary titles, the promotion of servant leadership, and the encouragement of lay participation. By fostering a culture of humility and service, the church can overcome the divisions caused by the quest for power and prestige and better fulfill its mission to be a unified body of believers.

Chapter 6: The Poison of Higher Criticism

The Emergence and Impact of Biblical Criticism

The rise of biblical criticism, particularly higher criticism, represents one of the most significant challenges to the authority and integrity of the Bible in modern times. Emerging in the Enlightenment era and flourishing in the 19th and 20th centuries, higher criticism seeks to analyze the Bible through the lens of historical and literary methodologies. While these approaches aim to uncover the historical context and development of the biblical texts, they often result in undermining the divine inspiration and reliability of Scripture. This chapter will examine the origins, methodologies, and profound impact of higher criticism, highlighting its weaknesses and the dangers it poses to Christian faith and doctrine.

The Emergence of Higher Criticism

Higher criticism, also known as the historical-critical method, emerged during the Enlightenment, a period characterized by a strong emphasis on reason, scientific inquiry, and skepticism of traditional authorities, including the Bible. Influential figures in the development of higher criticism include German scholars such as Johann Salomo Semler, Julius Wellhausen, and Rudolf Bultmann.

Johann Salomo Semler (1725-1791): Often regarded as the father of historical criticism, Semler introduced the idea that the Bible should be studied like any other ancient document. He distinguished between the divine content of Scripture and the human elements that he believed had been added over time.

Julius Wellhausen (1844-1918): Wellhausen is best known for his Documentary Hypothesis, which proposed that the Pentateuch (the first five books of the Bible) was not authored by Moses but was a compilation of four distinct sources (J, E, P, and D) written by different authors over several centuries. This hypothesis challenged the traditional view of Mosaic authorship and suggested that the Pentateuch was a product of evolving religious ideas rather than divine revelation.

Rudolf Bultmann (1884-1976): Bultmann advocated for "demythologizing" the New Testament, arguing that the supernatural elements of the biblical narratives should be stripped away to reveal the existential truths they contain. His approach questioned the historical reliability of the Gospels and the reality of the miracles and resurrection of Jesus.

Methodologies of Higher Criticism

Higher criticism employs several methodologies, each with its own assumptions and objectives. These methodologies often reflect a naturalistic and secular worldview, which can lead to biased interpretations of the biblical text.

Source Criticism: This method seeks to identify the various sources that were allegedly combined to form the biblical books. The Documentary Hypothesis is a prime example of source criticism. By dissecting the text into hypothetical sources, source criticism often undermines the unity and coherence of Scripture.

Form Criticism: Form criticism analyzes the literary forms and genres within the biblical text to uncover the pre-literary traditions that supposedly influenced its composition. Scholars like Hermann Gunkel applied this method to the Psalms and the Genesis narratives, arguing that these texts evolved from earlier oral traditions and communal practices.

Redaction Criticism: Redaction criticism focuses on the editorial process that shaped the final form of the biblical text. It examines how redactors (editors) may have altered or combined sources to promote particular theological agendas. This method can lead to the conclusion that the biblical text is a product of human manipulation rather than divine inspiration.

Tradition Criticism: This approach seeks to trace the development of theological ideas and traditions within the biblical text. It often assumes that these traditions evolved over time and were influenced by the surrounding cultures, thereby questioning the originality and uniqueness of biblical revelation.

The Impact of Higher Criticism

The methodologies of higher criticism have had profound and often detrimental effects on biblical interpretation, Christian theology, and the faith of believers.

Undermining Biblical Authority: By approaching the Bible as a purely human document, higher criticism undermines its divine authority. If the Bible is seen as a product of human authors with varying agendas, its claim to be the inspired Word of God is weakened. This erosion of authority can lead to skepticism and doubt about the reliability and truthfulness of Scripture.

Erosion of Doctrinal Foundations: Higher criticism challenges key doctrines of the Christian faith, such as the inspiration of Scripture, the historicity of biblical events, and the divinity of Jesus Christ. For example, if the resurrection of Jesus is interpreted as a myth rather than a historical event, the foundation of Christian hope and salvation is compromised (1 Corinthians 15:14).

Distancing Believers from Truth: By promoting a skeptical and naturalistic view of the Bible, higher criticism can distance believers from the truth of God's Word. It encourages an approach to Scripture that prioritizes human reason and scholarly consensus over faith and divine revelation. This can lead to a weakened faith and a diminished confidence in the transformative power of Scripture.

Reinforcing Scholar Biases: Higher criticism often reflects the biases and presuppositions of its proponents. Scholars who approach the Bible with a naturalistic worldview are likely to interpret it in ways that align with their assumptions. This can result in interpretations that are more reflective of modern scholarly trends than the intended message of the biblical authors.

Weaknesses of Higher Criticism

Despite its influence, higher criticism has several significant weaknesses that call into question its validity and usefulness.

Speculative Nature: Much of higher criticism is based on speculation and hypothetical reconstructions. The identification of sources, editorial processes, and pre-literary traditions often relies on subjective judgments rather than concrete evidence. This speculative nature makes higher criticism inherently unstable and open to continual revision.

Lack of Consensus: Higher criticism has not led to a scholarly consensus on many issues. Competing theories and interpretations abound, with scholars often disagreeing on key points. This lack of consensus highlights the subjective and uncertain nature of higher criticism, undermining its claim to provide definitive insights into the biblical text.

Dismissal of Supernatural Elements: Higher criticism's naturalistic bias leads to a dismissal of the supernatural elements of the Bible. Miracles, prophecies, and divine interventions are often explained away or reinterpreted in naturalistic terms. This approach fails to take seriously the Bible's own claims about the supernatural work of God in history.

Disconnection from the Church: Higher criticism is often practiced in academic settings that are disconnected from the faith and life of the church. This can result in interpretations that are more aligned with secular scholarship than with the theological and pastoral needs of the Christian community. The gap between academic biblical criticism and the church's reading of Scripture can lead to confusion and disillusionment among believers.

The Conservative Response

In response to the challenges posed by higher criticism, conservative scholars and theologians emphasize the importance of a historical-grammatical approach to biblical interpretation. This method seeks to understand the text in its original context, considering the historical, cultural, and linguistic factors that shaped its composition. However, it does so with a commitment to the divine inspiration and authority of Scripture.

Affirming Inspiration and Inerrancy: Conservative scholars affirm the inspiration and inerrancy of the Bible, holding that the Scriptures are God's Word and are therefore true and trustworthy in all they affirm. This belief provides a foundation for interpreting the Bible with confidence in its reliability and relevance.

Emphasizing Contextual Understanding: The historical-grammatical method prioritizes understanding the Bible in its historical and literary context. By considering the original audience, cultural background, and literary forms, interpreters can uncover the intended meaning of the text without imposing modern biases.

Engaging with Scholarship: Conservative scholars engage critically with the findings of higher criticism, recognizing the value of historical and literary analysis while rejecting the naturalistic assumptions that often underlie it. This balanced approach allows for rigorous scholarship that respects the divine nature of the Bible.

Strengthening Faith and Practice: By affirming the authority and reliability of Scripture, conservative interpretation seeks to strengthen the faith and practice of believers. It encourages a reading of the Bible that is both intellectually rigorous and spiritually nourishing, fostering a deeper relationship with God and a greater commitment to living out His Word.

The emergence and impact of higher criticism have posed significant challenges to the authority and integrity of the Bible. By treating Scripture as a purely human document, higher criticism undermines its divine inspiration and fosters skepticism and doubt. Despite its influence, higher criticism is marked by speculation, a lack of consensus, and a dismissal of the supernatural. In response, conservative scholars advocate for a historical-grammatical approach that affirms the inspiration and inerrancy of the Bible, emphasizing contextual understanding and engaging critically with scholarship. By upholding the authority of Scripture and promoting a faithful interpretation, the church can counter the divisive effects of higher criticism and remain steadfast in its commitment to the truth of God's Word.

Turning God's Word into Man's Word

The fundamental issue with higher criticism is its transformation of God's Word into man's word. This approach, rooted in Enlightenment thinking and modernist philosophy, fundamentally shifts the understanding of Scripture from divine revelation to a human product. Such a shift undermines the Bible's authority, reliability, and spiritual power. It distances believers from the truth and replaces divine inspiration with human interpretation. This section will explore how higher criticism accomplishes this transformation and the profound implications it has for Christian faith and practice.

The Philosophical Foundations of Higher Criticism

Higher criticism is deeply influenced by Enlightenment principles, which emphasize human reason, empirical evidence, and skepticism of traditional authorities. These principles laid the groundwork for questioning the supernatural elements of Scripture and treating it as a purely human artifact.

Rationalism and Naturalism: Enlightenment rationalism asserts that human reason is the primary source of knowledge and truth. Naturalism, which denies the supernatural, posits that all phenomena can be explained by natural causes and laws. These philosophies underpin higher criticism's approach to the Bible, leading scholars to scrutinize biblical texts with a skeptical eye, often rejecting miracles, prophecies, and divine inspiration.

Secularism and Humanism: The rise of secularism and humanism further contributed to the development of higher criticism. Secularism seeks to separate religious faith from public life and scholarship, while humanism places humanity at the center of all inquiry. This shift in focus encourages an interpretation of the Bible that prioritizes human perspectives and historical context over theological and spiritual truths.

Methodologies that Undermine Divine Inspiration

The methodologies employed by higher criticism often reflect these philosophical biases, treating the Bible as a collection of human writings rather than the inspired Word of God.

Source Criticism: This method attempts to identify the various sources that compose biblical texts. For example, the Documentary Hypothesis suggests that the Pentateuch is derived from four distinct sources (J, E, P, and D), each with its own theological agenda. This approach implies that the Bible is a patchwork of human documents rather than a unified divine revelation. By focusing on hypothetical sources, source criticism undermines the integrity and coherence of the biblical text.

Form Criticism: Form criticism analyzes the literary forms and genres within the Bible, seeking to reconstruct the pre-literary traditions that supposedly influenced its composition. This method often assumes that biblical narratives evolved from earlier myths, legends, or communal practices. By emphasizing these supposed human origins, form criticism diminishes the Bible's claim to divine revelation and historical reliability.

Redaction Criticism: Redaction criticism examines how editors (redactors) shaped and modified biblical texts to promote specific theological viewpoints. This approach suggests that the final form of the Bible is the result of human editing and manipulation rather than divine inspiration. It casts doubt on the authenticity and authority of the biblical message, portraying it as the product of human agendas.

Tradition Criticism: Tradition criticism traces the development of theological ideas within the Bible, often suggesting that these ideas evolved over time under the influence of surrounding cultures. This perspective implies that biblical theology is not unique or divinely revealed but is instead a human construct shaped by historical circumstances.

The Consequences of Turning God's Word into Man's Word

The transformation of God's Word into man's word through higher criticism has far-reaching consequences for the church and individual believers.

Erosion of Authority: When the Bible is viewed as a human product, its authority is significantly weakened. If Scripture is merely a collection of ancient writings subject to human error and revision, it loses its power to command belief and obedience. This erosion of authority leads to a relativistic approach to truth, where biblical teachings are seen as one option among many rather than the definitive revelation of God's will.

Undermining Faith: Higher criticism fosters skepticism and doubt about the Bible's reliability. By questioning the historicity of biblical events and the authenticity of its teachings, higher criticism can lead believers to doubt the foundational truths of their faith. This doubt undermines confidence in the Bible's promises and diminishes its role as a source of spiritual guidance and comfort.

Fragmentation of Doctrine: The emphasis on human sources and editorial processes often results in a fragmented view of Scripture. Higher criticism encourages the belief that different parts of the Bible reflect conflicting theological perspectives, leading to doctrinal confusion and division. This fragmentation undermines the unity and coherence of Christian doctrine, making it difficult for believers to discern and uphold the core truths of their faith.

Secularization of Theology: By prioritizing human reason and historical analysis over divine revelation, higher criticism contributes to the secularization of theology. This approach encourages theologians to interpret the Bible through a secular lens, often downplaying or rejecting its supernatural elements. The result is a theology that is more concerned with cultural relevance and academic respectability than with faithfully proclaiming the gospel.

Distancing from Truth: Higher criticism's naturalistic and humanistic assumptions distance biblical interpretation from the truth.

By rejecting the Bible's own claims about its divine origin and supernatural content, higher criticism leads scholars and believers away from the true meaning and purpose of Scripture. This distancing from truth weakens the transformative power of the Bible and diminishes its role in the life of the church.

A Conservative Response to Higher Criticism

To counter the negative impact of higher criticism, conservative scholars and theologians advocate for a return to the historical-grammatical method of biblical interpretation. This approach seeks to understand the text in its original context while affirming its divine inspiration and authority.

Affirming Divine Inspiration: Conservative scholars uphold the belief that the Bible is the inspired Word of God, true and trustworthy in all it affirms. This conviction provides a foundation for interpreting Scripture with confidence in its reliability and relevance. By affirming divine inspiration, conservative interpreters resist the tendency to view the Bible as a mere human product.

Contextual Understanding: The historical-grammatical method emphasizes understanding the Bible in its historical and literary context. This approach considers the original audience, cultural background, and linguistic features of the text, allowing interpreters to uncover the intended meaning of the biblical authors. By prioritizing context, conservative scholars avoid speculative reconstructions and maintain the integrity of the biblical message.

Respect for the Text: Conservative interpretation respects the unity and coherence of Scripture. Rather than dissecting the Bible into hypothetical sources and editorial layers, conservative scholars approach it as a unified and divinely inspired whole. This respect for the text fosters a holistic understanding of biblical theology and doctrine.

Engaging with Scholarship: While rejecting the naturalistic assumptions of higher criticism, conservative scholars engage critically with its findings. They recognize the value of historical and literary analysis while maintaining a commitment to the divine nature of

Scripture. This balanced approach allows for rigorous scholarship that respects both the human and divine aspects of the Bible.

Strengthening Faith: By affirming the authority and reliability of Scripture, conservative interpretation seeks to strengthen the faith and practice of believers. It encourages a reading of the Bible that is both intellectually rigorous and spiritually nourishing, fostering a deeper relationship with God and a greater commitment to living out His Word.

Higher criticism represents a significant challenge to the authority and integrity of the Bible, transforming God's Word into man's word through its naturalistic and humanistic methodologies. This approach undermines the divine inspiration and reliability of Scripture, fostering skepticism, doctrinal fragmentation, and secularization. In response, conservative scholars advocate for the historical-grammatical method, which affirms the Bible's divine inspiration, respects its unity, and engages critically with scholarship. By upholding the authority of Scripture and promoting a faithful interpretation, the church can counter the divisive effects of higher criticism and remain steadfast in its commitment to the truth of God's Word.

Interpretive Translations and Their Detrimental Effects

The task of Bible translation carries immense responsibility, as it involves conveying the inspired words of God accurately and faithfully. However, the rise of interpretive translations has introduced significant challenges and detrimental effects on how the Bible is understood and applied. Interpretive translations, also known as dynamic equivalence or thought-for-thought translations, prioritize conveying the meaning or intent behind the original text rather than translating the exact words. While this approach aims to make the Bible more accessible and understandable, it often leads to distortions of the original message and undermines the authority of Scripture. This chapter will explore the nature of interpretive translations, their detrimental effects, and the importance of adhering to a literal translation philosophy.

The Nature of Interpretive Translations

Interpretive translations seek to render the ideas and concepts expressed in the original text in a way that is thought to be more comprehensible to contemporary readers. This approach contrasts with formal equivalence, or word-for-word translation, which strives to stay as close as possible to the original wording and structure of the biblical text.

Dynamic Equivalence: Dynamic equivalence, pioneered by Eugene Nida, emphasizes the need to translate the "meaning" or "message" of the text rather than its exact wording. This method allows translators to adjust the language, idioms, and expressions to fit the cultural and linguistic context of the target audience. While it aims to make the Bible more readable, it often involves significant interpretive decisions that can introduce bias and subjectivity.

Paraphrasing: Paraphrasing takes dynamic equivalence a step further by rephrasing entire passages to capture what the translator believes is the underlying message. Paraphrased translations, such as The Message by Eugene Peterson, prioritize readability and relatability over fidelity to the original text. This approach can significantly alter the nuances and details of Scripture, leading to misinterpretations and doctrinal errors.

Detrimental Effects of Interpretive Translations

Interpretive translations can have several detrimental effects on the understanding and application of Scripture. These effects include the introduction of translator bias, loss of textual precision, and erosion of biblical authority.

Introduction of Translator Bias: By prioritizing the translator's interpretation of the text's meaning, interpretive translations inevitably introduce the translator's theological and cultural biases. These biases can shape how key doctrines and teachings are presented, potentially leading readers away from the intended message of the biblical authors. For example, interpretations of gender roles, eschatology, and soteriology can vary widely based on the translator's perspective, resulting in a skewed presentation of Scripture.

Loss of Textual Precision: Interpretive translations often sacrifice the precision and specificity of the original text for the sake of readability. This can lead to the loss of important theological and doctrinal nuances. For instance, the Greek word "logos" in John 1:1 is rich with philosophical and theological meaning, yet interpretive translations might simplify it to "word" without capturing its full depth. Such simplifications can obscure the richness of biblical revelation and hinder a deeper understanding of Scripture.

Erosion of Biblical Authority: When translations prioritize the translator's interpretation over the exact words of the text, the authority of Scripture is undermined. Readers may come to see the Bible as a flexible document open to various interpretations rather than the definitive Word of God. This erosion of authority can lead to relativism, where personal interpretations are valued over the objective truth of Scripture. It also weakens the church's ability to teach and defend sound doctrine based on the clear and authoritative words of the Bible.

Confusion and Division: The proliferation of interpretive translations contributes to confusion and division within the church. With so many versions offering different interpretations, believers may struggle to discern which translation accurately represents the original text. This can lead to disputes over doctrinal matters and hinder the church's unity. It also makes it challenging for believers to engage in meaningful Bible study and theological discussions when different translations present conflicting messages.

The Importance of Literal Translation Philosophy

To counter the detrimental effects of interpretive translations, it is essential to adhere to a literal translation philosophy. Literal translations, also known as formal equivalence translations, strive to convey the exact words and structure of the original text as closely as possible. This approach respects the inspiration and authority of

Scripture and ensures that the translator's role is to faithfully transmit God's Word rather than interpret it.

Accuracy and Fidelity: Literal translations prioritize accuracy and fidelity to the original text. By staying close to the original wording and syntax, literal translations preserve the nuances and details that are essential for sound exegesis and theological understanding. This approach allows readers to engage with the text in a way that is faithful to the intentions of the biblical authors and the divine inspiration behind their words.

Respect for Divine Inspiration: A literal translation philosophy recognizes the divine inspiration of Scripture and respects the original languages in which the Bible was written. By faithfully rendering the text, translators acknowledge that the Bible's words are not merely human expressions but the very words of God. This respect for divine inspiration reinforces the authority of Scripture and upholds its role as the ultimate standard for faith and practice.

Consistency and Clarity: Literal translations provide consistency and clarity in biblical interpretation. By avoiding interpretive paraphrasing, literal translations present a clear and consistent message that allows readers to develop a coherent understanding of Scripture. This consistency is crucial for systematic theology, doctrinal teaching, and personal Bible study. It ensures that believers can rely on their translation as a trustworthy guide for understanding and applying God's Word.

Empowerment of Readers: A literal translation philosophy empowers readers to engage directly with the biblical text. By providing a faithful rendering of the original words, literal translations enable readers to interpret Scripture for themselves under the guidance of the Holy Spirit. This approach fosters a deeper and more personal relationship with God's Word and encourages believers to seek the truth with diligence and discernment.

Interpretive translations, while aiming to make the Bible more accessible, often introduce significant distortions and undermine the authority of Scripture. By prioritizing the translator's interpretation over the exact words of the text, these translations introduce bias, sacrifice textual precision, and erode biblical authority. To counter these detrimental effects, it is essential to adhere to a literal translation philosophy that respects the divine inspiration of Scripture and faithfully conveys its original words. By upholding the accuracy and fidelity of the biblical text, the church can ensure that believers have a trustworthy guide for understanding and living out God's Word.

Chapter 7: Textual Criticism and the Search for Original Words

The Importance of Textual Integrity

Textual integrity is fundamental to understanding and interpreting the Bible accurately. The Bible, as the divinely inspired Word of God, must be preserved and transmitted with utmost fidelity to its original manuscripts. Textual criticism, when properly applied, seeks to recover the original words of the biblical authors, ensuring that contemporary readers can access the true message intended by Jehovah. This chapter will delve into the importance of textual integrity, the role of textual criticism, and the challenges and principles involved in preserving the purity of the biblical text.

The Foundation of Textual Integrity

The doctrine of textual integrity is based on the belief that the Scriptures, as originally written, are the inspired and infallible Word of God. This conviction is grounded in several biblical assertions and theological principles:

Divine Inspiration: The Bible claims divine inspiration, asserting that its authors were moved by the Holy Spirit to write God's words. As 2 Timothy 3:16 (UASV) states, "All Scripture is inspired by God and beneficial for teaching, for reproof, for correction, for instruction in righteousness." This divine origin necessitates that the text be preserved accurately to maintain its authority and trustworthiness.

Infallibility and Inerrancy: The belief in the infallibility and inerrancy of Scripture holds that the original manuscripts (autographs) were without error and fully trustworthy in all they affirm. Jesus affirmed this in John 17:17, saying, "Sanctify them in the truth; your word is truth." To uphold this truth, textual integrity must be a priority in the transmission and translation of the Bible.

Preservation: Jehovah's commitment to preserving His Word is evident throughout Scripture. Psalm 12:6-7 (UASV) states, "The words of Jehovah are pure words, as silver tried in a furnace on the earth, refined seven times. You, O Jehovah, will keep them; you will preserve him from this generation forever." This divine promise underscores the importance of maintaining textual integrity.

The Role of Textual Criticism

Textual criticism is the scholarly discipline dedicated to examining and evaluating the manuscript evidence of the biblical text to determine its original wording. This process involves several key tasks and principles:

Collation of Manuscripts: Textual critics collect and compare the numerous manuscript copies of the Bible, including papyri, uncials, minuscules, and lectionaries. By examining the variations among these manuscripts, scholars can identify textual changes, both intentional and unintentional.

Evaluation of Variants: Textual variants arise due to scribal errors, such as misspellings, omissions, or additions, as well as deliberate alterations made to clarify or harmonize the text. Textual critics evaluate these variants to determine which readings are most likely original. This evaluation involves both external evidence (the age, quality, and geographical distribution of manuscripts) and internal evidence (the context, style, and theological consistency of the readings).

Principles of Textual Criticism: Several key principles guide textual critics in their work. These include the preference for older manuscripts, the criterion of difficulty (more challenging readings are often preferred as scribes were more likely to simplify than complicate the text), and the consideration of geographical distribution (widespread readings are more likely to be original).

Restoration of the Text: The ultimate goal of textual criticism is to restore the biblical text as closely as possible to its original form. This restoration is vital for ensuring that contemporary translations and interpretations are based on the most accurate and reliable text.

Challenges in Preserving Textual Integrity

Despite the meticulous efforts of textual critics, several challenges complicate the task of preserving textual integrity:

Scribal Errors: Human error is inevitable in the process of copying manuscripts. Common scribal errors include dittography (repetition of a letter or word), haplography (omission of a letter or word), and homoioteleuton (skipping text due to similar word endings). While many of these errors are minor and easily corrected, they can still impact the text.

Intentional Alterations: Some scribes intentionally modified the text to clarify ambiguities, harmonize discrepancies, or support theological views. These alterations can be more challenging to identify and correct, as they may be subtle and contextually motivated.

Manuscript Diversity: The sheer number and diversity of biblical manuscripts present both an opportunity and a challenge. While a large number of manuscripts increases the likelihood of preserving the original text, the variations among these manuscripts require careful analysis and comparison.

Theological Biases: Textual critics, like all scholars, are not immune to biases that can influence their work. Theological, denominational, and personal beliefs can impact the evaluation and selection of textual variants. Ensuring objectivity and impartiality is essential for maintaining textual integrity.

The Conservative Approach to Textual Criticism

A conservative approach to textual criticism emphasizes the importance of adhering to the original text as closely as possible, recognizing the divine inspiration and authority of Scripture. Key aspects of this approach include:

Commitment to Originality: Conservative textual critics prioritize restoring the text to its original form, avoiding interpretive alterations or modernizing changes. This commitment ensures that the biblical message remains authentic and unaltered.

Respect for Manuscript Evidence: While recognizing the value of early and high-quality manuscripts, conservative scholars also consider the broader manuscript tradition. They avoid over-reliance on a single manuscript or text type, seeking a balanced evaluation of the evidence.

Theological Integrity: Conservative textual criticism upholds the theological integrity of the Bible, resisting changes that could compromise doctrinal truths. This approach maintains a high view of Scripture, recognizing its role as the ultimate authority for faith and practice.

Engagement with Scholarship: Conservative textual critics engage critically with the broader field of textual criticism, incorporating valuable insights while rejecting methods and conclusions that undermine the authority of Scripture. This balanced engagement ensures rigorous scholarship that respects the divine nature of the Bible.

The Impact of Textual Integrity on Faith and Practice

Maintaining textual integrity has profound implications for both individual believers and the church as a whole:

Confidence in Scripture: A faithful and accurate biblical text provides believers with confidence in the reliability and authority of God's Word. This confidence is essential for faith, as it assures believers that they can trust the Bible's teachings and promises.

Sound Doctrine: Textual integrity is crucial for developing and maintaining sound doctrine. Accurate translations and interpretations based on the original text ensure that theological teachings are grounded in the true message of Scripture. This foundation is vital for the church's teaching, preaching, and discipleship.

Unity in the Church: A unified and accurate biblical text fosters unity within the church. When believers share a common foundation in the Word of God, they can more easily come to a consensus on doctrinal matters and work together in ministry and mission.

Spiritual Growth: Accurate and faithful engagement with Scripture is essential for spiritual growth. By studying the true words of God, believers can deepen their understanding of His character, will, and purposes. This growth leads to greater maturity, obedience, and transformation in the life of the believer.

Textual integrity is foundational to preserving the divine inspiration and authority of the Bible. Through the disciplined work of textual criticism, scholars strive to recover the original words of Scripture, ensuring that contemporary readers can access the true message intended by Jehovah. Despite the challenges posed by scribal errors, intentional alterations, and manuscript diversity, a conservative approach to textual criticism upholds the theological integrity and authority of the Bible. By maintaining textual integrity, the church can provide believers with a trustworthy guide for faith and practice, fostering confidence, sound doctrine, unity, and spiritual growth.

Abandoning Core Principles

The abandonment of core principles in biblical textual criticism has led to significant consequences for the integrity and authority of Scripture. Textual criticism, when conducted with a commitment to the original text, is a crucial discipline that helps preserve the accuracy of the Bible. However, deviations from these core principles undermine the reliability of the biblical text and introduce theological and interpretive errors. This chapter explores the consequences of abandoning core principles in textual criticism, emphasizing the need for a return to a rigorous and faithful approach to maintaining the integrity of Scripture.

The Core Principles of Textual Criticism

Textual criticism involves several fundamental principles that guide scholars in their efforts to reconstruct the original text of the Bible. These principles include the following:

Preservation of Original Wording: The primary goal of textual criticism is to preserve the original wording of the biblical text as closely as possible. This involves analyzing manuscript evidence, evaluating textual variants, and making informed decisions to determine the most likely original reading.

Respect for Manuscript Evidence: Textual critics must respect the manuscript evidence available, considering the age, quality, and geographical distribution of manuscripts. Older and more widely attested manuscripts generally hold greater weight in determining the original text.

Minimization of Interpretive Bias: Textual critics must strive to minimize interpretive bias, focusing on objective evaluation of the evidence rather than allowing theological or doctrinal preferences to influence their decisions.

Recognition of Scribal Tendencies: Understanding common scribal tendencies and errors, such as omissions, additions, and harmonizations, is essential for identifying and correcting textual variants.

Consequences of Abandoning Core Principles

When textual critics abandon these core principles, the consequences for the integrity and authority of the biblical text are severe. The following are some of the most significant consequences:

Introduction of Theological Bias: When textual critics allow their theological biases to influence their decisions, they risk altering the text to support specific doctrinal views. This undermines the objectivity of textual criticism and compromises the authenticity of the biblical message. For example, altering texts to downplay or emphasize certain theological concepts can lead to a distorted understanding of Scripture.

Erosion of Textual Integrity: Abandoning the core principle of preserving the original wording leads to the erosion of textual integrity. When critics prioritize interpretive translations or paraphrasing over faithful reproduction of the original text, they introduce inaccuracies and distortions that can mislead readers.

Loss of Trust in Scripture: When the integrity of the biblical text is compromised, believers may lose trust in the reliability and authority of Scripture. This can weaken their faith and undermine the foundational truths of Christianity. A compromised text raises doubts about the authenticity and accuracy of the Bible's teachings.

Confusion and Division: Deviations from core principles in textual criticism contribute to confusion and division within the church. When different translations and interpretations of Scripture proliferate, believers may struggle to discern which versions are accurate and trustworthy. This can lead to doctrinal disputes and fragmentation within the Christian community.

Undermining of Sound Doctrine: Theological integrity is compromised when the text of Scripture is altered or distorted. Sound doctrine relies on an accurate and faithful understanding of the biblical text. When textual criticism fails to uphold core principles, the foundation for sound doctrine is weakened, leading to erroneous teachings and practices.

Examples of Abandoning Core Principles

Several historical and contemporary examples illustrate the consequences of abandoning core principles in textual criticism:

The Comma Johanneum: The inclusion of the Comma Johanneum (1 John 5:7-8) in the King James Version and other early translations is a notable example. This passage, which explicitly supports the doctrine of the Trinity, is absent from the earliest and most reliable Greek manuscripts. Its inclusion likely resulted from a later theological insertion rather than being part of the original text. The addition of this text introduced theological bias and compromised textual integrity.

The Long Ending of Mark: The longer ending of Mark (Mark 16:9-20) is another example. While it appears in many manuscripts, it is absent from the earliest and most reliable sources, such as Codex

Vaticanus and Codex Sinaiticus. The inclusion of this ending, which includes details not found in the rest of the New Testament, raises questions about its authenticity and the motivations behind its insertion.

The Pericope Adulterae: The story of the woman caught in adultery (John 7:53-8:11) is a well-known passage that is absent from many early manuscripts. Its inclusion in later manuscripts suggests that it may have been a later addition, possibly based on oral tradition. This passage, while beloved by many, presents challenges for textual critics seeking to preserve the original text.

The Call to Return to Core Principles

To address the consequences of abandoning core principles, textual critics and the broader Christian community must commit to a rigorous and faithful approach to textual criticism. This involves the following:

Adherence to Original Texts: Textual critics must prioritize the preservation of the original wording of the biblical text. This requires a careful and objective evaluation of manuscript evidence, with a commitment to maintaining the integrity of Scripture.

Minimization of Bias: Textual critics must strive to minimize interpretive and theological biases in their work. This involves recognizing and setting aside personal and doctrinal preferences to focus on the objective task of reconstructing the original text.

Respect for Manuscript Evidence: Textual critics must respect the manuscript evidence available, giving appropriate weight to older and more reliable manuscripts. This involves a balanced and comprehensive evaluation of the textual tradition.

Education and Awareness: The Christian community must be educated about the importance of textual criticism and the need to uphold core principles. This includes promoting an understanding of the history and transmission of the biblical text and encouraging a commitment to preserving its integrity.

Engagement with Scholarly Work: Textual critics must engage with the broader field of biblical scholarship, incorporating valuable insights while maintaining a commitment to core principles. This balanced engagement ensures that textual criticism remains a rigorous and faithful discipline.

Abandoning core principles in textual criticism has led to significant consequences for the integrity and authority of Scripture. The introduction of theological bias, erosion of textual integrity, loss of trust in Scripture, confusion and division, and undermining of sound doctrine are among the most serious outcomes. To address these challenges, textual critics and the Christian community must commit to a rigorous and faithful approach to preserving the original text of the Bible. By adhering to core principles, respecting manuscript evidence, and minimizing bias, textual criticism can continue to play a vital role in maintaining the integrity and authority of Scripture.

Strategies for Restoring Biblical Accuracy

Restoring biblical accuracy is essential for maintaining the integrity and authority of Scripture. As we navigate the complexities of textual criticism, we must employ strategies that prioritize fidelity to the original text and ensure that contemporary readers have access to the true message of the Bible. This chapter explores various strategies for restoring biblical accuracy, emphasizing the importance of rigorous scholarship, respect for manuscript evidence, and a commitment to upholding the divine inspiration of Scripture.

Rigorous Scholarly Methodology

A disciplined and methodical approach is crucial for accurate textual criticism. This involves several key practices:

Collation and Comparison of Manuscripts: Textual critics must gather and compare a wide array of manuscripts. By examining differences and similarities, scholars can identify and assess textual variants. This comprehensive collation helps in reconstructing the original text.

Critical Evaluation of Variants: Not all textual variants are created equal. Scholars must critically evaluate variants by considering both external and internal evidence. External evidence includes the age, quality, and geographical distribution of manuscripts, while internal evidence involves assessing the context, style, and coherence of the readings.

Use of Textual Families: Manuscripts are often grouped into textual families based on shared characteristics. Understanding these families—such as the Alexandrian, Byzantine, and Western text types—can provide insights into the transmission history of the text and help identify the most reliable readings.

Prioritizing Early and Reliable Manuscripts

One of the fundamental strategies for restoring biblical accuracy is prioritizing early and reliable manuscripts. These manuscripts are closer in time to the original writings and are less likely to have accumulated significant errors or alterations.

Age and Proximity: Manuscripts that date back to the earliest centuries of Christianity are generally more valuable for textual criticism. The closer a manuscript is to the time of the original writing, the fewer opportunities there have been for errors to creep in.

Quality and Reliability: Not all early manuscripts are equally reliable. Textual critics must assess the quality of manuscripts based on factors such as the skill of the scribe, the condition of the manuscript, and the consistency of the text with other reliable sources.

Geographical Distribution: Manuscripts from diverse geographical regions can provide a broader perspective on the text's transmission. Widely distributed readings are more likely to reflect the original text than those confined to a single region.

Minimizing Interpretive Bias

Maintaining objectivity and minimizing interpretive bias is crucial for textual criticism. Scholars must strive to separate their theological and doctrinal views from their analysis of the text.

Objective Analysis: Textual critics must focus on the evidence without allowing personal beliefs to influence their decisions. This requires a commitment to impartiality and a rigorous evaluation of the data.

Peer Review and Collaboration: Engaging with the broader scholarly community through peer review and collaboration helps ensure that conclusions are not driven by individual biases. Diverse perspectives can provide valuable insights and help identify potential biases.

Transparency and Documentation: Documenting the rationale behind textual decisions and being transparent about the evidence considered promotes accountability and allows others to evaluate and verify the conclusions reached.

Leveraging Technological Advancements

Technological advancements have significantly enhanced the field of textual criticism, providing new tools and methods for analyzing and comparing manuscripts.

Digital Imaging and Databases: High-resolution digital images of manuscripts and extensive databases of textual variants enable scholars to study the text in unprecedented detail. These resources facilitate comprehensive collation and comparison.

Computer-Assisted Analysis: Advanced software can assist in identifying and analyzing textual variants, recognizing patterns, and predicting likely original readings. These tools augment the capabilities of textual critics and enhance the accuracy of their work.

Online Collaboration: The internet allows scholars from around the world to collaborate and share insights. Online platforms and forums foster a global community of textual critics who can contribute to the restoration of biblical accuracy.

Emphasizing the Historical-Grammatical Method

The Historical-Grammatical Method is a cornerstone of conservative textual criticism. This method emphasizes understanding the text in its historical and linguistic context, ensuring that interpretations align with the intended meaning of the original authors.

Historical Context: Understanding the historical setting of the biblical text is crucial for accurate interpretation. This involves studying the cultural, political, and social background of the time when the text was written.

Linguistic Analysis: Analyzing the original languages of the Bible—Hebrew, Aramaic, and Greek—provides insights into the nuances and meanings of the text. This analysis helps ensure that translations and interpretations remain faithful to the original wording.

Authorial Intent: The goal of the Historical-Grammatical Method is to uncover the intended meaning of the biblical authors. This requires a careful examination of the text's grammar, syntax, and literary features to understand what the authors meant to convey.

Commitment to Theological Integrity

Maintaining theological integrity is paramount for restoring biblical accuracy. Textual critics must ensure that their work upholds the doctrines and teachings of Scripture without introducing distortions or biases.

Doctrinal Consistency: Textual decisions should not undermine core doctrines of the Christian faith. Ensuring that the text remains consistent with established theological truths is essential for preserving the integrity of Scripture.

Respect for Divine Inspiration: Recognizing the Bible as the inspired Word of God, textual critics must approach their work with reverence and a commitment to faithfully transmitting the divine message.

Guarding Against Theological Agendas: Textual critics must be vigilant against the influence of theological agendas that seek to alter the text to support specific views. Objectivity and a commitment to the original text are crucial for maintaining theological integrity.

Engaging with the Broader Christian Community

Restoring biblical accuracy is not solely the responsibility of textual critics; it involves the broader Christian community. Educating and engaging believers in the importance of textual integrity can foster a collective commitment to preserving the Word of God.

Educational Initiatives: Churches, seminaries, and Christian organizations should provide education on the principles of textual criticism and the importance of maintaining biblical accuracy. This helps believers understand and appreciate the significance of preserving the original text.

Encouraging Biblical Literacy: Promoting biblical literacy among believers equips them to engage with the text critically and discern accurate translations and interpretations. A well-informed Christian community is better positioned to uphold the integrity of Scripture.

Fostering Unity: A unified commitment to biblical accuracy can strengthen the church and foster a shared foundation of faith. By working together to preserve the integrity of Scripture, believers can build a stronger and more cohesive Christian community.

Restoring biblical accuracy is a vital task that requires a rigorous and faithful approach to textual criticism. By adhering to core principles, prioritizing early and reliable manuscripts, minimizing interpretive bias, leveraging technological advancements, emphasizing the Historical-Grammatical Method, and maintaining theological integrity, textual critics can ensure that the Bible remains a trustworthy and authoritative guide for faith and practice. Engaging the broader Christian community in this effort fosters a collective commitment to preserving the Word of God and upholding the truths of Scripture.

Chapter 8: The Failure to Evangelize

The Early Church's Evangelism Model

The early church's model of evangelism provides a powerful example of effective and faithful witness to the world. From Pentecost in 33 C.E. onward, the first-century Christians demonstrated a commitment to spreading the gospel that led to remarkable growth and influence. This chapter examines the principles, methods, and outcomes of early church evangelism, highlighting the lessons that contemporary Christians can learn to overcome current evangelistic failures.

The Foundation of Early Church Evangelism

The early church's evangelism was rooted in the Great Commission given by Jesus Christ. Before his ascension, Jesus instructed his disciples: "Go therefore and make disciples of all nations, baptizing them in the name of the Father and of the Son and of the Holy Spirit, teaching them to observe all that I have commanded you. And behold, I am with you always, to the end of the age" (Matthew 28:19-20, UASV). This command established the framework for the church's mission, emphasizing the universal scope of the gospel and the need for teaching and discipleship.

The Role of the Holy Spirit

At Pentecost, the Holy Spirit empowered the apostles to preach the gospel with boldness and clarity. Acts 2:1-4 (UASV) describes the outpouring of the Spirit: "When the day of Pentecost arrived, they were all together in one place. And suddenly there came from heaven a sound like a mighty rushing wind, and it filled the entire house where they were sitting. And divided tongues as of fire appeared to them and rested on each one of them. And they were all filled with the Holy Spirit and began to speak in other tongues as the Spirit gave them utterance." This divine empowerment enabled the apostles to communicate the gospel effectively to people from diverse linguistic and cultural backgrounds.

Core Principles of Early Church Evangelism

Several core principles underpinned the early church's evangelistic efforts:

1. Reliance on Scripture: The apostles and early Christians grounded their message in the Scriptures, demonstrating how Jesus fulfilled the prophecies and promises of the Old Testament. Peter's sermon at Pentecost (Acts 2:14-36) is a prime example, where he quotes extensively from the Psalms and the prophet Joel to validate Jesus' messianic identity and resurrection.

2. Bold Proclamation: The early church boldly proclaimed the gospel, undeterred by opposition or persecution. Acts 4:29 (UASV) records the prayer of the early believers: "And now, Lord, look upon their threats and grant to your servants to continue to speak your word with all boldness." This boldness stemmed from their conviction in the truth of the gospel and their reliance on the Holy Spirit's power.

3. Personal Testimony: Personal testimony played a significant role in early church evangelism. The apostles and other believers shared their experiences of encountering Jesus and the transformative impact of the gospel in their lives. Paul's conversion story, recounted multiple times in Acts (e.g., Acts 22:1-21), exemplifies the power of personal testimony in witnessing.

4. Community Witness: The early church's communal life and mutual love served as a powerful testimony to the gospel. Acts 2:42-47 (UASV) describes the early Christian community: "And they devoted themselves to the apostles' teaching and the fellowship, to the breaking of bread and the prayers. And awe came upon every soul, and many wonders and signs were being done through the apostles. And all who believed were together and had all things in common. And they were selling their possessions and belongings and distributing the proceeds to all, as any had need. And day by day, attending the temple together and breaking bread in their homes, they received their food with glad and generous hearts, praising God and having favor with all the people. And the Lord added to their number day by day those who were being saved." This vibrant community life attracted many to the faith.

Methods of Early Church Evangelism

The early church employed various methods to spread the gospel, adapting their approach to different contexts and audiences:

1. Public Preaching: Public preaching was a primary method of evangelism. The apostles often preached in synagogues, marketplaces, and other public venues. Peter's sermon at Pentecost (Acts 2), Paul's address at the Areopagus in Athens (Acts 17:22-34), and his defense before King Agrippa (Acts 26:1-29) are notable examples of public evangelistic efforts.

2. House-to-House Evangelism: The early Christians also engaged in house-to-house evangelism, sharing the gospel in more intimate settings. Acts 5:42 (UASV) notes, "And every day, in the temple and from house to house, they did not cease teaching and preaching that the Christ is Jesus." This method allowed for personal interaction and in-depth discussion of the faith.

3. Use of Miracles: Miraculous signs and wonders accompanied the preaching of the gospel, authenticating the message and drawing attention to the power of God. Acts 3:1-10 recounts the healing of a lame beggar by Peter and John, which led to an opportunity to preach to a gathered crowd. Miracles served as a powerful tool for evangelism, demonstrating the reality of God's kingdom.

4. Written Correspondence: The apostles and early church leaders also used written correspondence to spread the gospel and strengthen the faith of believers. The letters of Paul, Peter, John, and others provided doctrinal instruction, encouragement, and exhortation to the early Christian communities. These epistles were circulated among the churches and played a crucial role in the growth and unity of the early church.

Outcomes of Early Church Evangelism

The early church's evangelistic efforts yielded remarkable results, as evidenced by the rapid growth and spread of Christianity:

1. Numerical Growth: From an initial group of about 120 believers (Acts 1:15), the church grew exponentially. On the day of Pentecost alone, about 3,000 people were added to the church (Acts 2:41). Acts 4:4 (UASV) records that "many of those who had heard the word believed, and the number of the men came to about five thousand." This growth continued as the gospel spread beyond Jerusalem to Judea, Samaria, and the Gentile world.

2. Geographical Expansion: The gospel spread rapidly beyond the confines of Jerusalem, reaching major cities and regions throughout the Roman Empire. Acts records the missionary journeys of Paul and his companions, who established churches in places such as Antioch, Ephesus, Corinth, and Rome. By the end of the first century, Christianity had a significant presence in many parts of the known world.

3. Cultural Impact: The early church's evangelism led to a profound cultural impact, challenging and transforming societal norms and values. The Christian message of love, equality, and justice resonated with people from diverse backgrounds and brought about significant social change. The abolition of infanticide, the elevation of the status of women, and the establishment of charitable institutions are some examples of the early church's influence on society.

4. Persecution and Perseverance: Despite facing intense persecution from Jewish and Roman authorities, the early Christians persevered in their evangelistic mission. Their willingness to suffer and even die for their faith served as a powerful witness to the truth of the gospel. The martyrdom of Stephen (Acts 7), James (Acts 12:1-2), and countless others demonstrated the unwavering commitment of the early church to the Great Commission.

Lessons for Contemporary Evangelism

The early church's model of evangelism offers valuable lessons for contemporary Christians seeking to overcome current evangelistic failures:

1. Embrace the Great Commission: Modern Christians must take seriously the call to make disciples of all nations. This requires a renewed commitment to evangelism as a core mission of the church, grounded in the authority of Jesus' command.

2. Rely on the Holy Spirit: Effective evangelism depends on the empowerment and guidance of the Holy Spirit. Contemporary believers should seek the Spirit's leading and empowerment, trusting that He will provide the boldness, wisdom, and opportunities needed for witnessing.

3. Ground Evangelism in Scripture: The early church's reliance on Scripture provides a model for contemporary evangelism. Sharing the gospel must be rooted in the biblical narrative, demonstrating how Jesus fulfills God's redemptive plan and offers salvation to all.

4. Utilize Diverse Methods: Modern evangelism should employ a variety of methods, including public preaching, personal testimony, community witness, and digital outreach. Adapting to different contexts and utilizing available technologies can enhance the reach and effectiveness of evangelistic efforts.

5. Foster a Vibrant Community: A healthy and loving Christian community serves as a powerful testimony to the gospel. By living out the values of the kingdom of God, believers can attract others to the faith and provide a compelling witness to the transformative power of the gospel.

6. Persevere in the Face of Opposition: Just as the early Christians faced persecution and opposition, contemporary believers must be prepared to endure challenges and remain steadfast in their evangelistic mission. Perseverance and faithfulness are essential for long-term impact.

The early church's evangelism model provides a blueprint for effective and faithful witness to the world. By embracing the Great Commission, relying on the Holy Spirit, grounding evangelism in Scripture, utilizing diverse methods, fostering a vibrant community, and persevering in the face of opposition, contemporary Christians can overcome current evangelistic failures and fulfill their mission to make disciples of all nations. The lessons from the early church remind us of the transformative power of the gospel and the importance of faithfully proclaiming it to a lost and dying world.

Modern Failures and Their Causes

The contemporary church faces significant challenges in fulfilling the Great Commission. Despite unprecedented access to resources and technology, modern evangelistic efforts often fall short of the early church's fervor and effectiveness. This section explores the causes behind these failures, emphasizing the need for a return to biblically grounded, Spirit-empowered evangelism.

Dilution of the Gospel Message

One of the primary causes of modern evangelistic failure is the dilution of the gospel message. In an attempt to appeal to broader audiences, some churches have compromised the core truths of the Christian faith, presenting a watered-down version of the gospel that lacks the power to transform lives.

1. Avoidance of Sin and Repentance: Many contemporary evangelistic messages shy away from addressing sin and the need for repentance. This omission undermines the gospel's call for individuals to recognize their sinful state and turn to God for forgiveness and transformation. Without acknowledging sin, the message loses its urgency and depth.

2. Emphasis on Prosperity and Self-Improvement: The rise of the prosperity gospel and self-help theology has shifted the focus from spiritual renewal to material success and personal fulfillment. This shift distorts the gospel's true purpose and leads individuals to seek temporary, worldly benefits rather than eternal salvation.

3. Relativism and Inclusivism: In a culture that increasingly values relativism and inclusivism, some churches have adopted a stance that minimizes the exclusivity of Christ's redemptive work. By suggesting that all paths lead to God or downplaying the necessity of faith in Jesus, these churches compromise the gospel's essential truth and hinder effective evangelism.

Lack of Personal Evangelism

The early church's explosive growth was largely due to the active participation of all believers in evangelism. In contrast, modern Christianity often relegates evangelism to church leaders and professionals, resulting in a passive laity.

1. Professionalization of Ministry: The professionalization of ministry has created a divide between clergy and laity, leading many believers to view evangelism as the responsibility of pastors and missionaries. This mindset diminishes the biblical teaching that all Christians are called to be witnesses (Acts 1:8).

2. Fear of Rejection and Persecution: Fear of rejection, ridicule, or persecution prevents many Christians from sharing their faith. In societies that value tolerance and political correctness, the fear of being labeled intolerant or offensive can stifle evangelistic efforts.

3. Lack of Training and Confidence: Many believers feel ill-equipped to share the gospel effectively. A lack of training in evangelism, coupled with inadequate biblical knowledge, leads to a lack of confidence and a reluctance to engage in spiritual conversations.

Cultural and Societal Barriers

Modern cultural and societal dynamics present significant barriers to effective evangelism. Understanding and addressing these barriers is crucial for revitalizing evangelistic efforts.

1. Secularism and Atheism: The rise of secularism and atheism has created an environment where religious beliefs are often dismissed or ridiculed. Evangelistic efforts must navigate a cultural landscape that is increasingly skeptical of spiritual claims and resistant to the idea of absolute truth.

2. Moral Relativism: Moral relativism, which denies absolute moral standards, undermines the gospel's message of sin and redemption. In a culture where "what's true for you may not be true for me," the call to repentance and faith in Jesus can be perceived as judgmental or intolerant.

3. Pluralism and Religious Diversity: The prevalence of religious pluralism and the coexistence of multiple faiths within a society can create confusion and hesitation among believers. The fear of offending others or appearing intolerant can discourage Christians from sharing the exclusivity of the gospel.

Internal Church Issues

Internal issues within the church contribute significantly to the failure of modern evangelistic efforts. These issues include division, complacency, and a focus on internal rather than external mission.

1. Division and Disunity: The fragmentation of the church into numerous denominations and sects weakens the collective witness of Christianity. Jesus prayed for the unity of his followers (John 17:21), and division undermines the credibility and impact of the church's evangelistic mission.

2. Complacency and Comfort: In many parts of the world, Christians enjoy relative comfort and security. This comfort can lead to complacency, where believers become more focused on maintaining their lifestyles than advancing the kingdom of God. A lack of urgency and passion for evangelism is a significant hindrance to effective outreach.

3. Inward Focus: Many churches prioritize internal programs and activities over outward mission. While discipleship and community building are essential, an inward focus can result in neglecting the church's mandate to reach the lost. Churches must strike a balance between nurturing their members and engaging in active evangelism.

The Role of Modern Technology

While modern technology offers unprecedented opportunities for evangelism, it also presents challenges that can hinder effective outreach.

1. Superficial Engagement: Social media and digital platforms can facilitate superficial engagement rather than meaningful, deep conversations. The brevity and transient nature of online interactions often prevent substantive discussions about faith and salvation.

2. Information Overload: The vast amount of information available online can lead to confusion and misinformation about Christianity. Competing voices and conflicting messages can make it difficult for seekers to discern the truth of the gospel.

3. Isolation and Individualism: The digital age has fostered a sense of isolation and individualism, reducing face-to-face interactions and community involvement. Effective evangelism often requires personal connections and relationships, which can be challenging to develop in an increasingly digital world.

Strategies for Overcoming Modern Failures

To overcome these modern failures, the church must adopt a comprehensive and strategic approach to evangelism. This involves recommitting to the core principles of the gospel, empowering all believers to participate in evangelism, and addressing cultural and societal barriers with wisdom and discernment.

1. Reclaiming the Full Gospel: The church must reclaim and boldly proclaim the full gospel message, including the reality of sin, the need for repentance, and the exclusive nature of salvation through Jesus Christ. This requires a commitment to biblical fidelity and a rejection of diluted or compromised versions of the gospel.

2. Equipping and Empowering Believers: Churches must invest in training and equipping their members for evangelism. This includes providing resources, workshops, and practical tools to help believers share their faith confidently and effectively. Empowering all believers to see themselves as evangelists is crucial for revitalizing evangelistic efforts.

3. Engaging with Culture: The church must engage with culture thoughtfully and respectfully, addressing secularism, relativism, and pluralism with the truth of the gospel. This involves understanding cultural dynamics, building bridges, and presenting the gospel in a way that resonates with contemporary seekers.

4. Fostering Unity and Collaboration: Overcoming internal divisions and fostering unity within the body of Christ is essential for a credible and powerful witness. Churches and denominations must work together, emphasizing their common mission to reach the lost and advancing the kingdom of God.

5. Utilizing Technology Wisely: While modern technology presents challenges, it also offers significant opportunities for evangelism. Churches should leverage digital platforms to reach a broader audience, while also emphasizing the importance of personal relationships and community engagement.

6. Cultivating a Sense of Urgency: Reigniting a sense of urgency and passion for evangelism is vital. Churches must continually remind their members of the eternal significance of the gospel and the urgent need to share it with a lost and dying world.

The failure to evangelize effectively in the modern era stems from a combination of diluted gospel messages, lack of personal evangelism, cultural and societal barriers, internal church issues, and the challenges posed by modern technology. By addressing these causes head-on and adopting strategic measures, the church can overcome these failures and fulfill its mandate to make disciples of all nations. The early church's example serves as a powerful reminder of the transformative power of the gospel and the importance of faithful, Spirit-empowered evangelism.

Edward D. Andrews

Solutions for Effective Evangelism Today

In addressing the modern failures of evangelism, it is essential to return to the foundational principles that characterized the early church while also adapting to the unique challenges and opportunities of the contemporary world. This section will explore various strategies and solutions for effective evangelism today, focusing on a return to biblical fidelity, the empowerment of all believers, and the utilization of modern tools and methods.

Reclaiming Biblical Evangelism

To restore effective evangelism, churches must first reclaim the biblical message of the gospel. This involves a clear and uncompromising presentation of the core truths of Christianity, as outlined in Scripture.

1. Preaching the Full Gospel: Evangelistic efforts must emphasize the full message of the gospel, including the reality of sin, the need for repentance, and the exclusive salvation through Jesus Christ. This means avoiding diluted messages that focus solely on God's love without addressing His justice and the necessity of faith and repentance.

2. Upholding Biblical Authority: Churches must uphold the authority of the Bible as the inspired Word of God. This involves a commitment to sound doctrine and the rejection of theological liberalism that undermines biblical truth. Effective evangelism is rooted in a high view of Scripture, which provides the foundation for faith and practice.

3. Emphasizing Discipleship: Evangelism should not end with conversion but should include discipleship, helping new believers grow in their faith and understanding of God's Word. This ensures that converts are grounded in biblical truth and equipped to share their faith with others.

124

Empowering Every Believer

The early church's evangelistic success was due in large part to the active participation of all believers in sharing the gospel. To replicate this success, modern churches must empower every believer to be an evangelist.

1. Training and Equipping: Churches should provide regular training and equipping sessions for their members, teaching them how to share their faith effectively. This includes practical instruction on how to initiate spiritual conversations, present the gospel clearly, and respond to common objections.

2. Encouraging Personal Evangelism: Every believer should be encouraged to see evangelism as a personal responsibility. This involves creating a church culture that values and prioritizes evangelism, celebrating stories of evangelistic success, and providing opportunities for members to engage in outreach activities.

3. Utilizing Spiritual Gifts: Recognizing that God has gifted every believer uniquely, churches should help members identify and utilize their spiritual gifts in evangelism. Whether through teaching, hospitality, service, or other gifts, every believer has a role to play in the church's evangelistic mission.

Engaging with Contemporary Culture

Effective evangelism today requires an understanding of and engagement with contemporary culture. This involves addressing cultural barriers and finding ways to communicate the gospel in a way that resonates with modern audiences.

1. Addressing Secularism and Relativism: In a culture increasingly influenced by secularism and relativism, churches must be prepared to engage with these worldviews. This involves presenting the gospel as the objective truth and addressing the philosophical and moral questions that arise in a secular context.

2. Building Relationships: Evangelism is most effective within the context of relationships. Churches should encourage their members to build genuine relationships with unbelievers, demonstrating the love of Christ through their actions and providing opportunities for meaningful spiritual conversations.

3. Leveraging Technology: While technology presents challenges, it also offers significant opportunities for evangelism. Churches should leverage digital platforms to reach a broader audience, using social media, websites, podcasts, and other tools to share the gospel and connect with seekers.

Fostering Unity and Collaboration

The credibility of the church's witness is strengthened by unity and collaboration among believers. Overcoming divisions and working together can enhance evangelistic efforts.

1. Promoting Doctrinal Unity: While recognizing the diversity of thought within Christianity, churches should strive for unity on essential doctrines. This involves focusing on the core truths of the gospel and minimizing divisive issues that do not pertain to salvation.

2. Encouraging Inter-Church Cooperation: Churches should look for opportunities to collaborate with other congregations and denominations in evangelistic efforts. Joint outreach events, community service projects, and evangelistic campaigns can demonstrate the unity of the body of Christ and amplify the impact of evangelism.

3. Resolving Conflicts Biblically: Internal conflicts and divisions can hinder evangelistic efforts. Churches must be committed to resolving conflicts biblically, following the principles of reconciliation and forgiveness outlined in Scripture.

Developing a Strategic Evangelism Plan

Effective evangelism requires intentional planning and strategy. Churches should develop comprehensive evangelism plans that outline their goals, methods, and resources.

1. Setting Clear Goals: Churches should set clear, measurable goals for their evangelistic efforts. This includes numerical targets for conversions and baptisms, as well as goals for training and equipping members.

2. Identifying Target Audiences: Understanding the demographics and needs of the surrounding community can help churches tailor their evangelistic efforts. This involves identifying target audiences and developing strategies to reach them effectively.

3. Mobilizing Resources: Churches should allocate sufficient resources to support their evangelistic initiatives. This includes budget allocations, staffing, and the provision of materials and training for evangelism.

4. Evaluating and Adjusting: Regular evaluation of evangelistic efforts is essential for continuous improvement. Churches should assess the effectiveness of their strategies, gather feedback, and make necessary adjustments to enhance their impact.

Cultivating a Heart for the Lost

Ultimately, effective evangelism is driven by a genuine love and concern for the lost. Churches must cultivate a heart for evangelism among their members, motivating them to share the gospel out of compassion and obedience to Christ.

1. Prayer for the Lost: Prayer is a vital component of evangelism. Churches should regularly pray for the lost, asking God to soften hearts, open doors for the gospel, and empower believers to witness boldly.

2. Sharing Testimonies: Sharing personal testimonies of how God has transformed lives can inspire and motivate others to engage in evangelism. Testimonies provide powerful evidence of the gospel's impact and encourage believers to share their own stories.

3. Encouraging a Missional Lifestyle: Evangelism should not be seen as an occasional activity but as a lifestyle. Churches should encourage their members to live missionally, looking for opportunities to share the gospel in their daily lives and viewing every interaction as a potential opportunity for evangelism.

The modern church faces significant challenges in fulfilling the Great Commission, but by reclaiming biblical evangelism, empowering all believers, engaging with contemporary culture, fostering unity, developing strategic plans, and cultivating a heart for the lost, the church can overcome these challenges and effectively share the gospel. By following the example of the early church and relying on the guidance of the Spirit-inspired Word of God, the church can once again become a powerful force for evangelism in the world today.

Chapter 9: The Independent Spirit and Its Consequences

The Rise of Independent Churches

The emergence of independent churches is a significant phenomenon in the landscape of modern Christianity. This movement has roots in the desire for autonomy, doctrinal purity, and a reaction against perceived corruption and institutional rigidity within established denominations. However, the rise of independent churches has brought about both positive and negative consequences, which must be carefully examined.

Historical Context of Independent Churches

The rise of independent churches can be traced back to various historical movements that emphasized the need for personal faith, scriptural purity, and congregational autonomy. Key moments include:

1. The Radical Reformation: During the 16th century, the Radical Reformation birthed groups such as the Anabaptists, who sought to return to the New Testament model of church governance. They rejected the state-church model and emphasized believer's baptism, congregational governance, and separation from worldly influences.

2. The Great Awakenings: The religious revivals of the 18th and 19th centuries in America, known as the Great Awakenings, fueled the rise of numerous independent and non-denominational churches. These movements stressed personal conversion experiences, the authority of Scripture, and a decentralized church structure.

3. 20th-Century Fundamentalism and Evangelicalism: The 20th century saw the rise of fundamentalist and evangelical movements that often criticized mainline denominations for theological liberalism and compromise. This led to the formation of many independent churches that sought to preserve doctrinal purity and a high view of Scripture.

The Appeal of Independence

The appeal of independent churches is multifaceted, rooted in both theological convictions and practical considerations.

1. Doctrinal Purity: Many believers are drawn to independent churches because of their commitment to maintaining doctrinal purity. Independent churches often emphasize adherence to a literal interpretation of Scripture, rejecting modernist or liberal theological trends.

2. Autonomy: Independent churches offer autonomy from denominational structures, allowing congregations to govern themselves according to their interpretation of biblical principles. This autonomy is appealing to those who value local church governance and the freedom to adapt ministry practices to their specific context.

3. Reaction to Corruption: The perception of corruption or spiritual decay within established denominations has driven many to seek refuge in independent churches. Historical scandals, theological drift, and bureaucratic inefficiency in denominations have contributed to this exodus.

Consequences of Independence

While the rise of independent churches has brought about positive developments, such as the preservation of doctrinal purity and the fostering of dynamic faith communities, it has also led to several challenges and negative consequences.

1. Lack of Accountability: One of the primary concerns with independent churches is the lack of accountability. Without denominational oversight, there is a risk of unbalanced leadership, doctrinal errors, and ethical lapses. Independent churches can become insular, with leaders who wield unchecked authority.

2. Doctrinal Fragmentation: The proliferation of independent churches has contributed to the fragmentation of Christian doctrine. Without a unifying doctrinal standard, independent churches often develop unique interpretations and practices, leading to confusion and division within the broader Christian community.

3. Isolation: Independent churches can become isolated from the larger body of Christ. This isolation can hinder cooperation with other churches, reduce opportunities for mutual support, and limit the influence of broader Christian movements. It can also lead to a lack of exposure to diverse theological perspectives and practices.

4. Resource Limitations: Independent churches may struggle with limited resources. Without the support of a denomination, they may face challenges in funding, staffing, and accessing educational and training resources. This can impact the quality of ministry and the ability to engage in larger-scale missions and outreach efforts.

Addressing the Challenges

To address the challenges associated with the rise of independent churches, several strategies can be employed:

1. Establishing Accountability Structures: Independent churches should seek to establish internal accountability structures. This can include creating elder boards, advisory councils, and fostering relationships with other churches for mutual accountability and support.

2. Emphasizing Doctrinal Soundness: Independent churches must prioritize doctrinal soundness by adhering to a conservative, historical-grammatical method of biblical interpretation. They should engage with reputable theological resources and ensure that their teachings align with the core tenets of the Christian faith.

3. Fostering Cooperation: Despite their autonomy, independent churches should seek opportunities for cooperation with other like-minded churches. This can include participating in regional associations, joint mission projects, and inter-church fellowship events to foster unity and shared ministry efforts.

4. Leveraging Technology: To overcome resource limitations, independent churches can leverage technology to access educational and training materials. Online courses, webinars, and digital libraries can provide valuable resources for church leaders and members.

5. Encouraging Transparency: Transparency in governance and financial matters can help build trust within the congregation and the broader community. Independent churches should practice open communication and involve members in decision-making processes to foster a sense of ownership and accountability.

6. Prioritizing Discipleship: Independent churches should prioritize discipleship, ensuring that members are grounded in biblical truth and equipped to share their faith. This includes providing robust teaching, small group opportunities, and mentoring relationships.

The Way Forward

The rise of independent churches is a complex phenomenon with both positive and negative aspects. By recognizing the strengths and addressing the weaknesses of independent churches, the broader Christian community can work towards greater unity and effectiveness in fulfilling the Great Commission. Independent churches must balance their desire for autonomy with a commitment to accountability, doctrinal soundness, and cooperation with the larger body of Christ. Through intentional efforts to address these challenges, independent churches can contribute to the health and vitality of the Christian faith in the modern world.

Balancing Denominational Control and Individual Freedom

The rise of independent churches has significantly impacted the landscape of modern Christianity. This movement is characterized by congregations that operate autonomously, free from the control and oversight of larger denominational structures. While the pursuit of doctrinal purity and autonomy has driven the establishment of many independent churches, it has also led to notable challenges and consequences.

Historical Context of Independent Churches

The historical roots of independent churches can be traced back to several key movements and events:

1. The Radical Reformation: The Radical Reformation of the 16th century was a critical period that saw the emergence of groups like the Anabaptists. These groups rejected the state-church model and emphasized believers' baptism, congregational governance, and a return to New Testament Christianity. Their emphasis on personal faith and scriptural authority laid the groundwork for the independent church movement.

2. The Great Awakenings: The religious revivals of the 18th and 19th centuries, known as the Great Awakenings, further fueled the rise of independent churches. These revivals emphasized personal conversion experiences, the authority of Scripture, and a rejection of established religious institutions perceived as corrupt or spiritually dead. Many revival leaders and their followers formed independent congregations to maintain the purity and fervor of their newfound faith.

3. 20th-Century Fundamentalism and Evangelicalism: The 20th century saw the rise of fundamentalist and evangelical movements that often criticized mainline denominations for theological liberalism and compromise. Leaders within these movements sought to preserve doctrinal purity and a high view of Scripture, leading to the formation of numerous independent churches. These churches aimed to remain faithful to biblical teachings without the perceived constraints of denominational oversight.

The Appeal of Independence

The appeal of independent churches is rooted in several key factors:

1. Doctrinal Purity: Many believers are drawn to independent churches because of their commitment to maintaining doctrinal purity. Independent churches often emphasize adherence to a literal interpretation of Scripture, rejecting modernist or liberal theological trends. This commitment to doctrinal soundness attracts those who seek a church that aligns closely with their understanding of biblical truth.

2. Autonomy: Independent churches offer autonomy from denominational structures, allowing congregations to govern themselves according to their interpretation of biblical principles. This autonomy is appealing to those who value local church governance and the freedom to adapt ministry practices to their specific context. It allows churches to respond quickly to the needs of their congregations and communities without bureaucratic delays.

3. Reaction to Corruption: The perception of corruption or spiritual decay within established denominations has driven many to seek refuge in independent churches. Historical scandals, theological drift, and bureaucratic inefficiency in denominations have contributed to this exodus. Independent churches are seen as a haven where faith can be practiced free from the influence of compromised institutions.

Consequences of Independence

While the rise of independent churches has brought about positive developments, such as the preservation of doctrinal purity and the fostering of dynamic faith communities, it has also led to several challenges and negative consequences:

1. Lack of Accountability: One of the primary concerns with independent churches is the lack of accountability. Without denominational oversight, there is a risk of unbalanced leadership, doctrinal errors, and ethical lapses. Independent churches can become insular, with leaders who wield unchecked authority. This can lead to abuses of power and a lack of transparency in decision-making processes.

2. Doctrinal Fragmentation: The proliferation of independent churches has contributed to the fragmentation of Christian doctrine.

Without a unifying doctrinal standard, independent churches often develop unique interpretations and practices, leading to confusion and division within the broader Christian community. This doctrinal diversity can make it challenging for believers to find common ground on essential theological issues.

3. Isolation: Independent churches can become isolated from the larger body of Christ. This isolation can hinder cooperation with other churches, reduce opportunities for mutual support, and limit the influence of broader Christian movements. It can also lead to a lack of exposure to diverse theological perspectives and practices, which can enrich a congregation's faith experience.

4. Resource Limitations: Independent churches may struggle with limited resources. Without the support of a denomination, they may face challenges in funding, staffing, and accessing educational and training resources. This can impact the quality of ministry and the ability to engage in larger-scale missions and outreach efforts. Smaller congregations may particularly feel the strain of these limitations.

Addressing the Challenges

To address the challenges associated with the rise of independent churches, several strategies can be employed:

1. Establishing Accountability Structures: Independent churches should seek to establish internal accountability structures. This can include creating elder boards, advisory councils, and fostering relationships with other churches for mutual accountability and support. Transparent governance practices and regular financial audits can also enhance accountability.

2. Emphasizing Doctrinal Soundness: Independent churches must prioritize doctrinal soundness by adhering to a conservative, historical-grammatical method of biblical interpretation. They should engage with reputable theological resources and ensure that their teachings align with the core tenets of the Christian faith. Regular theological training for church leaders and members can help maintain doctrinal integrity.

3. Fostering Cooperation: Despite their autonomy, independent churches should seek opportunities for cooperation with other like-minded churches. This can include participating in regional associations, joint mission projects, and inter-church fellowship events to foster unity and shared ministry efforts. Collaboration can also enhance the church's impact on the community.

4. Leveraging Technology: To overcome resource limitations, independent churches can leverage technology to access educational and training materials. Online courses, webinars, and digital libraries can provide valuable resources for church leaders and members. Virtual platforms can also facilitate networking and collaboration with other churches and ministries.

5. Encouraging Transparency: Transparency in governance and financial matters can help build trust within the congregation and the broader community. Independent churches should practice open communication and involve members in decision-making processes to foster a sense of ownership and accountability. Regular updates on church activities, finances, and strategic plans can enhance transparency.

6. Prioritizing Discipleship: Independent churches should prioritize discipleship, ensuring that members are grounded in biblical truth and equipped to share their faith. This includes providing robust teaching, small group opportunities, and mentoring relationships. A strong discipleship program can foster spiritual growth and encourage members to take an active role in ministry.

The Way Forward

The rise of independent churches is a complex phenomenon with both positive and negative aspects. By recognizing the strengths and addressing the weaknesses of independent churches, the broader Christian community can work towards greater unity and effectiveness in fulfilling the Great Commission. Independent churches must balance their desire for autonomy with a commitment to accountability, doctrinal soundness, and cooperation with the larger body of Christ. Through intentional efforts to address these challenges, independent churches can contribute to the health and vitality of the Christian faith in the modern world.

Biblical Principles for Unity and Cooperation

The independent spirit that characterizes many contemporary churches has both benefits and challenges. Autonomy can foster a strong sense of local identity and doctrinal purity, but it can also lead to isolation and fragmentation within the broader body of Christ. Understanding and applying biblical principles for unity and cooperation is crucial for overcoming these challenges and promoting a healthier and more unified Christian community.

Unity in the Early Church

The early church provides a model of unity and cooperation despite the diversity of its members. The New Testament emphasizes the importance of unity among believers:

1. Jesus' Prayer for Unity: In John 17:21, Jesus prayed, "that they may all be one, just as you, Father, are in me, and I in you, that they also may be in us, so that the world may believe that you have sent me." This prayer highlights the critical role of unity in the witness of the church to the world. Jesus' desire for His followers to be united reflects the unity within the Trinity and sets a high standard for the church.

2. The Early Church's Practice: Acts 2:42-47 describes the early believers as being devoted to the apostles' teaching, fellowship, breaking of bread, and prayers. They shared their possessions and supported one another, creating a community that was both spiritually and materially united. This early example demonstrates that unity involves both doctrinal agreement and practical support.

3. Paul's Exhortation: In Ephesians 4:3-6, Paul urges believers to "be eager to maintain the unity of the Spirit in the bond of peace. There is one body and one Spirit—just as you were called to the one hope that belongs to your call—one Lord, one faith, one baptism, one

God and Father of all, who is over all and through all and in all." Paul emphasizes that unity is grounded in shared beliefs and the work of the Holy Spirit. Maintaining this unity requires effort and a commitment to peace.

Biblical Principles for Unity

Several key principles from Scripture can guide churches in pursuing unity and cooperation:

1. Humility and Selflessness: Philippians 2:3-4 instructs believers, "Do nothing from selfish ambition or conceit, but in humility count others more significant than yourselves. Let each of you look not only to his own interests but also to the interests of others." Humility and selflessness are foundational to unity. When believers prioritize others' needs and perspectives, it fosters a cooperative spirit.

2. Love and Forgiveness: Colossians 3:13-14 encourages believers to bear with one another and forgive each other, adding, "And above all these put on love, which binds everything together in perfect harmony." Love and forgiveness are essential for maintaining unity, especially in the face of disagreements and offenses. Love acts as the glue that holds the church together in harmony.

3. Doctrinal Soundness: While unity is important, it must not come at the expense of truth. Jude 1:3 urges believers to "contend for the faith that was once for all delivered to the saints." Churches should strive for unity in essential doctrines while allowing for diversity in non-essential matters. Doctrinal soundness provides a common foundation upon which unity can be built.

4. Cooperative Efforts: Romans 12:4-5 teaches that just as the body has many members with different functions, so the church is one body in Christ with diverse gifts. Cooperation among different parts of the body is crucial for effective ministry. Churches should recognize and value the unique contributions of each member and work together for the common good.

Practical Steps for Promoting Unity

To foster unity and cooperation, churches can take several practical steps:

1. Establish Clear Doctrinal Foundations: Churches should have clear statements of faith that outline essential doctrines. This helps to prevent doctrinal drift and ensures that all members are united around core beliefs. Regular teaching and catechism can reinforce these foundations.

2. Foster Inter-Church Relationships: Building relationships with other like-minded churches can enhance unity. This can include joint worship services, community service projects, and inter-church prayer meetings. These activities promote mutual support and understanding.

3. Promote Open Communication: Effective communication is vital for maintaining unity. Churches should encourage open dialogue about doctrinal issues, ministry initiatives, and any concerns that arise. Transparency and a willingness to listen can prevent misunderstandings and foster trust.

4. Emphasize Discipleship and Spiritual Growth: A focus on discipleship helps to ensure that all members are growing in their faith and understanding of Scripture. This spiritual maturity can contribute to greater unity as believers are better equipped to handle differences and work together effectively.

5. Encourage Humility and Servant Leadership: Church leaders should model humility and a servant's heart. This includes being open to feedback, admitting mistakes, and prioritizing the well-being of the congregation. Leaders who serve with humility set a tone that fosters unity.

6. Address Conflicts Biblically: When conflicts arise, they should be addressed according to biblical principles. Matthew 18:15-17 provides a clear process for resolving disputes within the church. Addressing conflicts directly and with a spirit of reconciliation can prevent divisions from taking root.

7. Cultivate a Culture of Prayer: Prayer is a powerful tool for promoting unity. Churches should regularly pray for unity within their congregation and the broader body of Christ. Corporate prayer meetings and prayer partnerships can strengthen bonds among members.

The Role of Denominations and Independent Churches

While independent churches value their autonomy, cooperation with denominational bodies can also be beneficial. Denominations provide resources, support, and accountability that can enhance the ministry of independent churches. At the same time, denominations can learn from the flexibility and innovative approaches of independent churches.

1. Balancing Autonomy and Accountability: Independent churches should seek to balance their autonomy with appropriate accountability structures. This can include forming associations with other independent churches or joining networks that provide mutual support and oversight.

2. Learning from Each Other: Both denominational and independent churches have valuable insights to offer. Denominational churches can learn from the entrepreneurial spirit and adaptability of independent churches, while independent churches can benefit from the stability and resources of denominational structures.

3. Promoting Unity Across Divides: Efforts should be made to promote unity across denominational and independent lines. This can include joint conferences, shared mission projects, and collaborative training programs. Such initiatives can help to bridge gaps and foster a sense of common purpose.

The independent spirit in modern Christianity presents both opportunities and challenges. By adhering to biblical principles for unity and cooperation, churches can overcome the divisive tendencies of independence and work together for the glory of God and the advancement of His kingdom. Through humility, love, doctrinal soundness, and practical cooperation, the church can reflect the unity that Jesus prayed for and effectively fulfill its mission in the world.

Chapter 10: The Role of Human Nature in Church Division

Understanding Genesis 6:5; 8:21; Jeremiah 17:9; and Romans 7:18

The issue of human nature is central to understanding the divisions within the church. The Bible provides profound insights into the inherent flaws and tendencies of humanity that contribute to discord and separation. Key scriptural passages such as Genesis 6:5, 8:21, Jeremiah 17:9, and Romans 7:18 offer a foundation for analyzing the intrinsic weaknesses of human nature and their impact on the unity of the church.

Genesis 6:5 – The Depth of Human Wickedness

Genesis 6:5 states: "Jehovah saw that the wickedness of man was great in the earth, and that every intention of the thoughts of his heart was only evil continually." This verse captures the pervasive corruption and moral depravity that characterized humanity before the Flood. It underscores the extent of human sinfulness, indicating that every intention and thought of man's heart was persistently evil.

This profound declaration highlights the intrinsic tendency of humans toward wickedness. The repeated emphasis on the continuous nature of evil thoughts reflects an unrelenting inclination toward sin. This inherent depravity disrupts not only the individual's relationship with God but also the harmony within the community of believers. When the hearts of individuals within the church are dominated by selfish and evil inclinations, unity is inevitably compromised.

Genesis 8:21 – Post-Flood Realities

Genesis 8:21 says: "And when Jehovah smelled the pleasing aroma, Jehovah said in his heart, 'I will never again curse the ground because of man, for the intention of man's heart is evil from his youth. Neither will I ever again strike down every living creature as I have done.'" This verse reveals God's acknowledgment of the enduring nature of human sinfulness even after the Flood. Despite this, He expresses a commitment to refrain from cursing the ground or destroying all living creatures again.

This passage underscores the persistent nature of human depravity from youth. The innate tendency toward evil persists throughout human life. This intrinsic corruption remains a significant barrier to unity within the church. As long as individuals are inclined to follow their sinful desires, achieving and maintaining unity requires constant vigilance and reliance on God's grace.

Jeremiah 17:9 – The Deceitfulness of the Human Heart

Jeremiah 17:9 declares: "The heart is deceitful above all things, and desperately sick; who can understand it?" This verse presents a stark picture of the human heart's deceitful and incurably sick nature. It emphasizes the profound difficulty in comprehending the full extent of human wickedness.

The deceitfulness and sickness of the heart contribute significantly to the divisions within the church. When individuals are driven by deceitful desires and intentions, trust and genuine fellowship are undermined. This internal corruption fosters misunderstandings, conflicts, and divisions as people pursue their selfish agendas rather than the collective good of the church.

Romans 7:18 – The Struggle with Sin

In Romans 7:18, Paul writes: "For I know that nothing good dwells in me, that is, in my flesh. For I have the desire to do what is right, but not the ability to carry it out." This passage encapsulates the apostle Paul's personal struggle with sin. He acknowledges the inherent weakness of the flesh and the difficulty of consistently doing what is right despite the desire to do so.

Paul's admission of his struggle with sin highlights the universal human experience of battling internal corruption. This struggle is not unique to Paul but is a common reality for all believers. The recognition of this ongoing battle with sin is crucial for understanding the divisions within the church. The inability to consistently do what is right, even when there is a desire to do so, contributes to the fractures and conflicts within the Christian community.

Implications for Church Unity

Understanding these scriptural insights into human nature provides a framework for addressing the divisions within the church. The recognition of inherent sinfulness, deceitfulness, and the struggle with the flesh underscores the need for several critical approaches to foster unity:

1. Dependence on Divine Grace: Recognizing the pervasive nature of human sinfulness should drive believers to rely on God's grace for transformation and unity. Human efforts alone are insufficient to overcome the intrinsic tendencies toward division. It is through God's grace and the work of the Holy Spirit that believers can experience genuine change and foster unity.

2. Emphasis on Humility and Repentance: Humility and repentance are essential responses to the recognition of one's sinful nature. Believers must continually acknowledge their weaknesses and seek God's forgiveness and strength. This posture of humility and repentance fosters a spirit of cooperation and reconciliation within the church.

3. Commitment to Scriptural Principles: The authority of Scripture must guide the church's efforts toward unity. By adhering to biblical teachings on love, forgiveness, and community, believers can counteract the divisive tendencies of their sinful nature. Scriptural principles provide a clear and objective standard for resolving conflicts and maintaining unity.

4. Accountability and Support: Recognizing the deceitfulness of the heart and the struggle with sin highlights the need for accountability within the church. Believers must support one another through mutual encouragement, correction, and accountability. This communal support helps individuals resist the temptations of their sinful nature and promotes unity.

5. Focus on Spiritual Growth: Spiritual growth and maturity are vital for overcoming the weaknesses of human nature. Through regular study of Scripture, prayer, and participation in the sacraments, believers can grow in their faith and develop the character necessary for fostering unity. Spiritual disciplines help to align the heart and mind with God's will, counteracting the innate tendencies toward division.

The scriptural understanding of human nature as depicted in Genesis 6:5, 8:21, Jeremiah 17:9, and Romans 7:18 provides a sobering yet essential foundation for addressing the divisions within the church. Recognizing the inherent sinfulness, deceitfulness, and struggles of the human heart underscores the need for divine intervention, humility, adherence to Scripture, accountability, and spiritual growth. By applying these biblical principles, the church can work towards overcoming the barriers to unity and fostering a community that reflects the love and grace of God.

The Sinful Nature and Its Impact on Unity

The sinful nature of humanity is a fundamental issue that has a significant impact on the unity of the church. The Bible provides clear insights into the extent of human sinfulness and the implications of this condition for the community of believers. From the early recognition of human depravity in the Old Testament to the New Testament reflections on the nature of sin, the scriptures offer a comprehensive examination of the challenge posed by human sin and its effects on church unity.

The Nature of Sin in the Old Testament

The Old Testament provides a foundational understanding of the sinful nature of humanity. In Genesis 3:1-7, we find the first instance of human disobedience: "Then the eyes of both were opened, and they knew that they were naked. And they sewed fig leaves together and made themselves loincloths." The consequences of this act were immediate and profound, introducing sin into the human condition and leading to the separation of humanity from God.

The ripple effects of this initial act of disobedience are immense, manifesting in the progressive corruption of human society. By the time of Noah, the moral degradation had reached such a level that Jehovah had to intervene drastically. As recorded in Genesis 6:5: "Jehovah saw that the wickedness of man was great in the earth, and that every intention of the thoughts of his heart was only evil continually." This passage highlights the depth of human depravity, as the thoughts of humanity were perpetually inclined towards evil.

The persistent nature of human sin is further emphasized after the Flood. Despite the divine judgment and the destruction of the wicked, the condition of human hearts remained largely unchanged. Genesis 8:21 makes this clear: "And when Jehovah smelled the pleasing aroma, Jehovah said in his heart, 'I will never again curse the ground because of man, for the intention of man's heart is evil from his youth. Neither will I ever again strike down every living creature as I have done.'" This declaration underscores the enduring nature of human sinfulness, highlighting the inclination of human hearts to evil from a young age.

The implications of this persistent sinfulness are dire for the community of believers. The sinful nature of individuals poses a constant threat to the unity and integrity of the church. As the Old Testament illustrates, the consequences of sin are severe and far-reaching, affecting not only the individuals involved but also the entire community.

The Perspective of the Prophets

The prophets of the Old Testament offer further insights into the consequences of human sinfulness. Jeremiah, in particular, provides a compelling depiction of the deceitful nature of human hearts. In Jeremiah 17:9, he writes: "The heart is deceitful above all things, and desperately sick; who can understand it?" This passage highlights the pervasive and insidious nature of human sin, suggesting that the deceit interventions by human means.

The prophets also emphasize the inevitability of divine judgment as a consequence of human sin. From the declarations of judgment in the books of Isaiah and Jeremiah to the admonishments of the minor prophets, the message is clear: sin incurs the wrath of God, and the persistence of sin within the community necessitates divine intervention. The implications of this perspective are crucial for the church, as it underscores the need for a constant vigilance and a deep reliance on the mercy and grace of God to counteract the tendencies of human nature.

The New Testament: The Continuation of the Sinful Condition

The New Testament continues to address the issue of human sinfulness and its implications for the community of believers. In Romans 3:23, Paul encapsulates the universal nature of sin: "For all have sinned and fall short of the glory of God." This statement, definitive and encompassing, reminds us that no one is exempt from the condition of sin. It underscores the pervasive nature of sin and the necessity of divine grace for salvation.

Paul's reflections on the struggle with sin in Romans 7:15-20 further elucidate the complexities of human nature: "For I do not understand my own actions. For I do not do the things that I want, and then I do the things that I don't want." This passage from Paul's epistle is a candid confession of the internal battle against sin that continues even for those who are redeemed. This struggle, as depicted by Paul, remains a constant challenge for individuals and poses a significant obstacle to the unity of the church.

The New Testament also emphasizes the community's responsibility to address the persistence of sin within the church. In Matthew 18:15-17, Jesus provides instructions for dealing with sin within the community: "If your brother or sister sins, go and point out the fault." This passage highlights the importance of accountability and the necessity of addressing sin directly to maintain the integrity and unity of the church.

Theological Reflections on Sin and Unity

The theological implications of human sin for the unity of the church are profound. The recognition of the sinful nature of humanity necessitates a theological framework that emphasizes the grace of God as the essential means of salvation and the maintenance of community. This recognition also requires a robust theological understanding of the doctrines of sin, redemption, and sanctification.

The doctrine of original sin, as articulated by theologians such as Augustine, provides a foundational understanding of the inherited nature of human sinfulness. This doctrine emphasizes the pervasive impact of the original sin of Adam and Eve on all humanity, highlighting the necessity of divine intervention for salvation.

The doctrine of redemption, central to Christian theology, underscores the redemptive work of Christ as the only means of overcoming the condition of sin. This doctrine emphasizes the necessity of the sacrificial death of Christ and the transformative power of the Holy Spirit in the lives of believers.

The doctrine of sanctification, as articulated by theologians such as John Wesley, emphasizes the process of becoming holy and the necessity of living a life of righteousness. This doctrine highlights the importance of spiritual disciplines, such as prayer, fasting, and the study of scriptures, as means of cultivating a life of holiness and counteracting the tendencies of the sinful nature.

Edward D. Andrews

Practical Implications for the Church

The practical implications of understanding the sinful nature and its impact on the unity of the church are numerous. The church must recognize the persistent nature of human sin and the necessity of divine grace for the maintenance of community. This recognition requires a theological framework that emphasizes the doctrines of sin, redemption, and sanctification.

The church must also prioritize the spiritual formation of its members, emphasizing the importance of spiritual disciplines and the cultivation of a life of holiness. This prioritization requires a robust theological education that emphasizes the importance of living a life of righteousness and the cultivation of a life of holiness.

The church must also recognize the necessity of accountability and the importance of addressing sin directly within the community. This recognition requires a theological framework that emphasizes the importance of accountability and the necessity of addressing sin directly to maintain the integrity and unity of the church.

Finally, the church must recognize the importance of theological reflection on the doctrines of sin, redemption, and sanctification. This recognition requires a theological framework that emphasizes the importance of living a life of righteousness and the cultivation of a life of holiness.

The recognition of the sinful nature of humanity and its impact on the unity of the church is a crucial theological issue that requires a robust theological framework that emphasizes the doctrines of sin, redemption, and sanctification. The church must recognize the persistent nature of human sin and the necessity of divine grace for the maintenance of community. This recognition requires a theological framework that emphasizes the importance of living a life of righteousness and the cultivation of a life of holiness.

Overcoming Human Flaws Through Biblical Teachings

Understanding and addressing the flaws inherent in human nature is vital for overcoming division within the church. The Bible provides not only an accurate diagnosis of the sinful nature of humanity but also prescribes a path for overcoming these flaws through adherence to biblical teachings. This section will explore how scriptural principles and teachings can help believers mitigate the impact of human weaknesses and foster unity within the church.

Recognizing the Depth of Human Flaws

The Bible clearly depicts the inherent flaws and sinful tendencies of humanity. From the very beginning, the Scriptures document the propensity for disobedience and rebellion against God's commands. Genesis 6:5 states: "Jehovah saw that the wickedness of man was great in the earth, and that every intention of the thoughts of his heart was only evil continually." This verse highlights the pervasiveness of human sin and the depth of moral corruption that characterizes humanity apart from divine intervention.

Similarly, Jeremiah 17:9 underscores the deceitful nature of the human heart: "The heart is deceitful above all things, and desperately sick; who can understand it?" This prophetic insight reveals the profound self-deception and moral sickness that plague humanity. Without recognizing these deep-seated flaws, any attempt at overcoming division within the church would be superficial and ineffective.

The Transformative Power of Biblical Teachings

The Bible offers a transformative remedy to the problem of human sinfulness. This transformation begins with the recognition of sin and the need for repentance. Acts 3:19 exhorts believers: "Repent therefore, and turn back, that your sins may be blotted out." Repentance is the first step toward overcoming human flaws, as it involves a conscious turning away from sin and a turning towards God.

Moreover, the teachings of Jesus Christ provide a foundation for overcoming human weaknesses. The Sermon on the Mount, recorded in Matthew 5-7, presents a radical reorientation of values and behaviors. For instance, Matthew 5:44 commands: "But I say to you, love your enemies and pray for those who persecute you." This teaching challenges believers to transcend natural inclinations toward hatred and retaliation, fostering a spirit of love and forgiveness that is essential for church unity.

The Role of the Holy Spirit in Transformation

While human effort is necessary, it is insufficient on its own to overcome the deep-seated flaws of human nature. The Bible emphasizes the crucial role of the Holy Spirit in the process of transformation. Galatians 5:16-17 states: "But I say, walk by the Spirit, and you will not gratify the desires of the flesh. For the desires of the flesh are against the Spirit, and the desires of the Spirit are against the flesh." This passage underscores the conflict between the sinful nature and the Spirit and highlights the necessity of reliance on the Holy Spirit to overcome the desires of the flesh.

The fruit of the Spirit, as described in Galatians 5:22-23, includes love, joy, peace, patience, kindness, goodness, faithfulness, gentleness, and self-control. These qualities are essential for maintaining unity within the church, as they counteract the divisive tendencies of human nature. By cultivating the fruit of the Spirit, believers can create an environment of mutual respect and cooperation, essential for church unity.

Scriptural Models of Unity and Cooperation

The Bible provides numerous examples of unity and cooperation that serve as models for the church. The early church in Acts 2:42-47 exemplifies a community characterized by unity and mutual support: "And they devoted themselves to the apostles' teaching and the fellowship, to the breaking of bread and the prayers. And awe came upon every soul, and many wonders and signs were being done through the apostles." This passage illustrates the importance of devotion to teaching, fellowship, and prayer in fostering unity.

Additionally, the Pauline epistles offer practical advice for maintaining unity within the church. Ephesians 4:1-3 urges believers to "walk in a manner worthy of the calling to which you have been called, with all humility and gentleness, with patience, bearing with one another in love, eager to maintain the unity of the Spirit in the bond of peace." This exhortation highlights the virtues necessary for preserving unity and emphasizes the active effort required to maintain it.

Addressing Specific Human Flaws Through Scripture

The Bible addresses specific human flaws that contribute to division within the church and provides guidance on how to overcome them. For example, pride is a significant source of conflict and division. Proverbs 16:18 warns: "Pride goes before destruction, and a haughty spirit before a fall." The New Testament reiterates this theme, with James 4:6 stating: "God opposes the proud but gives grace to the humble." By cultivating humility, as Jesus exemplified in His life and teachings, believers can mitigate the divisive effects of pride.

Similarly, selfishness is a common human flaw that disrupts unity. Philippians 2:3-4 advises: "Do nothing from selfish ambition or conceit, but in humility count others more significant than yourselves. Let each of you look not only to his own interests, but also to the interests of others." This teaching promotes a selfless attitude that prioritizes the well-being of others, fostering a spirit of cooperation and unity within the church.

The Importance of Forgiveness and Reconciliation

Forgiveness and reconciliation are critical for overcoming human flaws and maintaining unity within the church. Matthew 6:14-15 emphasizes the necessity of forgiveness: "For if you forgive others their trespasses, your heavenly Father will also forgive you, but if you do not forgive others their trespasses, neither will your Father forgive your trespasses." This teaching underscores the reciprocal nature of forgiveness and its importance for spiritual health and community harmony.

Furthermore, the process of reconciliation, as outlined in Matthew 18:15-17, provides a practical framework for addressing conflicts within the church. This passage advises believers to first address the issue privately, then with witnesses, and finally, if necessary, bring it before the church. This structured approach ensures that conflicts are addressed in a manner that promotes healing and restoration, rather than division.

Cultivating a Spirit of Unity Through Love

Ultimately, love is the foundational principle for overcoming human flaws and fostering unity within the church. 1 Corinthians 13:4-7 provides a comprehensive description of love: "Love is patient and kind; love does not envy or boast; it is not arrogant or rude. It does not insist on its own way; it is not irritable or resentful; it does not rejoice at wrongdoing, but rejoices with the truth. Love bears all things, believes all things, hopes all things, endures all things." This passage encapsulates the qualities of love that are essential for unity and cooperation within the church.

John 13:34-35 further emphasizes the centrality of love: "A new commandment I give to you, that you love one another: just as I have loved you, you also are to love one another. By this all people will know that you are my disciples, if you have love for one another." This commandment highlights love as the distinguishing mark of Christ's disciples and the key to maintaining unity within the church.

Practical Steps for Cultivating Unity

To cultivate unity within the church, believers must actively apply biblical teachings to their lives. This involves regular engagement with scripture, prayer, and participation in the community of believers. It also requires a commitment to personal spiritual growth and the development of Christlike virtues.

Church leaders play a crucial role in fostering unity by teaching and modeling biblical principles. They must also create an environment that encourages open communication, mutual support, and accountability. By addressing conflicts promptly and biblically, leaders can prevent the escalation of issues that threaten church unity.

Overcoming human flaws and fostering unity within the church is a challenging but essential task. By adhering to biblical teachings, cultivating the fruit of the Spirit, and prioritizing love, forgiveness, and reconciliation, believers can mitigate the divisive effects of human sinfulness. Through the transformative power of the Holy Spirit and a commitment to living out scriptural principles, the church can become a united body that effectively witnesses to the world the love and truth of Jesus Christ.

Chapter 11: A Balanced Approach to Church Governance

Avoiding the Extremes of Authoritarianism and Anarchy

A balanced approach to church governance is essential for maintaining both order and freedom within the Christian community. This requires avoiding the extremes of authoritarianism and anarchy, both of which can be detrimental to the spiritual health and unity of the church. Authoritarianism stifles individual growth and suppresses dissent, while anarchy leads to disorder and fragmentation. By adhering to biblical principles, churches can find a middle path that promotes healthy leadership and community involvement.

The Pitfalls of Authoritarianism

Authoritarianism in church governance often manifests as a concentration of power in the hands of a few leaders who exercise control over every aspect of church life. This can lead to an environment where questioning and dissent are discouraged, and members are expected to conform without critical engagement. Such a structure is contrary to the spirit of New Testament teachings, which emphasize mutual submission and servant leadership.

Jesus explicitly warned against authoritarian leadership among his followers. In Matthew 20:25-28, He said: "You know that the rulers of the Gentiles lord it over them, and their great ones exercise authority over them. It shall not be so among you. But whoever would be great among you must be your servant, and whoever would be first among you must be your slave, even as the Son of Man came not to be served but to serve, and to give his life as a ransom for many." This passage underscores the importance of servant leadership, where leaders prioritize the needs of others over their own authority.

Furthermore, 1 Peter 5:2-3 exhorts church leaders to "shepherd the flock of God that is among you, exercising oversight, not under compulsion, but willingly, as God would have you; not for shameful gain, but eagerly; not domineering over those in your charge, but being examples to the flock." The apostle Peter emphasizes that leaders should guide by example and not through domineering control, reflecting a model of leadership that is both humble and accountable.

The Dangers of Anarchy

On the opposite end of the spectrum, anarchy in church governance results in a lack of structure and accountability. Without clear leadership and established guidelines, churches can descend into chaos, where individual preferences and opinions overshadow collective goals and doctrinal integrity. This can lead to divisions and conflicts, undermining the unity and mission of the church.

The New Testament advocates for a structured and orderly approach to church life. In 1 Corinthians 14:40, Paul instructs the church in Corinth: "But all things should be done decently and in order." This directive highlights the necessity of maintaining order in church practices to avoid confusion and promote edification.

Moreover, the early church established clear roles and responsibilities for leaders to ensure effective governance. Ephesians 4:11-12 outlines the various roles within the church: "And he gave the apostles, the prophets, the evangelists, the shepherds and teachers, to equip the saints for the work of ministry, for building up the body of Christ." These roles are designed to equip believers for ministry and promote the growth and unity of the church.

The Biblical Model of Balanced Governance

A balanced approach to church governance involves a combination of strong, servant-oriented leadership and active participation from the congregation. This model ensures that leaders are accountable and that members are engaged in the life and mission of the church.

The New Testament provides a framework for such governance. The early church operated with a plurality of elders who shared the responsibility of leadership. Acts 14:23 records that Paul and Barnabas "appointed elders for them in every church, with prayer and fasting they committed them to the Lord in whom they had believed." The appointment of multiple elders ensured a distribution of power and prevented the concentration of authority in a single individual.

Additionally, the role of deacons in the early church, as described in Acts 6:1-6, illustrates the importance of delegating responsibilities to capable individuals within the congregation. The apostles appointed seven men of good repute, full of the Spirit and wisdom, to oversee the daily distribution of food, allowing the apostles to focus on prayer and the ministry of the word. This delegation of duties ensured that practical needs were met while maintaining the primary focus on spiritual leadership.

Implementing Balanced Governance Today

Implementing a balanced approach to church governance today requires a commitment to biblical principles and a willingness to adapt them to contemporary contexts. This involves selecting leaders based on spiritual qualifications rather than personal ambition or popularity. 1 Timothy 3:1-7 and Titus 1:5-9 provide detailed criteria for selecting elders, emphasizing qualities such as blamelessness, self-control, hospitality, and sound doctrine.

Churches should also foster a culture of mutual accountability and transparency. Regular meetings and open communication between leaders and members can help address issues before they escalate into major conflicts. Hebrews 13:17 encourages believers to "obey your leaders and submit to them, for they are keeping watch over your souls, as those who will have to give an account." This verse underscores the responsibility of leaders to care for their congregations and the importance of accountability in their roles.

Moreover, involving the congregation in decision-making processes can promote a sense of ownership and responsibility among members. Acts 15 provides an example of the early church convening a council in Jerusalem to address a doctrinal dispute. The apostles and elders, along with the whole church, deliberated and reached a consensus, demonstrating the value of collective discernment and decision-making.

The Role of Biblical Teaching in Governance

Sound biblical teaching is essential for maintaining balanced governance in the church. Leaders must be committed to teaching and upholding the truths of Scripture, ensuring that the church remains grounded in the Word of God. 2 Timothy 4:2 exhorts pastors to "preach the word; be ready in season and out of season; reprove, rebuke, and exhort, with complete patience and teaching." Consistent and faithful teaching helps to safeguard against doctrinal errors and provides a foundation for sound decision-making.

In addition to teaching, leaders must exemplify the character and conduct they wish to see in the congregation. Titus 2:7-8 instructs leaders to "show yourself in all respects to be a model of good works, and in your teaching show integrity, dignity, and sound speech that cannot be condemned." By living out the principles they teach, leaders can inspire trust and respect within the church, fostering an environment of mutual respect and cooperation.

Avoiding the extremes of authoritarianism and anarchy in church governance requires a balanced approach that combines strong, servant-oriented leadership with active participation from the congregation. By adhering to biblical principles, selecting qualified leaders, fostering mutual accountability, and maintaining a commitment to sound teaching, churches can create an environment that promotes unity, growth, and effective ministry. In doing so, the church can fulfill its mission and reflect the character of Christ to the world.

Establishing Effective Denominational Control

The establishment of effective denominational control is a critical aspect of maintaining order, unity, and doctrinal purity within the church. This approach balances the need for centralized authority with the necessity of local church autonomy, ensuring that while individual congregations have the freedom to minister effectively in their contexts, they remain aligned with broader denominational goals and teachings. This section will examine the principles and practices that contribute to effective denominational control, drawing from biblical examples and historical precedents.

The Biblical Basis for Denominational Control

The New Testament provides several examples of early church governance that emphasize the importance of both local and centralized control. One of the key passages is Acts 15, which describes the Jerusalem Council. When a doctrinal dispute arose regarding the necessity of circumcision for Gentile converts, representatives from various congregations gathered to discuss and resolve the issue. This meeting underscores the principle of collective decision-making and the role of central leadership in addressing theological controversies.

Paul's letters also reflect a balance between local autonomy and centralized oversight. While he established and nurtured individual congregations, he maintained a level of authority over them, offering guidance, correction, and instruction. For instance, in 1 Corinthians 16:1-2, Paul gives specific instructions on the collection for the saints, indicating a coordinated effort across multiple churches. Similarly, his letters to Timothy and Titus provide directives for church leadership, demonstrating an overarching concern for consistent governance and doctrine.

Historical Development of Denominational Structures

Throughout church history, various models of denominational control have emerged, each with its strengths and weaknesses. The early church fathers, such as Ignatius of Antioch, emphasized the importance of episcopal oversight, where bishops held authority over multiple congregations to maintain doctrinal purity and unity. This model evolved into more structured hierarchical systems, such as the Roman Catholic Church, which centralized authority in the papacy and the episcopal hierarchy.

The Reformation brought significant changes to denominational control, as reformers like Martin Luther and John Calvin sought to return to more scripturally based models of governance. Luther emphasized the priesthood of all believers, which reduced the hierarchical gap between clergy and laity, while Calvin's model of presbyterian polity established a system of elders and synods that balanced local and central authority.

In the contemporary context, various denominations have developed systems that reflect their theological convictions and historical backgrounds. For example, Baptist churches typically emphasize congregational autonomy, with local congregations retaining significant control over their affairs. In contrast, Methodist and Presbyterian denominations often have more structured systems of oversight, with conferences or synods providing leadership and accountability.

Principles for Effective Denominational Control

To establish effective denominational control, several key principles should be considered:

1. **Doctrinal Unity:** Central to effective control is the maintenance of doctrinal unity. Denominations must clearly define their core beliefs and ensure that all affiliated congregations adhere to these tenets. This requires a robust process for theological education and a mechanism for addressing deviations. As Paul instructed Timothy in 2 Timothy 1:13-14, "Follow the pattern of the sound words that you have heard from me, in the faith and love that are in Christ Jesus. By the Holy Spirit who dwells within us, guard the good deposit entrusted to you."

2. **Accountability Structures:** Establishing clear accountability structures is essential for maintaining integrity and preventing abuses of power. This includes regular reporting, audits, and oversight by denominational leaders. The early church's practice of sending representatives to oversee and report on the work of local congregations, as seen in Acts 14:23 and Titus 1:5, provides a biblical precedent for such structures.

3. **Training and Development:** Ongoing training and development for church leaders ensure that they are equipped to handle their responsibilities effectively. This includes theological education, leadership training, and practical ministry skills. Paul's letters to Timothy and Titus emphasize the importance of training leaders who can rightly handle the word of truth (2 Timothy 2:15).

4. **Conflict Resolution:** An effective system for conflict resolution is crucial for maintaining peace and unity. This involves clear processes for addressing grievances, mediating disputes, and enforcing disciplinary measures when necessary. Matthew 18:15-17 outlines a process for resolving conflicts within the church, emphasizing the importance of reconciliation and accountability.

5. **Local Autonomy:** While maintaining central oversight, denominations should respect the autonomy of local congregations to make decisions that best serve their communities. This balance allows for contextualized ministry while ensuring adherence to denominational standards. Paul's letters often addressed specific issues within local congregations, recognizing their unique contexts while providing apostolic guidance.

Implementing Effective Denominational Control

Implementing these principles requires intentionality and collaboration. Denominations must engage in continuous dialogue with their congregations, fostering a culture of mutual respect and shared vision. Practical steps for implementation include:

- **Regular Synods or Conferences:** Holding regular synods or conferences allows representatives from local congregations to gather, discuss, and make decisions on denominational matters. These gatherings should be inclusive, transparent, and focused on fostering unity and cooperation.

- **Clear Doctrinal Statements:** Developing and disseminating clear doctrinal statements ensures that all members understand the core beliefs of the denomination. These statements should be regularly reviewed and updated to address contemporary issues while remaining rooted in biblical truth.

- **Leadership Training Programs:** Establishing comprehensive leadership training programs equips current and future leaders with the necessary skills and knowledge. These programs should cover theological education, practical ministry skills, and ethical standards.

- **Effective Communication Channels:** Maintaining open and effective communication channels between denominational leaders and local congregations promotes transparency and trust. Regular newsletters, online platforms, and face-to-face meetings can facilitate this communication.

- **Robust Accountability Measures:** Implementing robust accountability measures, such as regular audits, peer reviews, and disciplinary processes, helps maintain integrity and prevent misconduct. These measures should be fair, transparent, and consistent with biblical principles.

The Role of Scripture in Denominational Control

Central to establishing effective denominational control is a commitment to Scripture as the ultimate authority. All governance structures and practices must be evaluated against the teachings of the Bible. As 2 Timothy 3:16-17 states, "All Scripture is breathed out by God and profitable for teaching, for reproof, for correction, and for training in righteousness, that the man of God may be complete, equipped for every good work." This commitment ensures that denominational control remains grounded in divine revelation rather than human tradition or innovation.

By adhering to these principles and practices, denominations can establish effective control that promotes unity, doctrinal purity, and effective ministry. This balanced approach respects the autonomy of local congregations while ensuring alignment with the broader goals and teachings of the denomination, ultimately contributing to the health and growth of the church as a whole.

Mechanisms for Doctrinal Accountability and Correction

Establishing mechanisms for doctrinal accountability and correction is essential to maintaining the integrity, unity, and purity of the church. As the body of Christ, it is vital that we adhere to sound doctrine and address deviations promptly and effectively. This section explores the biblical basis, historical precedents, and practical steps for implementing effective mechanisms for doctrinal accountability and correction within the church.

The Biblical Basis for Doctrinal Accountability

The New Testament provides clear instructions and examples regarding the importance of maintaining sound doctrine and addressing false teachings. Paul's epistles frequently emphasize the need for doctrinal purity and the responsibility of church leaders to guard against false teachings.

In 1 Timothy 4:16, Paul exhorts Timothy, "Pay close attention to yourself and to your teaching; persevere in these things, for as you do this you will ensure salvation both for yourself and for those who hear you." This passage highlights the critical role of church leaders in safeguarding doctrinal integrity.

Similarly, in Titus 1:9, Paul instructs Titus regarding the qualifications of an elder, stating that an elder must "hold firmly to the trustworthy message as it has been taught, so that he can encourage others by sound doctrine and refute those who oppose it." This underscores the dual responsibility of promoting sound doctrine and refuting error.

Historical Precedents for Doctrinal Accountability

Throughout church history, various mechanisms have been employed to maintain doctrinal purity and address deviations. The early church councils, such as the Council of Nicaea in 325 C.E., were convened to address heresies and establish clear doctrinal statements. These councils played a significant role in defining orthodoxy and correcting false teachings.

The Reformation also provides valuable lessons in doctrinal accountability. Reformers like Martin Luther and John Calvin emphasized the authority of Scripture and the necessity of doctrinal correction. Luther's 95 Theses, for example, were a call to correct doctrinal errors and abuses within the church, leading to significant theological reforms.

Principles for Effective Doctrinal Accountability

To establish effective mechanisms for doctrinal accountability and correction, several key principles must be considered:

1. **Scriptural Authority:** The foundation for doctrinal accountability is the authority of Scripture. All doctrinal positions and corrections must be based on a sound exegesis of the Bible, ensuring that the teachings align with the inspired Word of God. As 2 Timothy 3:16-17 states, "All Scripture is inspired by God and profitable for teaching, for reproof, for correction, and for training in righteousness, so that the man of God may be adequate, equipped for every good work."

2. **Qualified Leadership:** Church leaders must be well-trained in sound doctrine and equipped to identify and address doctrinal errors. This requires ongoing theological education and training. As Paul instructed Timothy in 2 Timothy 2:15, "Be diligent to present yourself approved to God as a

workman who does not need to be ashamed, accurately handling the word of truth."

3. **Clear Doctrinal Standards:** Establishing clear doctrinal standards and statements of faith helps ensure that all members understand the core beliefs of the church. These standards provide a basis for evaluating teachings and practices, facilitating accountability and correction.

4. **Transparency and Communication:** Effective doctrinal accountability requires transparent communication within the church. This includes regular teaching and discussion of doctrinal issues, as well as open channels for addressing concerns and questions.

5. **Disciplinary Procedures:** Implementing fair and consistent disciplinary procedures is essential for addressing doctrinal deviations. These procedures should be rooted in biblical principles, emphasizing restoration and reconciliation while maintaining doctrinal purity.

Practical Steps for Implementing Doctrinal Accountability

1. **Regular Theological Training:** Providing ongoing theological training for church leaders and members ensures that they are equipped to handle doctrinal issues effectively. This can include seminars, workshops, and study groups focused on sound doctrine and biblical exegesis.

2. **Doctrinal Reviews:** Conducting regular doctrinal reviews helps identify and address potential errors before they become widespread. These reviews can be carried out by a committee of qualified theologians and church leaders who evaluate teachings and practices in light of Scripture.

3. **Accountability Groups:** Establishing accountability groups within the church promotes mutual support and correction among leaders and members. These groups provide a safe

space for discussing doctrinal issues and holding one another accountable to biblical standards.

4. **Public Statements and Confessions:** Issuing public statements and confessions of faith reinforces the church's commitment to sound doctrine. These documents can be used as a reference point for evaluating teachings and practices, ensuring alignment with biblical truth.

5. **Formal Disciplinary Procedures:** Implementing formal disciplinary procedures for addressing doctrinal deviations is crucial for maintaining integrity and unity. These procedures should include steps for investigation, correction, and, if necessary, disciplinary action. Matthew 18:15-17 outlines a process for addressing sin within the church, emphasizing the importance of restoration and reconciliation.

6. **Engaging with Broader Church Networks:** Participating in broader church networks and associations can provide additional support and accountability. These networks often have established mechanisms for addressing doctrinal issues and can offer valuable resources and guidance.

Case Studies in Doctrinal Accountability

Examining case studies of doctrinal accountability within church history can provide valuable insights into effective practices and potential pitfalls. The Council of Nicaea, for instance, addressed the Arian heresy by clearly defining the doctrine of the Trinity and establishing a unified stance against Arianism. This council set a precedent for addressing doctrinal deviations through collective decision-making and clear doctrinal statements.

The Reformation also offers lessons in doctrinal accountability. The Reformers' emphasis on sola scriptura (Scripture alone) as the ultimate authority for faith and practice led to significant doctrinal corrections and the establishment of new confessions of faith, such as the Westminster Confession. These confessions provided a clear doctrinal framework for evaluating teachings and practices, promoting unity and doctrinal integrity.

The Role of Church Discipline in Doctrinal Accountability

Church discipline plays a crucial role in maintaining doctrinal purity and addressing errors. Biblical discipline is not merely punitive but aims to restore the erring individual and protect the integrity of the church. Galatians 6:1 instructs, "Brothers, if someone is caught in a sin, you who live by the Spirit should restore that person gently. But watch yourselves, or you also may be tempted." This verse highlights the restorative nature of church discipline and the importance of approaching it with humility and gentleness.

Implementing effective disciplinary measures involves several steps:

1. **Initial Warning and Instruction:** When a doctrinal error is identified, the first step is to provide clear instruction and warning. This involves explaining the error, referencing Scripture, and offering guidance for correction.

2. **Private Confrontation:** If the individual persists in error, private confrontation by a church leader or a small group of leaders is necessary. This step aims to address the issue directly and offer further opportunity for repentance and correction.

3. **Public Admonition:** If private confrontation fails, the matter may need to be addressed publicly within the church. This step involves informing the congregation of the issue and calling the individual to repentance, emphasizing the seriousness of maintaining doctrinal purity.

4. **Excommunication (if necessary):** In extreme cases where the individual remains unrepentant and continues to promote false teachings, excommunication may be necessary to protect the church's integrity. This step should be taken with great care and a heavy heart, always seeking the individual's eventual restoration.

The Importance of Humility and Love in Doctrinal Accountability

While maintaining doctrinal accountability is crucial, it must be approached with humility and love. The goal is not to create an atmosphere of suspicion and judgment but to foster a community committed to truth and unity. Ephesians 4:15-16 emphasizes the importance of speaking the truth in love, stating, "Instead, speaking the truth in love, we will grow to become in every respect the mature body of him who is the head, that is, Christ. From him, the whole body, joined and held together by every supporting ligament, grows and builds itself up in love, as each part does its work."

By grounding our efforts in humility and love, we can create an environment where doctrinal accountability promotes growth, unity, and spiritual maturity.

Establishing effective mechanisms for doctrinal accountability and correction is vital for the health and integrity of the church. By grounding these mechanisms in scriptural authority, qualified leadership, clear doctrinal standards, transparency, and fair disciplinary procedures, we can ensure that the church remains faithful to its calling and mission. As we strive to uphold sound doctrine and address errors with humility and love, we reflect the heart of Christ and build a stronger, more unified body of believers.

Chapter 12: Developing a Unified Evangelism Program

Implementing a Comprehensive Evangelism Strategy

Implementing a comprehensive evangelism strategy requires a structured approach that is rooted in biblical principles and designed to equip every church member with the tools and confidence needed to share the gospel effectively. Drawing from the principles laid out in "The Evangelism Handbook: How All Christians Can Effectively Share God's Word in Their Community," by Edward D. Andrews, this strategy emphasizes the importance of united doctrine, local engagement, and structured growth.

United Doctrine as the Foundation

A unified evangelism program begins with doctrinal consistency. All teachings must align with the Bible, ensuring that every member shares the same foundational beliefs. This unity is crucial for a cohesive evangelism effort, as it prevents doctrinal confusion and promotes a clear and consistent gospel message.

Starting from the Church Community

Evangelism should begin within the church community and expand outward. Each congregation must take responsibility for evangelizing their immediate surroundings. While some members may be called to distant missionary work, the primary focus should be on local outreach. This approach fosters strong community ties and ensures that the church remains relevant and engaged with those around them.

Structured Congregational Growth

To manage growth effectively, congregations should form new groups once they exceed 500 members. This process involves creating additional congregations within the same city, which helps maintain a sense of community and focus. As each new congregation reaches 500 members, the cycle continues, eventually covering the entire city. This method ensures sustainable growth and prevents any single congregation from becoming too large and impersonal.

Practical Training Components

The training program for evangelism should be comprehensive, covering both theological foundations and practical skills.

1. **Apologetic Evangelism:**

    o **Studying the Bible**: Emphasize the Historical-Grammatical Method to ensure accurate understanding and interpretation of Scripture.

    o **Effective Communication**: Teach members how to articulate the gospel clearly and persuasively, addressing common objections and questions.

    o **Social Media Evangelism**: Equip members to use social media platforms for outreach, expanding their reach while maintaining doctrinal integrity.

    o **Building Rapport**: Train members to establish trust and build relationships with non-believers, creating open doors for gospel conversations.

    o **Attitude in Evangelism**: Highlight the importance of humility, love, and respect in evangelistic efforts.

Edward D. Andrews

Equip and Proclaim: Evangelism Training School for All:

- o **Memory and Focus**: Enhance members' memory and focus through exercises that help them recall Scripture and key points during conversations.
- o **Public Speaking**: Develop public speaking skills, including clear articulation, effective modulation, and the use of visual aids.
- o **Continuous Spiritual Growth**: Encourage ongoing spiritual growth through diligent study, personal reflection, and active participation in church life.
- o **Practical Assignments**: Provide real-world assignments that allow members to practice their evangelism skills, receiving feedback and guidance.
- o **Effective Reading and Research**: Train members in accurate reading, pronunciation, and research methods to ensure effective study and presentation of the Bible.

Sustaining Evangelism Efforts

1. **Community Engagement**: Foster a culture of community involvement where members actively participate in local events and volunteer opportunities, building relationships for gospel sharing.

2. **Regular Evangelism Events**: Organize regular outreach programs, seminars, and workshops to maintain momentum and provide continuous opportunities for members to practice their skills.

3. **Mentorship Programs**: Establish mentorship systems where experienced evangelists guide and support newer members, offering encouragement and practical advice.

4. **Resource Utilization**: Use various resources and testimonies from individuals of different backgrounds to illustrate effective

cross-cultural evangelism, ensuring the gospel message is accessible to all.

5. **Feedback and Improvement**: Implement a feedback system where members can share their experiences, discuss challenges, and receive constructive criticism to enhance their efforts.

By following this comprehensive evangelism strategy, churches can ensure that all members are equipped and motivated to share the gospel effectively. This approach, grounded in biblical principles and practical training, aims to foster a strong, united church community dedicated to fulfilling the Great Commission.

Ensuring Consistent Doctrinal Teaching Across Congregations

Ensuring consistent doctrinal teaching across congregations is essential for maintaining unity and integrity within the church. A unified approach to doctrine helps prevent confusion, fosters a strong sense of community, and ensures that the gospel message remains clear and uncompromised. Drawing from "The Evangelism Handbook: How All Christians Can Effectively Share God's Word in Their Community," by Edward D. Andrews, this section outlines a comprehensive strategy to achieve doctrinal consistency.

Establishing a Strong Doctrinal Foundation

A consistent doctrinal foundation is built on a thorough understanding of the Bible, using the Historical-Grammatical Method of interpretation. This method emphasizes understanding the original context, grammar, and historical background of the Scriptures, ensuring that the intended meaning is accurately conveyed. Training programs should focus on equipping all members with the skills to study and interpret the Bible correctly. This approach helps to avoid personal biases and ensures that God's message is accurately communicated.

Doctrinal consistency begins with the leaders of the church. Pastors, elders, and teachers must be thoroughly trained in the

Historical-Grammatical Method. They should be able to discern the original intent of the biblical authors and communicate it effectively to their congregations. This requires a commitment to continuous learning and staying grounded in the Scriptures.

Unified Teaching Materials

To maintain consistency, all congregations should use the same teaching materials. These materials should be carefully developed and vetted to ensure they align with biblical principles and the church's doctrinal stance. Using standardized resources helps ensure that all members receive the same foundational teaching, regardless of their congregation. The teaching materials should include Bible study guides, sermon outlines, and educational programs that adhere strictly to the Historical-Grammatical Method.

Developing a centralized library of teaching resources is crucial. This library should be accessible to all congregations and contain approved books, articles, and study guides. Regular updates to these resources are necessary to address new theological insights and challenges while maintaining doctrinal purity.

Centralized Training for Leaders

Leaders play a crucial role in maintaining doctrinal consistency. A centralized training program for pastors, elders, and teachers ensures that all leaders are thoroughly equipped with a deep understanding of the church's doctrine and the skills to teach effectively. Regular training sessions, workshops, and seminars should be conducted to keep leaders updated and aligned with the church's teachings.

These training programs should cover various aspects of biblical interpretation, teaching methods, and practical ministry skills. They should emphasize the importance of adhering to the Historical-Grammatical Method and avoiding the pitfalls of subjective interpretation. Leaders should also be trained to identify and address doctrinal errors within their congregations promptly.

Regular Doctrinal Reviews

Regular doctrinal reviews help ensure that the church's teachings remain consistent and accurate. These reviews should involve a thorough examination of all teaching materials, sermons, and educational programs. Any discrepancies or deviations from the established doctrine should be addressed promptly. This process helps maintain the integrity of the church's teachings and prevents the spread of false doctrines.

A doctrinal review committee should be established to oversee this process. This committee should include experienced theologians and church leaders who are well-versed in the church's doctrinal positions. They should regularly audit the teachings of each congregation, provide feedback, and recommend corrective actions when necessary.

Communication and Feedback Channels

Effective communication channels between congregations and church leadership are vital for maintaining doctrinal consistency. Regular meetings, conferences, and forums allow leaders to discuss doctrinal issues, share insights, and address any concerns. A feedback system should also be in place, allowing members to raise questions and provide input on doctrinal matters.

Creating a robust communication network ensures that any doctrinal issues are identified and addressed promptly. This network should include online forums, newsletters, and regular updates from church leadership. Congregational leaders should be encouraged to share their experiences and insights, fostering a collaborative approach to doctrinal consistency.

Continuous Education and Growth

Doctrinal consistency is not a one-time achievement but an ongoing process. Continuous education and growth are essential for maintaining a unified understanding of the Scriptures. Congregations should be encouraged to engage in regular Bible studies, theological discussions, and personal study. Providing access to educational resources, such as books, articles, and online courses, supports this continuous learning process.

Church members should be encouraged to pursue formal theological education, attend Bible conferences, and participate in study groups. This commitment to lifelong learning helps to deepen their understanding of Scripture and reinforces the church's doctrinal positions. Leaders should also model this commitment by continuously expanding their theological knowledge and sharing their insights with their congregations.

Accountability and Discipline

Maintaining doctrinal consistency requires accountability and, when necessary, discipline. Leaders and members should be held accountable to the church's doctrinal standards. In cases where individuals promote teachings that deviate from the established doctrine, corrective measures should be taken. This may involve counseling, additional training, or, in extreme cases, disciplinary action to protect the integrity of the church's teachings.

A clear process for addressing doctrinal deviations should be established. This process should include steps for investigating doctrinal errors, providing corrective feedback, and implementing disciplinary actions when necessary. Ensuring that all leaders and members understand this process helps to maintain transparency and accountability within the church.

Practical Implementation

1. **Standardized Curriculum**: Develop a standardized curriculum that covers essential doctrinal topics and ensure that all congregations use this curriculum in their teaching programs.

2. **Leader Certification**: Implement a certification program for church leaders, requiring them to complete training and

demonstrate their understanding of the church's doctrine before assuming leadership roles.

3. **Doctrinal Audits**: Conduct regular doctrinal audits to review the teachings of each congregation, ensuring they align with the church's established doctrine.

4. **Inter-Congregational Conferences**: Organize inter-congregational conferences where leaders and members can come together to discuss doctrinal issues, share best practices, and strengthen their unity.

5. **Resource Library**: Create a resource library with approved books, articles, and study guides that members can use to deepen their understanding of the church's doctrine.

Implementing the Strategy

Standardized Curriculum

Developing a standardized curriculum is a foundational step in ensuring consistent doctrinal teaching. This curriculum should be comprehensive, covering essential topics such as the nature of God, salvation, the role of the church, and eschatology. Each topic should be explored in-depth, using the Historical-Grammatical Method to ensure that the original meaning of the Scriptures is accurately conveyed.

The curriculum should be designed to be used in various settings, including Sunday schools, Bible study groups, and discipleship programs. It should include detailed lesson plans, study guides, and supplementary materials that help teachers convey the material effectively. Regular updates to the curriculum should be made to address new theological insights and contemporary issues while maintaining doctrinal integrity.

Leader Certification Program

A leader certification program ensures that all church leaders are adequately trained and equipped to teach the church's doctrine. This program should include rigorous training in biblical interpretation, theology, and practical ministry skills. Leaders should be required to demonstrate their understanding of the church's doctrine and their ability to teach it effectively.

The certification program should be divided into several stages, with each stage focusing on different aspects of ministry and doctrinal teaching. Regular assessments should be conducted to ensure that leaders meet the required standards. Certification should be a prerequisite for all leadership positions within the church, ensuring that all leaders are qualified and committed to maintaining doctrinal consistency.

Doctrinal Audits

Regular doctrinal audits are essential for ensuring that the teachings of each congregation align with the church's established doctrine. These audits should be conducted by a doctrinal review committee, which should include experienced theologians and church leaders. The committee should review teaching materials, sermons, and educational programs to identify any deviations from the established doctrine.

Feedback from the doctrinal audits should be provided to congregational leaders, along with recommendations for corrective actions if necessary. Regular follow-up audits should be conducted to ensure that any issues are resolved and that doctrinal consistency is maintained. This process helps to prevent the spread of false doctrines and ensures that all congregations adhere to the church's doctrinal standards.

Inter-Congregational Conferences

Inter-congregational conferences provide an opportunity for leaders and members from different congregations to come together to discuss doctrinal issues, share best practices, and strengthen their unity. These conferences should be held regularly and include workshops, seminars, and discussion forums focused on doctrinal teaching and biblical interpretation.

The conferences should be designed to foster collaboration and mutual support among congregations. Leaders should be encouraged to share their experiences, insights, and challenges, creating a sense of community and shared purpose. The conferences should also provide opportunities for members to deepen their understanding of the church's doctrine and to engage in theological discussions.

Resource Library

Creating a centralized resource library with approved books, articles, and study guides is essential for supporting doctrinal consistency. This library should be accessible to all congregations and include resources that align with the church's doctrinal positions. The library should be regularly updated to include new publications and to address contemporary theological issues.

The resource library should include materials on various topics, such as biblical interpretation, theology, church history, and practical ministry. Providing access to these resources helps to ensure that all members have the tools they need to deepen their understanding of the Scriptures and to teach the church's doctrine effectively.

Ensuring consistent doctrinal teaching across congregations is crucial for maintaining the unity and integrity of the church. By implementing a structured approach that includes a standardized curriculum, centralized training for leaders, regular doctrinal reviews, effective communication channels, continuous education, and accountability measures, the church can foster a strong, unified community dedicated to sharing the gospel message accurately and effectively.

Developing a Unified Evangelism Program: Training and Equipping All Members for Evangelism

The foundation of a unified evangelism program lies in the consistent training and equipping of all church members. This initiative is not only about knowledge but also about fostering a deep commitment to the Great Commission, ensuring every member is prepared to share the gospel effectively within their community. Drawing from the principles laid out in "The Evangelism Handbook: How All Christians Can Effectively Share God's Word in Their Community," this section will detail how to implement a comprehensive training program that adheres to biblical teachings and practical strategies.

United in Doctrine, United in Mission

Before effective evangelism can occur, there must be unity in doctrine. Churches must ensure that all teachings are consistent with the Bible and that all members are equipped with the same understanding of key doctrinal points. This unity provides a strong foundation for evangelism efforts, as all members are aligned in their beliefs and approach.

Church Community as the Starting Point

The evangelism effort should begin within the church community and extend outward. While it is beneficial to have missionaries who reach out to distant areas, the primary focus should be on local evangelism. Each congregation should actively engage in reaching their immediate community, embodying the principle of evangelism starting "at home" and then expanding outward.

Structured Growth and Expansion

When a congregation exceeds 500 members, it should consider forming additional congregations within the same city. This strategy not only manages growth effectively but also ensures that each congregation remains closely knit and focused on community evangelism. As these new congregations grow, they continue the cycle, thereby covering the entire city with a strong network of biblically grounded churches. This process should then be replicated in other cities, states, and eventually across the country and internationally.

Practical Training Components

Apologetic Evangelism

1. **Importance of Studying the Bible**: Emphasize the necessity of understanding the Bible through the Historical-Grammatical Method. This approach ensures that members can accurately interpret Scripture and communicate its truths effectively.

2. **Effective Communication**: Teach members how to communicate the gospel clearly and persuasively, addressing common objections and questions with sound biblical reasoning.

3. **Social Media Evangelism**: Equip members with the skills to use social media as a platform for evangelism, helping them reach a broader audience while maintaining the integrity of their message.

4. **Building Rapport**: Train members on how to build relationships with non-believers, establishing trust and openness for gospel conversations.

5. **Right Attitude in Evangelism**: Instill the importance of humility, love, and respect when sharing the gospel, ensuring that the message is delivered with grace and truth.

Equip and Proclaim: Evangelism Training School for All

1. **Memory and Focus**: Enhance memory and focus through structured exercises, enabling members to recall Scripture and key points during evangelistic conversations.

2. **Public Speaking**: Develop public speaking skills, including clear articulation, effective modulation, and the use of visual aids to enhance presentations.

3. **Continuous Spiritual Growth**: Encourage ongoing spiritual growth through diligent study, personal reflection, and active participation in church life.

4. **Practical Assignments**: Provide practical assignments that allow members to practice their evangelism skills in real-world settings, receiving feedback and guidance for improvement.

5. **Effective Reading and Research**: Train members in accurate reading, pronunciation, and research methods, ensuring they can study the Bible effectively and present its truths accurately.

Strategies for Sustained Evangelism Efforts

1. **Community Engagement**: Foster a culture of community engagement, where members actively participate in local events, volunteer opportunities, and other community activities to build relationships and share the gospel.

2. **Regular Evangelism Events**: Organize regular evangelism events, such as outreach programs, seminars, and workshops, to maintain momentum and provide continuous opportunities for members to practice their skills.

3. **Mentorship Programs**: Establish mentorship programs where experienced evangelists can guide and support newer members, providing encouragement and practical advice.

4. **Resource Utilization**: Utilize various resources and testimonies from individuals of different backgrounds to illustrate effective evangelism across cultural boundaries, ensuring that the message of the gospel is accessible to all.

5. **Feedback and Improvement**: Implement a system of feedback and continuous improvement, where members can share their experiences, discuss challenges, and receive constructive criticism to enhance their evangelistic efforts.

By implementing a unified evangelism program that focuses on consistent doctrinal teaching and practical training, churches can equip all members to effectively share the gospel within their communities. This approach ensures that the message of salvation is communicated clearly, respectfully, and effectively, leading to the growth and strengthening of the church as a whole.

THE EVANGELISM HANDBOOK: How All Christians Can Effectively Share God's Word in Their Community (2017) Edward D. Andrews (Author)

"The Evangelism Handbook: How All Christians Can Effectively Share God's Word in Their Community" is an essential guide for every believer committed to fulfilling the Great Commission. This comprehensive manual equips Christians with practical tools and biblical strategies to confidently and effectively share the gospel in various contexts.

Book Contents Overview:

Section 1: Apologetic Evangelism

- Delve into the importance of studying the Bible and understanding its true meaning through the Historical-Grammatical Method.

- Learn how to communicate effectively, persuade others, and defend the faith with sound biblical reasoning.

- Discover methods for evangelizing on social media, building rapport, and sharing the gospel with tact and sensitivity.

- Gain insights into the power of body language, watchfulness from the apostles, and the right attitude in evangelism.

Section 2: Equip and Proclaim: Evangelism Training School for All

- Explore a structured training program designed to enhance your memory, focus, and public speaking skills for evangelism.

- Develop effective preparation and delivery of talks, engage in social media evangelism, and strive for continuous spiritual growth.

- Improve through targeted training on accurate reading, pronunciation, modulation, and the use of visual aids in evangelism.

Each chapter provides step-by-step instructions, real-life examples, and scriptural support to help you become a more effective witness for Christ. Whether you are a seasoned evangelist or just starting out, "The Evangelism Handbook" will inspire and guide you to share God's Word with clarity, confidence, and compassion.

Join us on this transformative journey and become a skilled, impactful evangelist in your community, bringing the light of the gospel to those in need.

Table of Contents

Book Description 11

Preface   13

Introduction   15

SECTION 1 Apologetic Evangelism   18

CHAPTER 1 The Importance of Studying the Bible   22

CHAPTER 2 Who Determines the Meaning?   26

CHAPTER 3 Introduction to the Historical-Grammatical Method   30

CHAPTER 4 The Importance of Personal Study 34

CHAPTER 5 Ways to Evangelize Others 38

CHAPTER 6 How to Effectively Communicate with Others   42

CHAPTER 7 Persuading Others to Become a Christian 48

CHAPTER 8 Mastering the Art of Biblical Reasoning and Defense   55

CHAPTER 9 Skilled Evangelists Using God's Word Aright   61

CHAPTER 10 Methods for Evangelizing on Social Media   65

CHAPTER 11 Building Bridges: Establishing Rapport in Evangelism   70

CHAPTER 12 Evangelizing with the Right Attitude   74

CHAPTER 13 Sharing the Gospel with Tact and Sensitivity   79

CHAPTER 14 The Modestly Dressed Evangelist: Reflecting Christ in Appearance and Behavior   84

CHAPTER 15 The Power of Body Language in Evangelism   88

CHAPTER 16 Reasoning from the Scriptures: Engaging Hearts and Minds   92

CHAPTER 17 Learn Watchfulness from Jesus' Apostles: Staying Spiritually Alert in Our Ministry   96

SECTION 2 Equip and Proclaim: Evangelism Training School for All 100

PART I Evangelism Training School   106

CHAPTER 18 Find Joy in the Inspired, Fully Inerrant Word of God   107

CHAPTER 19 Be Aware of How You're Listening   111

CHAPTER 20 Enhancing Your Memory for Effective Evangelism   115

CHAPTER 21 The Power of Focused Reading in Evangelism   119

CHAPTER 22 The Rewards of Diligent Study in Evangelism   124

CHAPTER 23 Mastering the Art of Bible Research   128

CHAPTER 24 Mastering the Art of Making an Outline   132

CHAPTER 25 Crafting Effective Student Assignments for Evangelism Training   136

Edward D. Andrews

CHAPTER 26 Effective Preparation of Talks for Evangelism Training School   140

CHAPTER 27 Developing Effective Public Discourses   144

CHAPTER 28 Cultivating the Skill of Teaching in Evangelism 148

CHAPTER 29 Enhancing Your Conversation Skills for Effective Evangelism 152

CHAPTER 30 Mastering the Art of Answering in Evangelism 157

CHAPTER 31 Engaging Effectively in Evangelism on Social Media 161

CHAPTER 32 Strive for Spiritual Growth: Making Advancement in Evangelism   165

CHAPTER 33 Cultivating Effective Reasoning Skills in Evangelism   169

PART II How to Improve Through the Evangelism Training School 173

CHAPTER 34 Enhancing Skills in Accurate Reading   180

CHAPTER 35 Articulate Your Words Clearly   183

CHAPTER 36 Mastering Accurate Pronunciation in Evangelism Training   186

CHAPTER 37 Learning Fluent Delivery in Evangelism   189

CHAPTER 38 Mastering the Art of Appropriate Pausing in Evangelism   192

CHAPTER 39 Enhancing Communication through Proper Sense Stress   195

CHAPTER 40 Mastering the Emphasis of Principal Ideas in Evangelism   198

CHAPTER 41 Achieving Suitable Volume in Evangelism 201

CHAPTER 42 Effective Modulation in Evangelism   204

CHAPTER 43 The Role of Enthusiasm in Effective Evangelism
207

CHAPTER 44 Conveying Warmth and Feeling in Evangelism
210

CHAPTER 45 The Power of Gestures and Facial Expressions in
Evangelism   213

CHAPTER 46 The Importance of Visual Contact in Evangelism
216

CHAPTER 47 Embracing Naturalness in Evangelism: Being
Yourself   219

CHAPTER 48 Maintaining Good Personal Appearance in
Evangelism   222

CHAPTER 49 Developing Poise in Evangelism: Standing with
Composure   225

CHAPTER 50 Mastering the Modulation of Voice in
Evangelism   228

CHAPTER 51 Effectively Using the Bible in Replying   231

CHAPTER 52 Encouraging Bible Use in Public Evangelism
Talks   234

CHAPTER 53 Effectively Introducing Scriptures in Evangelism
237

CHAPTER 54 Enhancing Evangelism with Proper Emphasis in
Scripture Reading   241

CHAPTER 55 Ensuring Correct Application of Scriptures in
Evangelism   244

CHAPTER 56 Making the Practical Value of Biblical Teaching
Clear in Evangelism   248

CHAPTER 57 The Power of Word Choice in Evangelism
252

Edward D. Andrews

CHAPTER 58 The Importance and Application of Using an Outline in Evangelism 255

CHAPTER 59 Structuring Evangelistic Messages with Logical Development 259

CHAPTER 60 Mastering Impromptu Delivery in Evangelism 263

CHAPTER 61 Developing a Conversational Manner in Evangelism 267

CHAPTER 62 Enhancing Voice Quality for Effective Evangelism 271

CHAPTER 63 Interest Shown in the Other Person 275

CHAPTER 64 Demonstrating Respect in Evangelism 279

CHAPTER 65 Speaking with Conviction: Strengthening Your Evangelistic Message 283

CHAPTER 66 Demonstrating Tact and Firmness in Evangelism 287

CHAPTER 67 Encouraging and Positive Evangelism 291

CHAPTER 68 Reiteration for Impact 295

CHAPTER 69 Developing a Unified Theme in Evangelistic Presentations 299

CHAPTER 70 Highlighting Main Points in Evangelistic Presentations 303

CHAPTER 71 Captivating Your Audience from the Start 307

CHAPTER 72 Crafting a Compelling Conclusion to Inspire Action 311

CHAPTER 73 Commitment to Accurate Statements in Evangelism 315

CHAPTER 74 Clarity in Evangelistic Communication 319

CHAPTER 75 Engaging and Informative Communication 322

CHAPTER 76 Building Your Talk Around Assigned Material 326

CHAPTER 77 Mastering the Art of Questions in Evangelism 330

CHAPTER 78 Using Illustrations and Examples to Teach Effectively   334

CHAPTER 79 Engaging Hearts: Illustrations from Familiar Situations   338

CHAPTER 80 Visual Aids for Evangelism: Enhancing Understanding and Retention 342

CHAPTER 81 The Power of a Reasoning Manner in Evangelism   346

CHAPTER 82 Convincing with Sound Arguments in Evangelism   350

CHAPTER 83 Appealing to the Heart in Evangelism   354

CHAPTER 84 Measured Moments, Balanced Deliverance 358

CHAPTER 85 Compelling Exhortation for Evangelistic Impact 362

CHAPTER 86 Inspiring and Strengthening the Audience 366

CHAPTER 87 Proclaiming the Gospel Message Effectively 370

CHAPTER 88 Instructions for School Evangelism Instructors for the Evangelism Training School   374

Bibliography   380

Chapter 13: Restoring Doctrinal Purity

Identifying Core Doctrines Based on Biblical Teaching

Restoring doctrinal purity within the church necessitates a return to the core doctrines based on a literal interpretation of the Bible. The Historical-Grammatical Method of interpretation serves as the most reliable approach, enabling us to understand what the biblical authors meant by the words they used. This method ensures that our interpretations are rooted in the original context, grammar, and historical setting of the Scriptures, thus preserving the intended meaning of the biblical text. Drawing insights from Edward D. Andrews' works, "INTERPRETING THE BIBLE: Introduction to Biblical Hermeneutics" and "BIBLICAL EXEGESIS: Biblical Criticism on Trial," we will explore how to identify and uphold these core doctrines.

The Historical-Grammatical Method

The Historical-Grammatical Method is both a science and an art that involves analyzing the grammar and historical context of the biblical text to uncover the author's original intent. This method stands in contrast to the subjective approaches of modern biblical criticism, which often impose contemporary ideologies onto the text. By focusing on the literal meaning of the text, the Historical-Grammatical Method maintains the integrity of Scripture and avoids the pitfalls of eisegesis—reading one's own ideas into the text.

Edward D. Andrews, in his book "INTERPRETING THE BIBLE: Introduction to Biblical Hermeneutics," emphasizes that understanding the Bible goes beyond surface reading. It requires a careful examination of the genres, historical contexts, and language used by the biblical authors. This foundational approach ensures that interpretations are not swayed by personal biases but are grounded in the actual words of Scripture.

Core Doctrines of the Christian Faith

1. **The Nature of God**: Understanding the nature of God as revealed in Scripture is paramount. God is described as one being in three persons—Father, Son, and Holy Spirit. This Trinitarian doctrine is foundational to Christian theology. Deuteronomy 6:4 states, "Hear, O Israel: Jehovah our God, Jehovah is one." This is further expanded in the New Testament, where the distinct persons of the Trinity are seen working in harmony (Matthew 28:19).

2. **The Authority of Scripture**: The Bible is the inspired, inerrant Word of God. 2 Timothy 3:16-17 asserts, "All Scripture is inspired by God and is profitable for teaching, for reproof, for correction, for instruction in righteousness, that the man of God may be complete, thoroughly equipped for every good work." Upholding the authority of Scripture is essential for maintaining doctrinal purity.

3. **Salvation through Faith in Jesus Christ**: The doctrine of salvation is central to the Christian faith. Ephesians 2:8-9 states, "For by grace you have been saved through faith, and that not of yourselves; it is the gift of God, not of works, lest anyone should boast." This doctrine underscores that salvation is a gift from God, received through faith in Jesus Christ, and not by human effort.

4. **The Deity of Christ**: Jesus Christ is fully God and fully man. John 1:1, 14 affirms, "In the beginning was the Word, and the Word was with God, and the Word was God... And the Word became flesh and dwelt among us, and we beheld his glory, the glory as of the only begotten of the Father, full of grace and truth." Recognizing the deity of Christ is essential for understanding the nature of the gospel.

5. **The Resurrection**: The resurrection of Jesus Christ is a cornerstone of Christian faith. 1 Corinthians 15:14-17 states, "And if Christ is not risen, then our preaching is empty and your faith is also empty... But now Christ is risen from the dead, and has become the firstfruits of those who have fallen asleep." The resurrection validates Jesus' victory over sin and death and assures believers of their future resurrection.

6. **The Second Coming of Christ**: The return of Jesus Christ is a fundamental belief. Acts 1:11 records the angels' words to the disciples, "This same Jesus, who was taken up from you into heaven, will so come in like manner as you saw him go into heaven." This doctrine provides hope and motivation for holy living.

Conservative Eisegesis and Its Role

While exegesis involves drawing out the meaning of the text, eisegesis involves reading meaning into the text. Conservative eisegesis, however, insists that any interpretation aligns with the broader theological framework established by Scripture. It avoids speculative interpretations and maintains fidelity to the historical and grammatical context of the biblical text. Edward D. Andrews, in "BIBLICAL EXEGESIS: Biblical Criticism on Trial," critiques the liberal-moderate approaches that often lead to doctrinal confusion and highlights the need for a return to conservative, biblically-grounded exegesis.

Implementing Doctrinal Purity in the Church

1. **Teaching and Preaching**: Consistent and accurate teaching and preaching of the core doctrines are vital. Pastors and teachers should be well-versed in the Historical-Grammatical Method and committed to conveying the original intent of the biblical authors. Regular doctrinal sermons and Bible studies help reinforce these truths within the congregation.

2. **Educational Programs**: Implement comprehensive educational programs that equip church members with the

skills to study the Bible accurately. Courses on biblical hermeneutics, theology, and church history can provide a solid foundation for understanding and defending the faith.

3. **Doctrinal Statements**: Develop clear and concise doctrinal statements that outline the church's beliefs based on Scripture. These statements serve as a guide for teaching and a standard for evaluating doctrinal purity. They should be readily available to all members and regularly reviewed to ensure alignment with biblical teaching.

4. **Accountability Structures**: Establish accountability structures to maintain doctrinal purity. This includes forming doctrinal review committees to oversee the teaching within the church and address any deviations from core doctrines. Regular audits and feedback mechanisms ensure that all teaching aligns with the church's doctrinal standards.

5. **Training Leaders**: Invest in the training and development of church leaders. Provide them with the resources and support needed to accurately interpret and teach the Bible. Encourage continuous learning and theological development to keep leaders grounded in the core doctrines.

6. **Resources and Tools**: Utilize reliable resources and tools that support accurate biblical interpretation. This includes scholarly commentaries, study Bibles, and educational materials that adhere to the Historical-Grammatical Method. Encourage the use of these resources in personal study and teaching.

Addressing Modern Challenges

The modern church faces numerous challenges that threaten doctrinal purity, including cultural pressures, theological liberalism, and misinformation. Addressing these challenges requires a firm commitment to the authority of Scripture and the core doctrines of the Christian faith.

1. **Cultural Pressures**: The church must resist the temptation to conform to cultural norms that contradict biblical teaching.

This requires a clear understanding of Scripture and a willingness to stand firm in the face of opposition. Regular teaching on the relevance and authority of the Bible helps equip members to navigate these pressures.

2. **Theological Liberalism**: The rise of theological liberalism has led to the erosion of core doctrines. Combatting this requires a return to conservative, biblically-grounded exegesis. Encouraging critical thinking and discernment within the congregation helps members recognize and reject false teachings.

3. **Misinformation**: In the age of information, misinformation about the Bible and Christian doctrine is rampant. Providing accurate, accessible resources and teaching helps counteract this. Encourage members to seek out reliable sources and to verify information against Scripture.

Practical Steps for Implementation

1. **Develop a Comprehensive Curriculum**: Create a curriculum that covers the core doctrines and provides in-depth study of the Bible using the Historical-Grammatical Method. This curriculum should be used in all teaching settings within the church, from Sunday schools to discipleship programs.

2. **Host Regular Training Sessions**: Conduct regular training sessions for church leaders and teachers. These sessions should focus on biblical hermeneutics, theology, and practical ministry skills. Encourage continuous learning and provide opportunities for leaders to deepen their understanding of Scripture.

3. **Form Doctrinal Review Committees**: Establish committees responsible for reviewing all teaching materials and ensuring they align with the church's doctrinal standards. These committees should regularly audit sermons, Bible studies, and educational programs, providing feedback and recommendations for improvement.

4. **Encourage Personal Study**: Promote personal Bible study among church members. Provide resources and tools that support accurate interpretation, such as study guides, commentaries, and online courses. Encourage members to engage with the Bible regularly and to seek out reliable sources for their studies.

5. **Foster a Culture of Accountability**: Create a culture of accountability within the church. Encourage open dialogue about doctrinal issues and provide a safe space for members to raise concerns. Establish clear processes for addressing doctrinal deviations and ensure that all leaders are held accountable to the church's doctrinal standards.

6. **Utilize Technology**: Leverage technology to support doctrinal teaching. Use online platforms to share sermons, teaching materials, and educational resources. Provide access to digital libraries and online courses that members can use to deepen their understanding of Scripture.

Restoring doctrinal purity within the church is a critical task that requires a return to the core doctrines based on a literal interpretation of the Bible. The Historical-Grammatical Method of interpretation provides a reliable framework for understanding what the biblical authors meant by the words they used. By implementing comprehensive educational programs, establishing accountability structures, and promoting continuous learning, the church can ensure that its teachings remain consistent and aligned with Scripture. This commitment to doctrinal purity will equip the church to navigate modern challenges and to faithfully proclaim the gospel message to the world.

Addressing and Correcting False Doctrines

Restoring doctrinal purity within the church is akin to a meticulous and committed physician diagnosing and treating a potentially terminal illness. In the spiritual context, this involves identifying, addressing, and correcting false doctrines that have infiltrated the church. Using the Historical-Grammatical Method of Interpretation and the principles outlined in Edward D. Andrews' books, "INTERPRETING THE BIBLE: Introduction to Biblical Hermeneutics" and "BIBLICAL EXEGESIS: Biblical Criticism on Trial," we will examine the steps necessary for this crucial task.

The Historical-Grammatical Method: Foundation of Truth

The Historical-Grammatical Method of interpretation is essential for understanding Scripture as the authors intended. This method focuses on the literal meaning of the text, considering its grammatical structure and historical context. This approach stands in stark contrast to modern biblical criticism, which often distorts the text by imposing contemporary biases and ideologies.

Edward D. Andrews emphasizes that understanding the Bible requires careful analysis of its genres, historical contexts, and language. This approach ensures that interpretations are rooted in the original meaning intended by the biblical authors, thus preserving the integrity of Scripture.

Identifying False Doctrines

The first step in restoring doctrinal purity is identifying false doctrines. False teachings often arise from misinterpretations or deliberate distortions of Scripture. These can be identified by their deviation from the core doctrines of Christianity as revealed in the Bible.

1. **The Nature of God**: Any teaching that contradicts the biblical portrayal of God as one being in three persons—Father, Son, and Holy Spirit—is a false doctrine. For instance, teachings that deny the deity of Christ or the personhood of the Holy Spirit must be corrected.

2. **The Authority of Scripture**: Teachings that undermine the authority of the Bible, suggesting it contains errors or is not

fully inspired, are false doctrines. The Bible must be upheld as the inerrant Word of God.

3. **Salvation through Faith in Jesus Christ**: Doctrines that promote salvation through works or any means other than faith in Jesus Christ are false. Ephesians 2:8-9 clearly states, "For by grace you have been saved through faith, and that not of yourselves; it is the gift of God, not of works, lest anyone should boast."

4. **The Resurrection**: Denying the physical resurrection of Jesus or the future resurrection of believers is a false doctrine. The resurrection is a cornerstone of Christian faith, as affirmed in 1 Corinthians 15.

Addressing False Doctrines

Once false doctrines are identified, they must be addressed with clarity and conviction. This involves both public refutation and private correction, always with the aim of restoring truth and unity within the church.

1. **Public Refutation**: False doctrines that have gained public traction must be publicly refuted. This can be done through sermons, Bible studies, and published materials that clearly outline the biblical truth and expose the errors of the false teachings. For example, Paul publicly refuted false teachers in his letters to the Galatians and Corinthians.

2. **Private Correction**: Individuals who have been influenced by false doctrines should be approached privately and lovingly corrected. This involves patient teaching and discussion, helping them to see the truth of Scripture. As Paul advised Timothy, "A servant of the Lord must not quarrel but be gentle to all, able to teach, patient, in humility correcting those who are in opposition" (2 Timothy 2:24-25).

3. **Educational Programs**: Implementing comprehensive educational programs that teach the core doctrines of the faith and the principles of sound biblical interpretation is essential.

This ensures that church members are well-equipped to discern truth from error.

Correcting Doctrines with Conservative Eisegesis

While exegesis involves drawing out the meaning of the text, conservative eisegesis involves ensuring that interpretations align with the broader theological framework established by Scripture. It maintains fidelity to the historical and grammatical context of the biblical text, avoiding speculative and ideologically driven interpretations.

Edward D. Andrews, in "BIBLICAL EXEGESIS: Biblical Criticism on Trial," critiques liberal-moderate approaches that lead to doctrinal confusion. He highlights the need for a return to conservative, biblically grounded exegesis. This involves:

1. **Faithful Interpretation**: Ensuring that all interpretations are consistent with the overall message of the Bible. This means interpreting difficult passages in light of clearer ones and maintaining the unity of Scripture.

2. **Rejecting Speculation**: Avoiding interpretations that rely on speculative theories or modern ideologies. The focus should always be on what the text actually says and means within its original context.

3. **Commitment to Truth**: Upholding the authority and inerrancy of Scripture in all teaching and preaching. This commitment ensures that the church remains grounded in the truth of God's Word.

Implementing Corrective Measures

To correct false doctrines and restore doctrinal purity, the church must implement specific measures that uphold the integrity of Scripture and promote sound teaching.

1. **Doctrinal Statements**: Develop clear and concise doctrinal statements that outline the church's beliefs based on Scripture.

These statements should be used as a guide for teaching and a standard for evaluating doctrinal purity.

2. **Doctrinal Review Committees**: Establish committees responsible for reviewing all teaching materials and ensuring they align with the church's doctrinal standards. These committees should regularly audit sermons, Bible studies, and educational programs, providing feedback and recommendations for improvement.

3. **Training Programs**: Implement training programs that equip church leaders and teachers with the skills to accurately interpret and teach the Bible. These programs should focus on the Historical-Grammatical Method, theology, and practical ministry skills.

4. **Accountability Structures**: Create structures that promote accountability within the church. This includes establishing processes for addressing doctrinal deviations and ensuring that all leaders are held accountable to the church's doctrinal standards.

5. **Promoting Personal Study**: Encourage personal Bible study among church members. Provide resources and tools that support accurate interpretation, such as study guides, commentaries, and online courses. Promote regular engagement with the Bible and the use of reliable sources for study.

6. **Using Technology**: Leverage technology to support doctrinal teaching. Use online platforms to share sermons, teaching materials, and educational resources. Provide access to digital libraries and online courses that members can use to deepen their understanding of Scripture.

Addressing and correcting false doctrines is a critical task for restoring doctrinal purity within the church. By using the Historical-Grammatical Method of Interpretation and adhering to conservative exegetical principles, the church can ensure that its teachings remain faithful to the original intent of the biblical authors. Implementing comprehensive educational programs, establishing accountability structures, and promoting personal study are essential steps in this process. This commitment to doctrinal purity will equip the church to navigate modern challenges and faithfully proclaim the gospel message to the world.

Encouraging Theological Education and Biblical Literacy

Restoring doctrinal purity in the church necessitates a commitment to theological education and biblical literacy. The task is not merely about imparting knowledge but about fostering a deep and abiding relationship with God's Word. This endeavor must be grounded in the Historical-Grammatical Method of interpretation and informed by conservative exegetical principles. Using insights from Edward D. Andrews' books, "INTERPRETING THE BIBLE: Introduction to Biblical Hermeneutics" and "BIBLICAL EXEGESIS: Biblical Criticism on Trial," this chapter will outline a comprehensive strategy for encouraging theological education and biblical literacy within the church.

The Necessity of Theological Education

Theological education is essential for ensuring that church leaders and members are well-equipped to understand and teach the Bible accurately. Theological education provides the tools needed to interpret Scripture correctly, defend the faith, and apply biblical principles to everyday life.

1. **Training Church Leaders**: Church leaders, including pastors, elders, and teachers, must receive thorough theological training. This training should cover biblical languages, hermeneutics, theology, church history, and practical ministry skills. Leaders must be able to interpret Scripture accurately and teach it effectively to their congregations.

2. **Equipping Lay Members**: Theological education should not be limited to church leaders. Lay members also need to be equipped with a solid understanding of biblical doctrine and

interpretation. Churches should offer classes and seminars on various theological topics, making them accessible to all members.

3. **Developing Curriculum**: Churches should develop a curriculum that covers essential theological topics. This curriculum should be structured to provide a comprehensive understanding of the Bible and its teachings. Topics might include the nature of God, salvation, sanctification, the end times, and the role of the church.

Implementing Biblical Literacy Programs

Biblical literacy is the foundation upon which sound theology is built. A biblically literate church is one where members read, understand, and apply Scripture in their daily lives. To foster biblical literacy, churches must implement programs that encourage regular and in-depth engagement with the Bible.

1. **Bible Study Groups**: Establish regular Bible study groups that meet to read and discuss Scripture. These groups should be led by knowledgeable leaders who can guide discussions and answer questions. The goal is to help members understand the text in its historical and grammatical context.

2. **Scripture Memorization**: Encourage members to memorize Scripture. Memorization helps internalize God's Word and provides a foundation for spiritual growth and doctrinal stability. Churches can organize memorization challenges and provide resources to assist with this practice.

3. **Daily Bible Reading Plans**: Promote daily Bible reading by providing reading plans that guide members through the entire Bible. Reading plans can be tailored to different levels of familiarity with Scripture, ensuring that everyone can participate.

4. **Biblical Literacy Workshops**: Host workshops focused on biblical literacy skills, such as how to study the Bible, understanding biblical genres, and using study tools like

concordances and commentaries. These workshops should be practical and interactive, equipping members with the skills they need to engage with Scripture independently.

Promoting the Historical-Grammatical Method

The Historical-Grammatical Method is the cornerstone of accurate biblical interpretation. It ensures that the meaning derived from Scripture is consistent with the intent of the original authors. Churches must promote this method as the standard approach to interpreting the Bible.

1. **Teaching the Method**: Offer classes on the Historical-Grammatical Method, explaining its principles and demonstrating how to apply them. These classes should cover topics such as understanding historical context, analyzing grammatical structures, and identifying literary genres.

2. **Using Reliable Resources**: Provide members with access to reliable resources that support the Historical-Grammatical Method. This includes study Bibles, commentaries, and online tools that align with conservative exegetical principles.

3. **Modeling in Preaching and Teaching**: Church leaders should model the use of the Historical-Grammatical Method in their preaching and teaching. Sermons and Bible studies should demonstrate how this method leads to accurate and meaningful interpretations of Scripture.

Encouraging a Love for God's Word

Beyond mere academic understanding, encouraging a deep love for God's Word is crucial. This love for Scripture motivates believers to study, internalize, and live out biblical truths.

1. **Personal Testimonies**: Share personal testimonies of how engagement with Scripture has transformed lives. Hearing how God's Word has impacted others can inspire members to seek similar experiences.

2. **Passionate Teaching**: Teach with passion and conviction, conveying the beauty and power of God's Word. When leaders demonstrate their love for Scripture, it can ignite a similar passion in their listeners.

3. **Spiritual Disciplines**: Encourage the practice of spiritual disciplines such as prayer, meditation, and fasting, alongside Bible study. These disciplines help cultivate a deeper relationship with God and a greater appreciation for His Word.

Addressing Modern Challenges

In today's world, biblical literacy faces numerous challenges, including secularism, relativism, and the proliferation of false teachings. Churches must be proactive in addressing these challenges to maintain doctrinal purity.

1. **Countering Secularism**: Teach members to recognize and refute secular ideologies that contradict biblical teachings. Provide resources that address common secular arguments and equip members to defend their faith.

2. **Standing Against Relativism**: Emphasize the absolute truth of Scripture in a culture that promotes relativism. Teach that God's Word is the ultimate authority and that its truths are timeless and unchanging.

3. **Refuting False Teachings**: Equip members to identify and refute false teachings. This includes understanding the characteristics of false doctrines and knowing how to respond biblically. Use examples of contemporary false teachings to illustrate these points.

Building a Supportive Community

Creating a supportive community that values theological education and biblical literacy is essential. This community should encourage one another in the pursuit of truth and provide accountability in maintaining doctrinal purity.

1. **Mentorship Programs**: Establish mentorship programs where mature believers can guide others in their theological education and spiritual growth. Mentors can provide personalized support, answer questions, and model faithful Christian living.

2. **Discussion Forums**: Create forums for open discussion and debate on theological issues. These forums should be guided by knowledgeable leaders who can ensure that discussions remain respectful and grounded in Scripture.

3. **Encouraging Accountability**: Promote accountability by encouraging members to study the Bible together, share insights, and hold one another accountable in their understanding and application of Scripture.

Leveraging Technology for Theological Education

In the digital age, technology offers numerous opportunities to enhance theological education and biblical literacy. Churches should leverage these tools to reach a wider audience and provide accessible resources.

1. **Online Courses**: Offer online courses on theological topics and biblical interpretation. These courses can reach members who may not be able to attend in-person classes and provide flexible learning options.

2. **Digital Libraries**: Provide access to digital libraries that include reliable theological resources. Members can use these libraries for personal study and research.

3. **Webinars and Podcasts**: Host webinars and podcasts that cover various theological topics and biblical studies. These formats allow for in-depth exploration of subjects and can be accessed at any time.

4. **Social Media Engagement**: Use social media platforms to share biblical content, promote theological discussions, and connect with a broader audience. This can include posting

articles, hosting live Q&A sessions, and sharing testimonies of how Scripture has impacted lives.

Encouraging theological education and biblical literacy is a vital task for restoring doctrinal purity within the church. By equipping leaders and members with a deep understanding of Scripture, promoting the Historical-Grammatical Method of interpretation, and fostering a love for God's Word, the church can stand firm against false doctrines and uphold the truth of the Bible. Implementing comprehensive educational programs, addressing modern challenges, and leveraging technology will ensure that the church remains grounded in sound doctrine and faithfully proclaims the gospel to the world.

Edward D. Andrews

Chapter 14: Creating a New Denomination for True Christians

Defining the Mission and Vision of the New Denomination

In establishing a new denomination dedicated to adhering strictly to biblical truths, it is crucial to define a clear mission and vision that guides all activities and decisions. This denomination should be rooted in the principles of the Historical-Grammatical Method of biblical interpretation, uphold conservative exegetical standards, and reject the fallacies of modern biblical criticism. The mission and vision must be grounded in Scripture, focusing on the purity of doctrine, the unity of believers, and the effective spread of the gospel.

The Mission

The mission of this new denomination is to restore and uphold the doctrinal purity of the Christian faith as revealed in the Holy Scriptures. This includes:

1. **Proclaiming the Gospel**: The primary mission is to proclaim the gospel of Jesus Christ to all nations, making disciples and baptizing them in the name of the Father, the Son, and the Holy Spirit. (Matthew 28:19-20)

2. **Teaching Sound Doctrine**: Ensuring that all teachings and practices are firmly rooted in the Bible, interpreted through the Historical-Grammatical Method, to maintain doctrinal integrity. (Titus 2:1)

3. **Promoting Biblical Literacy**: Encouraging deep and regular engagement with Scripture among all members to foster a thorough understanding of God's Word. (Psalm 1:2)

4. **Equipping the Saints**: Providing comprehensive theological education and practical training to equip believers for ministry and effective evangelism. (Ephesians 4:11-12)

5. **Maintaining Holiness and Integrity**: Upholding high standards of personal and corporate holiness, reflecting the character of Christ in all aspects of life. (1 Peter 1:15-16)

6. **Fostering Unity**: Striving for unity among believers through shared beliefs and practices, while avoiding ecumenism that compromises biblical truth. (John 17:21)

The Vision

The vision of this new denomination encompasses long-term goals and aspirations that align with its mission. The vision should inspire and direct the efforts of all members and leaders:

1. **A Biblically Grounded Community**: Building a community of believers who are deeply rooted in Scripture, demonstrating a commitment to understanding and living out biblical truths. (Colossians 3:16)

2. **Faithful Churches Worldwide**: Establishing churches that adhere strictly to biblical doctrines across cities, states, and countries, ensuring that the truth of the gospel reaches every corner of the globe. (Acts 1:8)

3. **Holistic Discipleship**: Developing a robust discipleship program that addresses spiritual growth, biblical knowledge, and practical application of faith in daily life. (2 Timothy 2:2)

4. **Effective Evangelism**: Implementing a comprehensive evangelism strategy that equips every member to share the gospel effectively in their communities and beyond, leading to widespread conversion and church growth. (2 Timothy 4:5)

5. **Strong Leadership**: Cultivating a new generation of church leaders who are well-versed in Scripture, capable of teaching sound doctrine, and committed to leading with integrity and humility. (1 Timothy 3:1-7)

6. **Cultural Engagement**: Engaging with the surrounding culture in a way that upholds biblical values, challenges secular ideologies, and presents the gospel as the ultimate truth and solution. (1 Peter 3:15)

7. **Resource Development**: Producing high-quality resources, including books, study guides, and digital content, that support theological education and evangelistic efforts. (Proverbs 4:7)

Implementation Strategy

To achieve the mission and vision of the new denomination, a strategic plan must be developed. This plan should include specific actions, timelines, and accountability measures:

1. **Establishing Doctrinal Standards**: Formulate and publish a comprehensive statement of faith that clearly articulates the core doctrines and theological positions of the denomination. This document will serve as the foundation for all teaching and practice. (2 Timothy 1:13-14)

2. **Developing Educational Programs**: Create theological training programs for church leaders and lay members, focusing on biblical interpretation, doctrine, and practical ministry skills. These programs should be accessible and rigorous, ensuring a high standard of theological education. (2 Timothy 2:15)

3. **Planting New Churches**: Launch church planting initiatives that follow a strategic plan for growth. Start by establishing a strong base in key cities and expand to surrounding areas. Each new church should adhere strictly to the denomination's doctrinal standards and be equipped to engage in effective evangelism. (Acts 14:21-23)

4. **Promoting Accountability**: Implement structures for accountability among church leaders and members. This includes regular doctrinal reviews, peer evaluations, and disciplinary measures for those who deviate from biblical teaching. (Galatians 6:1)

5. **Utilizing Technology**: Leverage modern technology to enhance theological education, evangelism, and community building. This includes online courses, webinars, social media engagement, and digital resources. (1 Corinthians 9:22)

6. **Encouraging Personal Holiness**: Promote a culture of personal holiness and integrity within the denomination. Encourage regular spiritual disciplines such as prayer, fasting, and Scripture meditation, and provide support for members struggling with sin. (James 1:22)

7. **Fostering Unity**: Work diligently to maintain unity within the denomination by addressing conflicts biblically, fostering open communication, and emphasizing shared beliefs and goals. Avoid practices that lead to division or compromise on essential doctrines. (Ephesians 4:3)

Commitment to Scriptural Authority

Central to the mission and vision of the new denomination is an unwavering commitment to the authority of Scripture. The Bible is the ultimate guide for faith and practice, and all doctrinal and ethical decisions must be based on its teachings. This commitment involves:

1. **Upholding Inerrancy**: Affirming that the Bible, in its original manuscripts, is without error and fully trustworthy in all it teaches. This includes historical, doctrinal, and ethical teachings. (Psalm 19:7-9)

2. **Promoting Expository Preaching**: Emphasizing the importance of expository preaching that systematically teaches through books of the Bible, allowing the text to speak for itself and ensuring that God's Word is faithfully communicated. (2 Timothy 4:2)

3. **Encouraging Biblical Interpretation**: Teaching members to interpret Scripture correctly using the Historical-Grammatical Method, which seeks to understand the original meaning of the text in its historical and cultural context. (Nehemiah 8:8)

4. **Rejecting Modern Critical Methods**: Rejecting the use of modern critical methods that undermine the authority of Scripture, such as form criticism, redaction criticism, and other approaches that question the reliability of the biblical text. (1 Timothy 6:20)

Defining the mission and vision of the new denomination is a critical step in ensuring that it remains faithful to biblical teaching and effective in its ministry. By grounding all activities in Scripture, promoting theological education, fostering unity, and leveraging modern technology, the denomination can fulfill its mission of restoring doctrinal purity and proclaiming the gospel to the world. This commitment to truth and integrity will serve as a guiding light, leading the denomination to impact lives and glorify God in all that it does.

Establishing Foundational Beliefs and Practices

Establishing a new denomination for true Christians involves laying down a clear and uncompromising foundation of beliefs and practices based on the unerring truths of the Bible. This new denomination must prioritize doctrinal purity, rooted in the Historical-Grammatical Method of interpretation, and reject the distortions brought by modern biblical criticism. Our foundational beliefs and practices must reflect an unwavering commitment to the authority of Scripture, the historical doctrines of the Christian faith, and a dedication to evangelizing the world with the gospel of Jesus Christ.

Foundational Beliefs

1. **Scriptural Inerrancy and Authority**: We affirm that the Bible, in its original manuscripts, is the inspired, infallible, and authoritative Word of God. Every word of Scripture is God-

breathed and must be the final authority in all matters of faith and practice. (2 Timothy 3:16-17)

2. **Historical-Grammatical Interpretation**: Our approach to interpreting the Bible is the Historical-Grammatical Method. This method seeks to understand the original intent of the biblical authors by considering the historical context, grammar, and literary form of the text. We reject subjective and modern critical methods that undermine the reliability of Scripture. (Nehemiah 8:8)

3. **The Trinity**: We believe in one God, eternally existing in three Persons: Father, Son, and Holy Spirit. Each Person of the Trinity is fully God, co-equal and co-eternal. (Matthew 28:19)

4. **The Deity and Humanity of Christ**: We affirm that Jesus Christ is fully God and fully man. He was conceived by the Holy Spirit, born of the virgin Mary, lived a sinless life, died on the cross for our sins, rose bodily from the dead, ascended to heaven, and will return in glory. (John 1:1, 14; Philippians 2:6-8)

5. **Salvation by Grace Through Faith**: Salvation is a gift of God's grace, received through faith in Jesus Christ alone. We are justified by faith apart from works, and this salvation is available to all who believe. (Ephesians 2:8-9; Romans 3:28)

6. **The Person and Work of the Holy Spirit**: The Holy Spirit is fully God and works to convict the world of sin, righteousness, and judgment. He regenerates, indwells, and empowers believers for godly living and service. (John 16:8-11; Titus 3:5)

7. **The Church**: The Church is the body of Christ, composed of all true believers. It exists to glorify God, edify believers, and evangelize the lost. We reject ecumenical movements that compromise doctrinal integrity. (Ephesians 4:4-6; Acts 2:42-47)

8. **The Ordinances**: We affirm two ordinances instituted by Christ: baptism and the Lord's Supper. Baptism is the outward sign of inward faith and identification with Christ, while the

Lord's Supper is a memorial of His death and anticipation of His return. (Matthew 28:19; 1 Corinthians 11:23-26)

9. **Eschatology**: We believe in the personal, visible return of Jesus Christ, the resurrection of the dead, the final judgment, and the eternal state of the righteous and the wicked. (Revelation 20:11-15; 1 Thessalonians 4:16-17)

Foundational Practices

1. **Expository Preaching and Teaching**: Our primary method of teaching the Scriptures will be expository preaching, where the message of the Bible is explained and applied in its context. This ensures that the congregation receives the full counsel of God. (2 Timothy 4:2)

2. **Doctrinal Education**: We will establish comprehensive programs for theological education to equip all members with a deep understanding of biblical doctrines and how to defend the faith. This includes regular Bible studies, discipleship programs, and training in apologetics. (1 Peter 3:15)

3. **Evangelism and Discipleship**: Every member of the church will be trained and encouraged to engage in personal evangelism and discipleship, following the model outlined in "The Evangelism Handbook" by Edward D. Andrews. This involves sharing the gospel in our communities and beyond, planting new churches, and nurturing new believers. (Matthew 28:19-20)

4. **Church Planting Strategy**: We will implement a strategic church planting initiative where new congregations are established once existing churches reach a certain size (e.g., 500 members). This strategy aims to spread the gospel efficiently and manage church growth effectively. (Acts 14:21-23)

5. **Prayer and Worship**: Our gatherings will emphasize heartfelt prayer and worship, recognizing the importance of seeking God's guidance and expressing our devotion through praise.

This includes regular corporate prayer meetings and worship services that honor God's holiness. (Acts 2:42; Psalm 95:6)

6. **Accountability and Discipline**: We will maintain structures for accountability among church leaders and members to ensure doctrinal purity and moral integrity. This involves regular doctrinal reviews, ethical oversight, and, when necessary, church discipline to address unrepentant sin. (Galatians 6:1-2; 1 Corinthians 5:12-13)

7. **Community Engagement**: While upholding doctrinal purity, we will engage with our communities to demonstrate Christ's love through acts of service and compassion. This includes outreach programs, charitable activities, and support for those in need, always pointing them to the gospel. (James 1:27; Matthew 5:16)

8. **Stewardship**: We will teach and practice biblical stewardship, encouraging members to use their time, talents, and resources for the glory of God and the advancement of His kingdom. This includes responsible financial giving, volunteer service, and wise management of church resources. (2 Corinthians 9:6-7; 1 Peter 4:10)

9. **Biblical Counseling**: We will offer counseling services based on biblical principles to support members facing personal, relational, or spiritual challenges. This ministry aims to bring healing and restoration through the application of God's Word. (2 Timothy 3:16-17; Galatians 6:2)

10. **Global Missions**: Committed to the Great Commission, we will actively support and send missionaries to unreached areas, partnering with like-minded organizations to extend the reach of the gospel worldwide. (Romans 10:14-15; Acts 1:8)

Establishing a new denomination for true Christians requires a steadfast commitment to the foundational beliefs and practices derived from Scripture. By adhering to the Historical-Grammatical Method of interpretation, rejecting modern critical approaches, and focusing on doctrinal purity, we can build a denomination that faithfully represents the teachings of the Bible and effectively fulfills the Great

Commission. This new denomination will stand as a beacon of truth in a world increasingly tolerant of doctrinal error and moral compromise, ensuring that the true gospel of Jesus Christ is proclaimed and preserved for generations to come.

Strategies for Attracting True Christians from Divided Denominations

In creating a new denomination that faithfully adheres to biblical truths, one of the crucial steps is to attract true Christians from currently divided denominations. This requires a clear, compelling vision grounded in the inerrant Word of God, coupled with a strategic approach that emphasizes unity in doctrine and practice. The following strategies will outline how to achieve this objective effectively.

Establishing a Clear Doctrinal Foundation

The first and foremost step in attracting true Christians is to establish a clear and uncompromising doctrinal foundation. This foundation must be rooted in the Historical-Grammatical Method of interpretation, ensuring that our beliefs are directly derived from the intended meaning of the biblical authors. We must clearly articulate our stance on key doctrines such as the Trinity, the deity and humanity of Christ, salvation by grace through faith, the authority of Scripture, and the role of the church. By providing a robust theological framework, we offer a stable and reliable alternative to the doctrinal confusion prevalent in many denominations.

Communicating the Vision

Effective communication of the new denomination's vision is essential. This vision should emphasize a return to biblical Christianity, free from the distortions of modern critical methods and the compromises of ecumenism. We must highlight the importance of doctrinal purity, the authority of Scripture, and the commitment to evangelizing the world with the gospel of Jesus Christ. Utilizing various platforms such as church meetings, conferences, social media, and printed materials, we can reach a wide audience and clearly convey our mission and values.

Building a Strong Online Presence

In today's digital age, having a strong online presence is crucial. A well-designed website should serve as a central hub for information about the new denomination. This website should include detailed statements of faith, explanations of our doctrinal positions, resources for theological education, and information on how to join the movement. Additionally, leveraging social media platforms can help spread our message and engage with believers who are searching for a church that remains true to biblical principles.

Offering Theological Education

Providing accessible and rigorous theological education is another key strategy. Through online courses, webinars, and local study groups, we can equip Christians with the knowledge and tools they need to understand and defend their faith. These educational programs should emphasize the Historical-Grammatical Method of interpretation, apologetics, and practical ministry skills. By investing in the spiritual and intellectual growth of our members, we not only strengthen our denomination but also empower believers to become effective witnesses for Christ.

Creating a Supportive Community

Many Christians feel isolated and unsupported in their current denominations due to doctrinal compromises and divisive practices. By creating a supportive and welcoming community, we can attract those who are seeking a more faithful expression of Christianity. This involves establishing local congregations that prioritize fellowship, mutual edification, and accountability. Small groups, prayer meetings, and discipleship programs can foster a sense of belonging and encourage spiritual growth.

Providing Practical Ministry Opportunities

Offering practical ministry opportunities is essential for engaging true Christians. This includes organizing evangelism outreaches, service projects, and mission trips. By actively involving members in hands-on ministry, we demonstrate our commitment to living out the Great Commission and provide tangible ways for believers to use their gifts and talents for God's glory. These opportunities also help to build a sense of purpose and camaraderie among members.

Addressing Contemporary Issues with Biblical Clarity

In a world where many churches are swayed by cultural trends and societal pressures, addressing contemporary issues with biblical clarity is paramount. We must provide clear, scripturally based teaching on topics such as marriage, sexuality, social justice, and moral ethics. By standing firm on the truths of Scripture, we offer a refuge for those who are disillusioned with the shifting moral landscape and are seeking a church that upholds biblical standards.

Emphasizing Evangelism and Discipleship

A key component of attracting true Christians is demonstrating a strong commitment to evangelism and discipleship. We must prioritize equipping our members to share their faith confidently and effectively. This involves training in personal evangelism, apologetics, and disciple-making strategies. By focusing on the Great Commission, we align ourselves with the core mission of the church and attract believers who are passionate about reaching the lost.

Maintaining Transparency and Accountability

Transparency and accountability are crucial for building trust and integrity within the new denomination. This includes clear governance structures, financial accountability, and open communication with members. Regularly publishing doctrinal statements, financial reports, and updates on ministry activities helps to build confidence and trust among those considering joining the denomination.

Networking with Like-Minded Ministries

Networking with other like-minded ministries and organizations can also help attract true Christians. By forming alliances and partnerships with groups that share our commitment to biblical truth, we can extend our reach and influence. Conferences, joint evangelism efforts, and collaborative projects can help to create a broader movement of believers committed to doctrinal purity and faithful ministry.

Encouraging Personal Holiness and Spiritual Growth

Attracting true Christians also involves emphasizing personal holiness and spiritual growth. Teaching on the importance of living a life that honors God, fostering spiritual disciplines such as prayer, Bible study, and fasting, and encouraging accountability relationships are vital. A church that prioritizes personal sanctification and spiritual maturity will naturally attract those who are serious about their faith.

In summary, attracting true Christians from divided denominations requires a multifaceted approach that emphasizes doctrinal clarity, effective communication, robust theological education, supportive community, practical ministry opportunities, biblical responses to contemporary issues, and a commitment to evangelism and discipleship. By establishing a new denomination that remains unwaveringly faithful to the truths of Scripture and the mission of the church, we can provide a haven for believers seeking a return to biblical Christianity and a community dedicated to glorifying God and proclaiming the gospel.

Chapter 15: Maintaining Unity and Addressing Disagreements

Principles for Maintaining Unity in the Congregation

In addressing the profound challenge of maintaining unity within the Christian congregation, it is essential to ground our approach in the immutable truths of Scripture. Unity in the church is not merely a desirable trait but a divine mandate that reflects the nature of God Himself. As Jesus prayed in John 17:21, "that they may all be one, just as you, Father, are in me, and I in you, that they also may be in us, so that the world may believe that you have sent me." The pursuit of unity is a testament to the authenticity of our faith and the transformative power of the gospel.

Biblical Foundations for Unity

The foundation of unity within the congregation is firmly rooted in the teachings of the New Testament. Paul's epistles, in particular, provide extensive instruction on this subject. In Ephesians 4:3, Paul urges believers to be "eager to maintain the unity of the Spirit in the bond of peace." This verse underscores the proactive effort required to preserve unity, emphasizing that it is the Spirit who unites us, and we are called to maintain what God has established.

In Philippians 2:2-4, Paul writes, "complete my joy by being of the same mind, having the same love, being in full accord and of one mind. Do nothing from selfish ambition or conceit, but in humility count others more significant than yourselves. Let each of you look not only to his own interests, but also to the interests of others." This passage highlights the attitudes necessary for unity: humility, selflessness, and a Christ-like regard for others.

The Role of Sound Doctrine

Sound doctrine is crucial for maintaining unity in the congregation. As Paul exhorts Timothy in 2 Timothy 4:2-3, "preach the word; be ready in season and out of season; reprove, rebuke, and exhort, with complete patience and teaching. For the time is coming when people will not endure sound teaching." Teaching that is firmly based on the Word of God provides a common foundation for belief and practice, reducing the potential for divisive errors.

The Historical-Grammatical Method of interpretation is essential in this regard. By seeking to understand the original intent of the biblical authors, we ensure that our teaching remains true to Scripture. This method avoids the subjective pitfalls of modern critical approaches, providing a stable and consistent framework for doctrine.

Cultivating a Spirit of Humility and Forgiveness

Humility and forgiveness are indispensable for unity. Ephesians 4:31-32 instructs, "Let all bitterness and wrath and anger and clamor and slander be put away from you, along with all malice. Be kind to one another, tenderhearted, forgiving one another, as God in Christ forgave you." A congregation that practices humility and forgiveness reflects the character of Christ and fosters an environment where unity can flourish.

Practical Steps for Maintaining Unity

To maintain unity, practical steps must be taken within the congregation. Regular teaching on the importance of unity, grounded in Scripture, helps to keep this priority at the forefront of congregational life. Leaders must model unity, demonstrating a commitment to resolving conflicts biblically and maintaining open, honest communication.

Developing clear processes for addressing disagreements is also vital. Matthew 18:15-17 provides a biblical blueprint for dealing with sin and conflict within the church. By following these steps—first addressing the issue privately, then with witnesses, and finally, if necessary, involving the church—unity can be preserved, and reconciliation can be pursued.

Encouraging Mutual Accountability

Mutual accountability is a key principle for maintaining unity. Hebrews 10:24-25 encourages believers to "consider how to stir up one another to love and good works, not neglecting to meet together, as is the habit of some, but encouraging one another, and all the more as you see the Day drawing near." Regular fellowship and accountability help to build strong relationships and prevent divisions from taking root.

Promoting a Culture of Service

A culture of service promotes unity by focusing the congregation on outward actions of love and support. Galatians 5:13 instructs, "For you were called to freedom, brothers. Only do not use your freedom as an opportunity for the flesh, but through love serve one another." When members of the congregation serve each other and their community, they build bonds of love and cooperation that strengthen unity.

Addressing Doctrinal Disagreements

When doctrinal disagreements arise, they must be addressed with wisdom and a commitment to truth. Acts 15 provides an example of how the early church dealt with a significant doctrinal issue. The Jerusalem Council brought together leaders to discuss the matter, and through careful deliberation and seeking the guidance of the Holy Spirit, they reached a consensus.

Today, we can follow this example by bringing together knowledgeable and respected leaders to address doctrinal disputes. Open forums for discussion, guided by Scripture, help to ensure that differing views are heard and considered. Ultimately, the goal is to arrive at a conclusion that is faithful to the Word of God and promotes unity within the body.

Emphasizing Common Ground

While doctrinal purity is essential, emphasizing common ground is also important for unity. Philippians 2:1-2 encourages believers to be "of the same mind, having the same love, being in full accord and of one mind." By focusing on the core beliefs that unite us—such as the deity of Christ, the authority of Scripture, and the message of salvation—we can build a strong foundation for unity.

Fostering a Spirit of Encouragement

Encouragement is a powerful tool for maintaining unity. 1 Thessalonians 5:11 exhorts, "Therefore encourage one another and build one another up, just as you are doing." Regularly affirming and encouraging one another fosters a positive and supportive environment where unity can thrive. This involves recognizing and celebrating the contributions of each member, providing support during difficult times, and encouraging spiritual growth and maturity.

Maintaining unity within the congregation is a complex and ongoing process that requires a commitment to biblical principles, sound doctrine, humility, forgiveness, and practical steps for resolving conflicts. By grounding our efforts in the Word of God and following the example of the early church, we can build a unified and effective body of believers that reflects the love and truth of Christ to the world.

Procedures for Addressing Doctrinal Disagreements

Doctrinal disagreements are an inevitable part of the Christian experience, given the diversity of thought and interpretation that arises within any community of believers. However, it is crucial to address these disagreements in a manner that is both biblical and effective, ensuring that unity is maintained and truth is upheld. The following procedures outline a comprehensive approach to addressing doctrinal disagreements, rooted in Scripture and guided by principles of humility, love, and a commitment to truth.

Biblical Foundation for Addressing Disagreements

The Bible provides clear guidance on how to address disagreements among believers. Matthew 18:15-17 offers a foundational framework: "If your brother sins against you, go and tell him his fault, between you and him alone. If he listens to you, you have gained your brother. But if he does not listen, take one or two others along with you, that every charge may be established by the evidence of two or three witnesses. If he refuses to listen to them, tell it to the church. And if he refuses to listen even to the church, let him be to you as a Gentile and a tax collector." While this passage specifically addresses personal offenses, the principles of private confrontation, the involvement of witnesses, and ultimately the church's role can be applied to doctrinal disagreements.

Step 1: Private Discussion

The first step in addressing a doctrinal disagreement is a private discussion between the parties involved. This approach allows for a respectful and personal dialogue, minimizing the risk of public conflict and misunderstanding. As Paul advises in Galatians 6:1, "Brothers, if anyone is caught in any transgression, you who are spiritual should restore him in a spirit of gentleness. Keep watch on yourself, lest you too be tempted." The goal is restoration and understanding, not condemnation.

During this private discussion, it is important to come prepared with relevant Scriptures and a clear articulation of the doctrinal issue. Both parties should approach the conversation with humility and a willingness to listen. As James 1:19 instructs, "let every person be quick to hear, slow to speak, slow to anger." By prioritizing understanding and mutual respect, many disagreements can be resolved at this stage.

Step 2: Involvement of Witnesses

If a private discussion does not lead to a resolution, the next step is to involve one or two witnesses. These witnesses should be mature believers who can provide objective perspectives and help mediate the discussion. Their role is to ensure that the conversation remains respectful and focused on seeking truth.

Witnesses can also help to clarify misunderstandings and provide additional biblical insight. As Paul writes in 2 Timothy 2:24-25, "And the Lord's servant must not be quarrelsome but kind to everyone, able to teach, patiently enduring evil, correcting his opponents with gentleness. God may perhaps grant them repentance leading to a knowledge of the truth." The involvement of witnesses can often bring about a resolution that was not possible through private discussion alone.

Step 3: Bringing the Issue Before the Church

If the involvement of witnesses does not lead to a resolution, the issue should be brought before the church. This step is in accordance with Matthew 18:17: "If he refuses to listen to them, tell it to the church." Bringing the issue before the church should be done in an orderly and respectful manner, ensuring that the congregation is fully informed of the nature of the disagreement and the steps that have already been taken to resolve it.

The church's leadership, typically the elders or pastors, should facilitate this process. They should provide a forum for both parties to present their views, supported by Scripture. The goal is to reach a consensus that aligns with biblical truth. The church's decision should be respected and upheld by all parties involved.

Step 4: Church Discipline

If one party refuses to accept the church's decision and continues to promote a doctrinal error, church discipline may be necessary. As Paul advises in Titus 3:10-11, "As for a person who stirs up division, after warning him once and then twice, have nothing more to do with him, knowing that such a person is warped and sinful; he is self-condemned." The purpose of church discipline is not punitive but restorative, aiming to bring the erring individual back to sound doctrine and fellowship.

Church discipline should be carried out with a spirit of love and humility, always seeking the repentance and restoration of the individual. Galatians 6:1 emphasizes the need for gentleness and self-awareness in this process. It is also important to provide ongoing support and counseling for those undergoing church discipline, helping them to understand and correct their doctrinal error.

Fostering a Culture of Doctrinal Soundness

To minimize doctrinal disagreements, it is essential to foster a culture of doctrinal soundness within the congregation. This involves regular teaching and preaching that is firmly grounded in Scripture, using the Historical-Grammatical Method of interpretation. By ensuring that the congregation is well-versed in biblical truth, the potential for doctrinal errors is significantly reduced.

Additionally, providing opportunities for theological education and discussion can help members to deepen their understanding of Scripture and develop discernment. This can be achieved through Bible studies, seminars, and training programs that focus on key doctrines and how to interpret the Bible accurately.

Encouraging Open Communication

Encouraging open communication within the congregation is also crucial for addressing doctrinal disagreements. Members should feel comfortable bringing their questions and concerns to the leadership, knowing that they will be heard and taken seriously. This can prevent misunderstandings from escalating into significant conflicts.

Regular forums for discussion and Q&A sessions can provide valuable opportunities for members to engage with doctrinal issues in a supportive environment. By promoting a culture of openness and mutual respect, the congregation can work together to uphold sound doctrine and maintain unity.

Addressing doctrinal disagreements requires a commitment to biblical principles, humility, and a willingness to seek truth together. By following the procedures outlined above—private discussion, involvement of witnesses, bringing the issue before the church, and, if necessary, church discipline—congregations can navigate doctrinal disagreements in a way that preserves unity and upholds the authority of Scripture. Fostering a culture of doctrinal soundness and open communication further strengthens the church's ability to address disagreements effectively and maintain the unity that Christ desires for His body.

Ensuring a Humble and Teachable Spirit Among Leaders and Members

Ensuring a humble and teachable spirit among church leaders and members is crucial for maintaining unity and addressing disagreements effectively. This chapter will explore the biblical foundation for humility and teachability, practical steps to cultivate these qualities, and the benefits of fostering a community that values humility and openness to learning.

Biblical Foundation for Humility and Teachability

The Bible consistently emphasizes the importance of humility and a teachable spirit. In Proverbs 11:2, it is written, "When pride comes, then comes disgrace, but with the humble is wisdom." Humility is foundational to wisdom and understanding, essential qualities for any church leader or member. Furthermore, James 4:6 states, "But he gives more grace. Therefore it says, 'God opposes the proud but gives grace to the humble.'" God's grace is bestowed upon those who are humble, making humility a vital characteristic for anyone seeking to grow in faith and understanding.

In the New Testament, Jesus serves as the ultimate example of humility. In Philippians 2:5-8, Paul writes, "Have this mind among yourselves, which is yours in Christ Jesus, who, though he was in the form of God, did not count equality with God a thing to be grasped, but emptied himself, by taking the form of a servant, being born in the likeness of men. And being found in human form, he humbled himself by becoming obedient to the point of death, even death on a cross."

Jesus' willingness to humble himself and serve others is a model for all believers.

A teachable spirit is closely related to humility. Proverbs 9:9 states, "Give instruction to a wise man, and he will be still wiser; teach a righteous man, and he will increase in learning." Being open to instruction and eager to learn are marks of wisdom and righteousness. In the New Testament, James 1:19 encourages believers to be "quick to hear, slow to speak, slow to anger," emphasizing the importance of listening and learning.

Practical Steps to Cultivate Humility and Teachability

1. **Model Humility and Teachability**: Leaders must exemplify humility and a teachable spirit. As Peter advises in 1 Peter 5:3, "not domineering over those in your charge, but being examples to the flock." When leaders demonstrate these qualities, they set a powerful example for the congregation to follow.

2. **Encourage Self-Examination**: Regularly encourage leaders and members to engage in self-examination. 2 Corinthians 13:5 instructs, "Examine yourselves, to see whether you are in the faith. Test yourselves." Self-examination helps individuals recognize areas where they need to grow and seek God's guidance in their spiritual journey.

3. **Foster an Environment of Open Dialogue**: Create a culture where open dialogue and respectful discussions are encouraged. Ephesians 4:15 highlights the importance of speaking "the truth in love," allowing for constructive conversations that promote growth and understanding.

4. **Provide Opportunities for Learning**: Offer regular teaching and training sessions on biblical principles, theology, and practical ministry skills. Colossians 1:28 emphasizes the goal of teaching: "that we may present everyone mature in Christ." Equipping the congregation with sound doctrine and practical knowledge fosters a teachable spirit.

5. **Encourage Accountability**: Establish systems of accountability where leaders and members can provide and receive constructive feedback. Proverbs 27:17 states, "Iron sharpens iron, and one man sharpens another." Accountability helps individuals stay humble and open to growth.

6. **Promote Prayer and Dependence on God**: Emphasize the importance of prayer and reliance on God for wisdom and guidance. James 1:5 promises, "If any of you lacks wisdom, let him ask God, who gives generously to all without reproach, and it will be given him." Regular prayer cultivates humility and a recognition of one's dependence on God.

Benefits of Fostering Humility and Teachability

1. **Enhanced Unity**: A humble and teachable spirit promotes unity within the congregation. Philippians 2:2 encourages believers to be "of the same mind, having the same love, being in full accord and of one mind." Humility helps to minimize conflicts and foster a spirit of cooperation and mutual respect.

2. **Spiritual Growth**: Individuals who are humble and teachable are more likely to experience spiritual growth. Proverbs 15:33 states, "The fear of Jehovah is instruction in wisdom, and humility comes before honor." A willingness to learn and grow leads to greater maturity in faith.

3. **Effective Leadership**: Leaders who embody humility and a teachable spirit are more effective in their roles. They are better equipped to guide and nurture the congregation, as they are open to God's leading and the input of others. Proverbs 16:18 warns, "Pride goes before destruction, and a haughty spirit before a fall." Humility protects leaders from the pitfalls of pride and ensures they remain effective and faithful in their ministry.

4. **Conflict Resolution**: A humble and teachable spirit aids in resolving conflicts. When individuals are open to listening and learning, they are more likely to find common ground and work towards reconciliation. Matthew 5:9 states, "Blessed are

the peacemakers, for they shall be called sons of God." Peacemaking requires humility and a willingness to understand others' perspectives.

5. **Witness to the World**: A congregation characterized by humility and teachability serves as a powerful witness to the world. John 13:35 declares, "By this all people will know that you are my disciples, if you have love for one another." Humility and a teachable spirit demonstrate the transformative power of the gospel and attract others to Christ.

Implementing a Humility and Teachability Program

To ensure that humility and teachability are integral to the church's culture, it is essential to implement a structured program that includes the following elements:

1. **Regular Teaching on Humility and Teachability**: Incorporate teaching on these topics into sermons, Bible studies, and training sessions. Use biblical examples and practical applications to illustrate the importance of these qualities.

2. **Mentorship and Discipleship**: Establish mentorship and discipleship programs where more mature believers can guide others in developing humility and a teachable spirit. Titus 2:3-4 advises older women to "train the young women," highlighting the value of mentorship.

3. **Workshops and Seminars**: Offer workshops and seminars focused on cultivating humility and teachability. These sessions can provide practical tools and techniques for self-examination, listening, and learning.

4. **Encouragement of Personal Reflection**: Encourage members to spend time in personal reflection and prayer, seeking God's guidance in their growth. Psalm 139:23-24 is a helpful prayer for this purpose: "Search me, O God, and know my heart! Try me and know my thoughts! And see if there be any grievous way in me, and lead me in the way everlasting!"

5. **Feedback and Evaluation**: Create opportunities for regular feedback and evaluation within the congregation. This can include anonymous surveys, suggestion boxes, and structured feedback sessions. Feedback helps individuals understand how they are perceived and where they can improve.

6. **Celebration of Growth**: Recognize and celebrate growth in humility and teachability. Publicly acknowledging individuals who demonstrate these qualities encourages others to aspire to the same. Romans 12:10 encourages believers to "outdo one another in showing honor."

Ensuring a humble and teachable spirit among church leaders and members is essential for maintaining unity and addressing disagreements effectively. By grounding this effort in biblical principles and implementing practical steps, the church can foster a culture that values humility and openness to learning. This culture not only enhances unity and spiritual growth but also serves as a powerful witness to the world. As believers commit to humility and teachability, they align themselves with God's will and create an environment where truth and love flourish.

Chapter 16: The Role of Church Leadership

Biblical Qualifications for Church Leaders

The role of church leadership is pivotal in maintaining the health and direction of a congregation. Church leaders are called to be shepherds of the flock, guiding and nurturing believers towards spiritual maturity. To ensure that church leaders fulfill their responsibilities effectively, the Bible provides clear qualifications that must be met. These qualifications are essential for preserving the integrity and unity of the church.

Scriptural Foundation for Leadership Qualifications

The qualifications for church leaders are primarily outlined in the New Testament, particularly in the pastoral epistles written by Paul to Timothy and Titus. These letters provide a comprehensive framework for evaluating potential leaders within the church.

1 Timothy 3:1-7 and Titus 1:5-9 are the key passages that detail the qualifications for overseers, also referred to as elders or bishops. These passages highlight the moral, spiritual, and practical attributes required of those who aspire to lead within the church.

1 Timothy 3:1-7 (UASV) "The saying is trustworthy: If anyone aspires to the office of overseer, he desires a noble task. Therefore an overseer must be above reproach, the husband of one wife, sober-minded, self-controlled, respectable, hospitable, able to teach, not a drunkard, not violent but gentle, not quarrelsome, not a lover of money. He must manage his own household well, with all dignity keeping his children submissive, for if someone does not know how to manage his own household, how will he care for God's church? He must not be a recent convert, or he may become puffed up with conceit and fall into the condemnation of the devil. Moreover, he must be well thought of by outsiders, so that he may not fall into disgrace, into a snare of the devil."

Titus 1:5-9 (UASV) "This is why I left you in Crete, so that you might put what remained into order, and appoint elders in every town as I directed you—if anyone is above reproach, the husband of one wife, and his children are believers and not open to the charge of debauchery or insubordination. For an overseer, as God's steward, must be above reproach. He must not be arrogant or quick-tempered or a drunkard or violent or greedy for gain, but hospitable, a lover of good, self-controlled, upright, holy, and disciplined. He must hold firm to the trustworthy word as taught, so that he may be able to give instruction in sound doctrine and also to rebuke those who contradict it."

Key Qualifications for Church Leaders

1. **Above Reproach**: A church leader must have a reputation for integrity and moral uprightness. This means living a life that is free from scandal or accusations that could harm the church's reputation. Being above reproach is a comprehensive qualification that encompasses all other attributes.

2. **Husband of One Wife**: This qualification underscores the importance of marital fidelity and commitment. It emphasizes the leader's faithfulness in his marriage, indicating a life of purity and devotion to one spouse.

3. **Sober-Minded and Self-Controlled**: A leader must exhibit clear thinking and sound judgment. Sober-mindedness involves being temperate and prudent, while self-control refers to the ability to manage one's desires and impulses.

4. **Respectable and Hospitable**: Respectability involves living a life that commands respect and admiration from others. Hospitality is the practice of being welcoming and generous to others, particularly strangers and those in need.

5. **Able to Teach**: A key responsibility of church leaders is to instruct and guide the congregation in sound doctrine. Therefore, they must be knowledgeable in Scripture and able to communicate its truths effectively.

6. **Not Given to Drunkenness or Violence**: Leaders must demonstrate self-control in all areas, including their use of alcohol. They should not be prone to violence or aggressive behavior, but rather exhibit gentleness and a peaceful demeanor.

7. **Not Quarrelsome or Greedy**: A leader should avoid contentiousness and a love of money. Instead, they should be gentle, content, and focused on serving others rather than pursuing personal gain.

8. **Good Manager of His Household**: Effective leadership begins at home. A leader must manage his household well, demonstrating his ability to lead and nurture his family. This includes maintaining order and respect within the home.

9. **Not a Recent Convert**: Leaders should be mature in their faith, having demonstrated consistency and growth over time. This helps prevent pride and ensures they have a solid foundation in their spiritual life.

10. **Good Reputation with Outsiders**: A leader's character should be evident not only within the church but also in the broader community. This ensures that the leader does not bring disrepute to the church.

Practical Application of These Qualifications

Implementing these biblical qualifications involves a thorough and prayerful selection process. Churches must be diligent in evaluating potential leaders against these criteria to ensure they meet the high standards set forth in Scripture. This process includes:

1. **Assessment of Personal Life**: The candidate's personal life, including their family relationships and conduct outside the

church, must be examined. This ensures that they live out their faith consistently in all areas of life.

2. **Doctrinal Soundness**: Leaders must be grounded in sound doctrine and able to teach it effectively. This requires a thorough understanding of Scripture and a commitment to upholding its truths.

3. **Spiritual Maturity**: The candidate's spiritual journey should be assessed to ensure they have grown and matured in their faith. This includes evaluating their ability to handle responsibility and maintain humility.

4. **Community Reputation**: The leader's reputation in the broader community is crucial. References from outside the church can provide insight into their character and integrity.

5. **Ongoing Accountability**: Even after a leader is appointed, there should be systems in place for ongoing accountability and support. This helps maintain high standards and provides a structure for addressing any issues that arise.

The Role of the Congregation in Supporting Leaders

The congregation also plays a vital role in supporting and upholding the standards for church leadership. This includes:

1. **Prayerful Support**: Regularly praying for church leaders is essential. The congregation should seek God's guidance and wisdom for their leaders, asking for protection and strength in their ministry.

2. **Encouragement and Feedback**: Constructive feedback and encouragement from the congregation can help leaders grow and remain accountable. Open communication fosters a healthy relationship between leaders and members.

3. **Commitment to Unity**: The congregation should strive for unity and cooperation, supporting their leaders' efforts to maintain doctrinal purity and spiritual growth. This unity strengthens the church and its mission.

4. **Active Participation**: Members should actively participate in the life of the church, including its teaching and discipleship programs. This engagement helps ensure that the entire congregation grows together in faith and understanding.

The Importance of Adhering to Biblical Qualifications

Adhering to the biblical qualifications for church leaders is not just a matter of maintaining standards; it is crucial for the health and effectiveness of the church. Leaders who embody these qualifications serve as role models for the congregation, guiding them in spiritual growth and maturity.

Moreover, leaders who meet these qualifications are better equipped to handle the challenges and responsibilities of ministry. They can provide wise counsel, teach sound doctrine, and lead with integrity and compassion. This, in turn, fosters a healthy, vibrant church that can effectively fulfill its mission to spread the gospel and make disciples.

The qualifications for church leaders outlined in the Bible provide a clear and comprehensive framework for ensuring that those who lead are well-suited to their roles. By adhering to these qualifications, the church can maintain its integrity, unity, and effectiveness. Church leaders must exemplify these qualities in their personal lives and ministry, serving as faithful shepherds of God's flock. As the congregation supports and upholds these standards, the church can thrive and grow, fulfilling its God-given mission with excellence and faithfulness.

Responsibilities of Pastors, Elders, and Deacons

Church leadership is a cornerstone of the Christian community, tasked with guiding, nurturing, and overseeing the spiritual growth and well-being of the congregation. The roles of pastors, elders, and deacons are biblically defined and encompass a wide range of responsibilities essential for maintaining doctrinal purity, fostering unity, and promoting effective ministry.

Pastors

Shepherding the Flock

The term "pastor" derives from the Latin word for shepherd, reflecting the primary role of pastors to tend to the spiritual needs of the congregation. As spiritual shepherds, pastors are responsible for leading the flock with care, compassion, and diligence.

Preaching and Teaching

Pastors bear the significant responsibility of preaching and teaching the Word of God. As Paul exhorted Timothy, "Preach the word; be ready in season and out of season; reprove, rebuke, and exhort, with complete patience and teaching" (2 Timothy 4:2, UASV). This involves not only delivering sermons that expound biblical truths but also ensuring that teaching within the church aligns with sound doctrine.

Spiritual Oversight

Pastors provide spiritual oversight, guiding the congregation in their walk with Christ. This includes offering counsel, prayer, and support to individuals, addressing spiritual concerns, and fostering an environment of spiritual growth and maturity. As shepherds, pastors must guard against false teachings and ensure that the church remains faithful to the gospel.

Equipping the Saints

Pastors are called to equip the saints for the work of ministry, as outlined in Ephesians 4:11-12: "And he gave the apostles, the prophets, the evangelists, the shepherds and teachers, to equip the saints for the work of ministry, for building up the body of Christ." This involves training and mentoring members to serve effectively in various ministries and encouraging them to use their spiritual gifts for the edification of the church.

Elders

Governing and Leading

Elders share in the governance and leadership of the church. They are entrusted with making important decisions regarding the direction, vision, and policies of the congregation. Elders must work collaboratively to discern God's will for the church and implement strategies that align with biblical principles.

Teaching and Exhortation

While all elders must be able to teach, not all may engage in regular preaching. Nonetheless, elders play a crucial role in teaching and exhorting the congregation, ensuring that members are well-grounded in Scripture. Titus 1:9 emphasizes the importance of this role: "He must hold firm to the trustworthy word as taught, so that he may be able to give instruction in sound doctrine and also to rebuke those who contradict it."

Pastoral Care

Elders assist in providing pastoral care, offering support and guidance to individuals and families within the church. This includes visiting the sick, counseling those in need, and addressing any issues that may arise within the congregation. The compassionate care of elders helps maintain the spiritual and emotional health of the church community.

Maintaining Doctrinal Integrity

Elders are tasked with maintaining doctrinal integrity within the church. They must be vigilant in guarding against false teachings and ensuring that all instruction aligns with biblical truth. As Paul warned the Ephesian elders, "I know that after my departure fierce wolves will come in among you, not sparing the flock; and from among your own selves will arise men speaking twisted things, to draw away the disciples after them" (Acts 20:29-30).

Deacons

Service and Administration

Deacons are primarily responsible for service and administration within the church. Their role is rooted in the early church's practice, as described in Acts 6:1-6, where deacons were appointed to oversee the distribution of food to the needy. This allowed the apostles to focus on prayer and the ministry of the word. Deacons today continue this tradition by managing practical aspects of church life, including finances, facilities, and benevolence ministries.

Supporting the Pastoral Staff

Deacons support the pastoral staff by taking on administrative and logistical responsibilities, freeing pastors and elders to concentrate on spiritual leadership and teaching. This partnership ensures that the church operates smoothly and that the needs of the congregation are met efficiently.

Promoting Unity and Service

Deacons play a vital role in promoting unity and fostering a spirit of service within the church. By organizing and overseeing various service projects and ministries, deacons encourage members to actively participate in the life of the church and to serve one another in love. This reflects the biblical mandate to "serve one another humbly in love" (Galatians 5:13).

Providing for Physical Needs

One of the key responsibilities of deacons is to address the physical needs of the congregation. This includes caring for the poor, the sick, and the vulnerable. Deacons are often involved in coordinating efforts to provide food, clothing, and other forms of assistance to those in need, both within the church and in the broader community.

Biblical Basis for Church Leadership Roles

The roles and responsibilities of pastors, elders, and deacons are firmly grounded in Scripture. The qualifications and duties for each role are clearly outlined in the New Testament, providing a framework for church governance that ensures the effective functioning of the body of Christ.

Pastors/Elders: The terms pastor, elder, and overseer are often used interchangeably in the New Testament, reflecting the overlapping responsibilities of these roles. Key passages include:

- 1 Timothy 3:1-7: Outlines the qualifications for overseers.

- Titus 1:5-9: Describes the qualifications and duties of elders.

- 1 Peter 5:1-4: Exhorts elders to shepherd the flock with humility and diligence.

Deacons: The role of deacons is introduced in Acts 6:1-6, with further qualifications provided in 1 Timothy 3:8-13. These passages emphasize the importance of integrity, faithfulness, and a servant's heart in those who serve as deacons.

Practical Application in the Church

To implement these biblical principles effectively, churches must adopt a thorough and prayerful approach to selecting and appointing leaders. This process includes:

Screening and Selection: Potential leaders should be carefully screened to ensure they meet the biblical qualifications. This involves assessing their personal character, spiritual maturity, doctrinal soundness, and ability to teach and lead.

Training and Development: Once selected, leaders should receive ongoing training and development to equip them for their roles. This includes theological education, practical ministry training, and opportunities for mentorship and accountability.

Ongoing Support and Accountability: Church leaders must be supported and held accountable to maintain high standards of integrity and faithfulness. Regular evaluations, peer support, and accountability structures help ensure that leaders remain effective and faithful in their ministry.

Encouraging Congregational Involvement: The congregation should be encouraged to actively support and pray for their leaders. This fosters a healthy relationship between leaders and members and helps maintain unity within the church.

The responsibilities of pastors, elders, and deacons are clearly defined in Scripture and are essential for the health and growth of the church. By adhering to these biblical principles, churches can ensure that their leaders are well-equipped to guide, nurture, and protect the congregation. This, in turn, fosters a vibrant and thriving church community that faithfully fulfills its mission to spread the gospel and make disciples.

Accountability and Transparency in Leadership

Accountability and transparency are foundational principles for effective church leadership. These concepts ensure that leaders maintain integrity, uphold biblical standards, and foster a trustful and harmonious relationship within the congregation. This section will explore the importance of accountability and transparency, grounded in Scripture, and provide practical steps for implementation.

Importance of Accountability

Biblical Mandate

Accountability is a biblical mandate. Leaders are called to a higher standard of conduct and responsibility. James 3:1 warns, "Not many of you should become teachers, my brothers, for you know that we who teach will be judged with greater strictness." This underscores the gravity of the leadership role and the necessity for leaders to be accountable to God and their congregation.

Protecting the Flock

The primary role of church leaders is to shepherd the flock, protecting them from false teachings and leading them in spiritual growth. Acts 20:28 advises, "Pay careful attention to yourselves and to all the flock, in which the Holy Spirit has made you overseers, to care for the church of God, which he obtained with his own blood." Accountability helps ensure that leaders are vigilant in this duty, safeguarding the spiritual well-being of the congregation.

Maintaining Integrity

Integrity is crucial for church leaders. Proverbs 11:3 states, "The integrity of the upright guides them, but the crookedness of the treacherous destroys them." Leaders must be examples of moral and ethical behavior. Accountability structures help maintain this integrity by providing checks and balances on leadership actions.

Importance of Transparency

Building Trust

Transparency builds trust within the congregation. When leaders are open about their decisions and actions, it fosters a culture of trust and respect. Proverbs 27:6 emphasizes the value of honesty, "Faithful are the wounds of a friend; profuse are the kisses of an enemy." Transparent leadership is akin to a faithful friend who speaks the truth in love.

Preventing Misunderstandings

Transparency helps prevent misunderstandings and miscommunications. Clear communication about church decisions, financial matters, and strategic directions reduces the potential for rumors and conflicts. 1 Corinthians 14:33 reminds us, "For God is not a God of confusion but of peace." Transparent leadership promotes peace and unity within the church.

Encouraging Participation

When church members understand the rationale behind decisions and policies, they are more likely to participate actively and support the church's mission. Transparency encourages a sense of ownership and involvement among the congregation, which is vital for a vibrant church community.

Practical Steps for Accountability and Transparency

Establishing Clear Structures

Eldership Accountability

The eldership should have clear structures for accountability. This can include regular meetings where elders review each other's conduct, decisions, and spiritual health. Mutual accountability among the eldership ensures that no single leader operates without oversight.

Financial Oversight

Transparent financial practices are essential. This includes regular financial reports to the congregation, external audits, and a finance committee composed of trusted members who oversee budgeting and expenditures. 2 Corinthians 8:21 advises, "For we aim at what is honorable not only in the Lord's sight but also in the sight of man."

Decision-Making Processes

Church decisions should involve input from a broad range of members. This can be facilitated through committees, open forums, and surveys that gather feedback from the congregation. Acts 6:3 illustrates this principle, "Therefore, brothers, pick out from among you seven men of good repute, full of the Spirit and of wisdom, whom we will appoint to this duty."

Regular Reporting

Leaders should regularly report to the congregation about the church's spiritual and operational state. This includes updates on ministry activities, financial status, and strategic plans. Regular reporting fosters a sense of transparency and keeps the congregation informed and engaged.

Conflict Resolution Mechanisms

Biblical Process for Addressing Sin

Leaders should follow the biblical process for addressing sin and conflicts within the church. Matthew 18:15-17 outlines a clear procedure: "If your brother sins against you, go and tell him his fault, between you and him alone. If he listens to you, you have gained your brother. But if he does not listen, take one or two others along with you, that every charge may be established by the evidence of two or three witnesses. If he refuses to listen to them, tell it to the church. And if he refuses to listen even to the church, let him be to you as a Gentile and a tax collector."

Third-Party Mediation

In some cases, it may be beneficial to involve an impartial third party to mediate conflicts. This ensures that all parties are heard and that the resolution is fair and just. Galatians 6:1 advises, "Brothers, if anyone is caught in any transgression, you who are spiritual should restore him in a spirit of gentleness. Keep watch on yourself, lest you too be tempted."

Training in Conflict Resolution

Leaders and members should be trained in biblical conflict resolution principles. This equips them to handle disputes effectively and maintain unity within the church. Ephesians 4:3 encourages, "Make every effort to keep the unity of the Spirit through the bond of peace."

Encouraging a Culture of Accountability and Transparency

Modeling by Leaders

Leaders must model accountability and transparency. Their example sets the tone for the entire congregation. 1 Timothy 4:12 exhorts, "Let no one despise you for your youth, but set the believers an example in speech, in conduct, in love, in faith, in purity."

Open Communication Channels

Churches should establish open communication channels where members feel comfortable voicing concerns and providing feedback. This can include suggestion boxes, regular town hall meetings, and a clear process for members to bring issues to the leadership.

Regular Training and Development

Regular training on the importance of accountability and transparency should be part of the church's leadership development program. This includes workshops, seminars, and retreats focused on ethical leadership and effective communication.

Fostering a Culture of Mutual Respect

A culture of mutual respect and support fosters transparency. When members and leaders respect and trust each other, they are more likely to engage in open and honest communication. Romans 12:10 encourages, "Love one another with brotherly affection. Outdo one another in showing honor."

Implementing Feedback Mechanisms

Surveys and Feedback Forms

Churches can use surveys and feedback forms to gather input from the congregation on various aspects of church life. This feedback helps leaders understand the needs and concerns of the members and make informed decisions.

Regular Review Meetings

Regular review meetings with ministry leaders and members provide an opportunity to discuss successes, challenges, and areas for improvement. These meetings should be conducted in a spirit of openness and constructive feedback.

Anonymous Reporting Channels

Providing anonymous reporting channels for ethical concerns and misconduct ensures that members can report issues without fear of retaliation. This reinforces a culture of accountability and transparency.

Accountability and transparency in church leadership are essential for maintaining integrity, building trust, and fostering unity within the congregation. By establishing clear structures, encouraging open communication, and modeling ethical behavior, church leaders can create an environment where accountability and transparency thrive. This, in turn, ensures that the church remains faithful to its mission and effectively ministers to the spiritual needs of its members.

Chapter 17: Effective Church Discipline

Biblical Principles of Church Discipline

Church discipline is an essential aspect of maintaining the purity and integrity of the Christian congregation. When done according to biblical principles, it serves as a means to correct, restore, and uphold the spiritual health of the church. This section will explore the biblical basis for church discipline, its purposes, and the methods to implement it effectively.

Biblical Basis for Church Discipline

Scriptural Foundation

The practice of church discipline is firmly rooted in Scripture. Jesus provided explicit instructions on how to handle sin within the church in Matthew 18:15-17: "If your brother sins against you, go and tell him his fault, between you and him alone. If he listens to you, you have gained your brother. But if he does not listen, take one or two others along with you, that every charge may be established by the evidence of two or three witnesses. If he refuses to listen to them, tell it to the church. And if he refuses to listen even to the church, let him be to you as a Gentile and a tax collector."

Paul also emphasized the necessity of church discipline in his letters. In 1 Corinthians 5:1-13, he addresses a case of sexual immorality in the Corinthian church, instructing them to remove the offender from their midst to maintain the church's purity. Similarly, in Galatians 6:1, Paul advises, "Brothers, if anyone is caught in any transgression, you who are spiritual should restore him in a spirit of gentleness. Keep watch on yourself, lest you too be tempted."

Purpose of Church Discipline

Restoration and Repentance

The primary goal of church discipline is the restoration of the sinner to fellowship with God and the church. The process is intended to bring the individual to repentance and spiritual renewal. James 5:19-20 states, "My brothers, if anyone among you wanders from the truth and someone brings him back, let him know that whoever brings back a sinner from his wandering will save his soul from death and will cover a multitude of sins."

Purity of the Church

Church discipline also serves to protect the purity and testimony of the church. Allowing sin to go unchecked can lead to spiritual decay and diminish the church's witness to the world. Paul's instruction in 1 Corinthians 5:6-7 underscores this: "Do you not know that a little leaven leavens the whole lump? Cleanse out the old leaven that you may be a new lump, as you really are unleavened."

Deterrence of Sin

Discipline acts as a deterrent to sin within the congregation. When members see that the church takes sin seriously, it promotes a culture of holiness and accountability. 1 Timothy 5:20 advises, "As for those who persist in sin, rebuke them in the presence of all, so that the rest may stand in fear."

Honor to God's Name

Ultimately, church discipline honors God's name by upholding His standards of righteousness and holiness. It demonstrates a commitment to living according to His Word and sets the church apart as a community dedicated to God's principles.

Methods of Church Discipline

Private Confrontation

The first step in the discipline process is private confrontation. This step involves one believer approaching another who has sinned, in a spirit of gentleness and humility, seeking to bring about repentance. This approach is based on Jesus' teaching in Matthew 18:15. The goal is to address the issue discreetly and restore the individual without involving others unnecessarily.

Small Group Confrontation

If private confrontation does not lead to repentance, the next step is to involve one or two others. This small group approach ensures that there is a witness to the proceedings and provides additional support and encouragement for the offending member to repent. Matthew 18:16 supports this step: "But if he does not listen, take one or two others along with you, that every charge may be established by the evidence of two or three witnesses."

Public Announcement

Should the small group confrontation fail, the matter is then brought before the church. This step is taken to emphasize the seriousness of the sin and the need for repentance. Matthew 18:17 states, "If he refuses to listen to them, tell it to the church." The public announcement is a call for the entire congregation to pray for and appeal to the offending member to turn from their sin.

Excommunication

As a last resort, if the individual remains unrepentant, the church must take the difficult step of excommunication, treating the person as an outsider. This action aims to show the gravity of unrepentant sin and protect the church's purity. Matthew 18:17 concludes, "And if he refuses to listen even to the church, let him be to you as a Gentile and a tax collector." Paul also supports this in 1 Corinthians 5:13, "Purge the evil person from among you."

Principles for Implementing Church Discipline

Biblical Grounds for Discipline

Moral Failures

Moral failures, such as sexual immorality, dishonesty, or other actions that violate God's commandments, are grounds for church discipline. Paul's letters to the Corinthians and Galatians provide clear examples of addressing moral lapses within the church.

Doctrinal Errors

Persistent teaching or adherence to false doctrine is another reason for discipline. In Titus 3:10-11, Paul instructs, "As for a person who stirs up division, after warning him once and then twice, have nothing more to do with him, knowing that such a person is warped and sinful; he is self-condemned."

Divisiveness and Rebellion

Members who cause division or refuse to submit to church authority also face discipline. Hebrews 13:17 exhorts believers, "Obey your leaders and submit to them, for they are keeping watch over your souls, as those who will have to give an account."

Process of Discipline

Gentleness and Humility

The process of church discipline must be conducted with gentleness and humility, always seeking the restoration of the sinner. Galatians 6:1 emphasizes this approach: "Brothers, if anyone is caught in any transgression, you who are spiritual should restore him in a spirit of gentleness."

Fairness and Impartiality

Discipline must be fair and impartial, without favoritism or prejudice. James 2:1 warns against partiality: "My brothers, show no partiality as you hold the faith in our Lord Jesus Christ, the Lord of glory."

Confidentiality and Discretion

Whenever possible, discipline should be handled confidentially to protect the dignity of the individual and avoid unnecessary scandal. Only when the sin is public or affects the broader congregation should it be addressed publicly.

Consistency and Firmness

Church discipline must be consistent and firm. Leaders must not waver in applying biblical principles, regardless of the individual's status within the church. 1 Timothy 5:19-20 underscores this need for consistency: "Do not admit a charge against an elder except on the evidence of two or three witnesses. As for those who persist in sin, rebuke them in the presence of all, so that the rest may stand in fear."

Challenges in Church Discipline

Cultural Resistance

In a culture that often values personal autonomy over communal accountability, implementing church discipline can be challenging. Leaders must educate the congregation on the biblical basis and necessity of discipline to overcome this resistance.

Fear of Conflict

Leaders may fear conflict or backlash when enforcing discipline. However, it is essential to prioritize obedience to God's Word over the desire to avoid discomfort. Acts 5:29 reminds us, "We must obey God rather than men."

Misunderstanding of Grace

Some may argue that discipline contradicts the message of grace. However, true grace includes the call to holiness and repentance. Titus 2:11-12 explains, "For the grace of God has appeared, bringing salvation for all people, training us to renounce ungodliness and worldly passions, and to live self-controlled, upright, and godly lives in the present age."

Encouraging a Culture of Accountability

Teaching and Preaching

Regular teaching and preaching on the biblical principles of church discipline help foster a culture of accountability. Leaders should not shy away from addressing this topic from the pulpit, using Scripture to explain its importance and benefits.

Modeling Accountability

Leaders must model accountability in their own lives. By being transparent and open to correction themselves, they set an example for the congregation to follow. Paul's exhortation in 1 Corinthians 11:1, "Be imitators of me, as I am of Christ," highlights the importance of leading by example.

Creating Safe Environments

Churches should create safe environments where members feel comfortable confessing sins and seeking help. This includes providing pastoral care, counseling, and support groups to assist those struggling with sin.

Regular Reviews and Assessments

Regularly reviewing and assessing the effectiveness of church discipline practices helps ensure that they remain biblically grounded and effectively implemented. This may involve feedback from the congregation and consultation with other church leaders.

Church discipline, when conducted according to biblical principles, serves as a vital tool for maintaining the spiritual health and integrity of the church. It aims to restore the sinner, protect the congregation, deter sin, and honor God. By adhering to scriptural guidelines and implementing practical steps with gentleness, fairness, and consistency, church leaders can effectively manage discipline within the church. This not only preserves the church's purity but also strengthens its witness to the world.

Procedures for Handling Disobedience and Division

Effective church discipline is essential to the health and purity of the church. The Bible provides clear guidelines for handling disobedience and division within the church. This section will explore the procedures for addressing these issues, based on biblical principles and the Historical-Grammatical method of interpretation.

Scriptural Basis for Discipline

The foundation for church discipline is found in the Bible. The primary passages that outline the process of discipline are Matthew 18:15-17, 1 Corinthians 5:1-13, and Galatians 6:1. These passages provide the framework for addressing disobedience and division within the church.

Matthew 18:15-17 outlines the steps for addressing personal offenses:

"If your brother sins, go and show him his fault in private; if he listens, the fault is corrected. But if he does not listen, take one or two others with you so that the matter may be established by the evidence of two or three witnesses. If he refuses to listen to them, tell the church; and if he refuses to listen to the church, treat him as a gentile and a tax collector."

This passage emphasizes the importance of confidentiality, due process, and the restoration of the individual.

1 Corinthians 5:1-13 addresses the issue of immorality within the church and the necessity of discipline to maintain the purity of the church. Paul admonishes the church to remove the unrepentant person from their fellowship to protect the church's reputation and moral integrity.

Galatians 6:1 provides guidance on how to handle transgressions: "Brothers, if someone is caught in a sin, you who are spiritual should restore him gently. But watch yourself; you also may be tempted."

The goal of discipline is not to punish but to restore the sinner to a right relationship with God and the church.

The Process of Church Discipline

The process of church discipline involves several steps, as outlined in Matthew 18:15- from private confrontation, to the involvement of witnesses, and finally to the involvement of the church. The goal is to restore the individual to a right relationship with God and the church.

Step 1: Private Confrontation

The first step in the discipline process is private: a private confrontation. This step involves one believer approaching the person who has committed the offense. The approach should be made in a spirit of love and concern, with the goal of restoring the individual to a right relationship with God and the church. This step is based on Matthew 18:15, which states, "If your brother sins, go and show him his fault in private; if he listens, the fault is corrected."

The emphasis here is on confidentiality and the opportunity for the individual from verse 15, which provides a model for addressing personal offenses:

"If your brother sins, go and show him his fault in private; if he listens, the fault is corrected."

The goal is to resolve the issue privately and to avoid public embarrassment or disgrace. This approach allows the, as established by biblical principles and the guidance of the Holy Spirit, to correct the error without causing unnecessary conflict or discord within the church.

Step 2: Involvement of Witnesses

If the person does not respond to the private confrontation, the next step is to involve one or two witnesses. This step ensures that the process is fair and impartial and that there is a record of the proceedings. Matthew 18:16 provides the basis for this step:

"If he does not listen, take one or two others with you so that the matter may be established by the evidence of two or three witnesses."

The involvement of witnesses also serves as a protective measure for both the, as established by biblical principles and the guidance of the Holy Spirit, and the person involved. It ensures that the process is conducted with due process and that the facts are documented and corroborated.

Step 3: Involvement of the Church

If the person continues to be unrepentant, the next step is to involve the entire church. This and the accountability of the entire church community. Matthew 18:17 outlines this step:

"If he refuses to listen to them, tell the church; and if he refuses to listen to the church, treat him as a gentile and a tax collector."

The involvement of the church serves as a final appeal to the person to repent and return to the faith. It also provides the church community with the opportunity to support and pray for the person.

Step 4: Excommunication

As a last resort, if the person remains unrepentant, the church must take the difficult step of excommunication. This involves treating the person as a gentile and a tax collector, meaning that the person is no longer considered a member of the church community. This step is based on Matthew 18:17 and 1 Corinthians 5:13, which states, "Remove the wicked person from among you."

The purpose of excommunication is not to punish but to protect the church community and to emphasize the seriousness of the person's actions. It also serves as a final call to repentance and a reminder of the consequences of unrepentant sin.

Addressing Division within the Church

Division within the church can be particularly damaging, as it can lead to discord, confusion, and the erosion of the church's unity and witness. The Bible provides guidance on how to address division and restore unity within the church.

Recognize the Source of Division

The first step in addressing division is to recognize the source of the division. The Bible identifies several sources of division, including:

False Teachings

False teachings can lead to confusion and division within the church. The Bible warns against false teachings and urges the church to remain faithful to the true gospel. Galatians 1:6-9 warns against false teachings:

"I am astonished that you are so quickly deserting the one who called you by the grace of Christ and are turning to a different gospel—which is really no gospel at all. Evidently, some people are throwing you into confusion and are trying to pervert the gospel of Christ. But even if we or an angel from heaven should preach a gospel other than the one we preached to you, let him be eternally condemned! As I said before, I say again: to you, if anybody preaches a gospel other than the one you received, let him be eternally condemned!"

The church must be vigilant in identifying and correcting false teachings to protect the integrity of the gospel and the unity of the church.

Personal Conflicts

Personal conflicts can also lead to division within the church. The Bible provides guidance on how to handle personal conflicts and restore relationships within the church. Matthew 18:15-17 outlines the process for addressing personal offenses, as discussed earlier.

The goal is to resolve conflicts privately and to restore relationships through reconciliation and forgiveness. Ephesians 4:26-27 advises, "In your anger do not sin: Do not let the sun go down while you are angry and do not give the devil a foothold."

The church must create a culture of forgiveness and reconciliation to prevent personal conflicts from leading to division.

Power Struggles

Power struggles and the pursuit of personal agendas can also lead to division within the church. The Bible emphasizes the importance of humility and servant leadership as the foundation of church leadership. Matthew 20:25-28 provides guidance on the attitude of leadership:

"Jesus called them together and said, 'You know that the rulers of the Gentiles lord it over them, and their high officials exercise authority over them. Not so with you. Instead, whoever wants to become great among you must be a servant, and whoever wants to be first must be a servant. Just as the Son of Man did not come to be served, but to serve, and to give his life as a ransom for many.'"

The church must cultivate a culture of servant leadership and humility to prevent power struggles and maintain unity.

Promote Unity and Reconciliation

The Bible provides several principles for promoting unity and reconciliation within the church.

Emphasize the Unity of the Body

The Bible emphasizes the unity of the body of Christ and urges the church to maintain that unity. Ephesians 4:3-6 urges, "Make every effort to keep the unity of the Spirit through the bond of peace. There is one body and one Spirit—just as you were called to one hope when you were called—one Lord, one faith, one baptism; one God and Father of all, who is over all and through all and in all."

The church must prioritize unity and make every effort to maintain it through the bond of peace.

Encourage Humility and Gentleness

The Bible emphasizes the importance of humility and gentleness in maintaining unity and resolving conflicts. Ephesians 4:1-2 advises, "As a prisoner for the Lord, then, I urge you to live a life worthy of the calling you have received. Be completely humble and gentle; be patient, bearing with one another in love."

The church must cultivate a culture of humility and gentleness to promote reconciliation and maintain unity.

Practice Forgiveness

The Bible emphasizes the importance of forgiveness in maintaining relationships and unity within the church. Colossians 3:13 advises, "Bear with each other and forgive whatever grievances you may have against one another. Forgive as the Lord forgave you."

The church must practice forgiveness and encourage members to forgive one another as the Lord has forgiven them.

Foster a Culture of Love

The Bible emphasizes the importance of love in maintaining unity and resolving conflicts. 1 Corinthians 13:4-7 describes the characteristics of love:

"Love is patient; love is kind. It does not envy; it does not boast. It is not proud. It is not rude; it is not self-seeking. It is not easily angered; it keeps no record of wrongs. Love does not delight in evil but rejoices with the truth. It always protects, always trusts, always hopes, always perseveres."

The church must foster a culture of love and encourage members to love one another as Christ has loved them.

Implementing Practical Steps

The church can implement several practical steps to address disobedience and division and promote unity.

Regular Teaching and Preaching

Regular teaching and preaching on biblical principles of discipline, unity, and reconciliation can help the church understand and apply these principles in their lives. Leaders should not shy away from addressing these topics from the pulpit.

Provide Training and Resources

The church can provide training and resources to help members understand and apply biblical principles of discipline and reconciliation. This may include workshops, seminars, and Bible studies on these topics.

Establish Clear Procedures

The church should establish clear procedures for addressing disobedience and division, based on biblical principles. These procedures should be communicated to the congregation so that everyone understands the process and knows what to expect.

Create Supportive Environments

The church should create supportive environments where members feel comfortable confessing sins, seeking help, and resolving conflicts. This may include providing pastoral care, counseling, and support groups.

Encourage Accountability

The church should encourage accountability among its members. This may include establishing accountability groups or partners who can provide support and encouragement in maintaining spiritual disciplines and addressing sin.

Effective church discipline is essential to the health and purity of the church. By following biblical principles and implementing practical steps, the church can address disobedience and division, promote unity, and maintain its witness to the world. The goal of discipline is not to punish but to restore individuals to a right relationship with God and the church, protect the church community, and honor God's name.

The Importance of Restoration and Reconciliation

Church discipline is often misunderstood as a punitive measure, but its primary purpose is to restore and reconcile the individual to the body of Christ. Effective discipline rooted in biblical principles aims at healing and strengthening the spiritual health of the church community. The goal is not merely to correct behavior but to foster a deeper relationship with Jehovah and with fellow believers. Understanding the importance of restoration and reconciliation is crucial for maintaining the integrity and unity of the church.

Biblical Foundation for Restoration and Reconciliation

The concept of restoration and reconciliation is deeply embedded in the Scriptures. The Bible consistently emphasizes the importance of bringing wayward members back into the fold with love and compassion.

Galatians 6:1

"Brothers, if anyone is caught in any transgression, you who are spiritual should restore him in a spirit of gentleness. Keep watch on yourself, lest you too be tempted."

This verse underscores the responsibility of spiritually mature believers to guide those who have strayed, emphasizing a gentle and humble approach. The term "restore" used here implies setting a broken bone, highlighting the care and precision needed to bring healing without causing further harm.

Matthew 18:15-17

"If your brother sins, go and show him his fault in private; if he listens, you have won your brother. But if he does not listen, take one or two others with you, so that by the mouth of two or three witnesses every fact may be confirmed. If he refuses to listen to them, tell it to the church; and if he refuses to listen even to the church, let him be to you as a Gentile and a tax collector."

These verses outline a step-by-step process for addressing sin within the church. The progression from private confrontation to involving the entire church community illustrates the effort that should be made to restore the individual. The ultimate aim is winning back the brother or sister to fellowship and faithfulness.

James 5:19-20

"My brothers, if anyone among you wanders from the truth and someone brings him back, let him know that whoever brings back a sinner from his wandering will save his soul from death and will cover a multitude of sins."

James highlights the eternal significance of restoration, portraying it as a life-saving act that covers a multitude of sins. This perspective underscores the gravity and the mercy involved in the process of reconciliation.

The Role of Love in Restoration

Restoration and reconciliation are inherently acts of love. The Bible instructs believers to love one another deeply, and this love should be the driving force behind church discipline.

1 Peter 4:8

"Above all, keep loving one another earnestly, since love covers a multitude of sins."

Love is patient and kind, not envious or boastful, and it seeks the best for others. In the context of church discipline, love motivates the church to pursue the errant member with a heart full of grace and truth. The aim is always to bring about healing and wholeness, reflecting the love of Christ.

John 13:34-35

"A new commandment I give to you, that you love one another: just as I have loved you, you also are to love one another. By this all people will know that you are my disciples, if you have love for one another."

The mark of true discipleship is love for one another, and this love should be evident in the way church discipline is administered. A loving approach to discipline will not only restore the individual but also strengthen the witness of the church to the watching world.

Practical Steps for Restoration and Reconciliation

Implementing effective church discipline involves practical steps that ensure the process is carried out in a way that promotes restoration and reconciliation.

Private Confrontation

The first step in the process of discipline, as outlined in Matthew 18:15, is private confrontation. This step involves one believer approaching the person who has committed the offense. The approach should be made in a spirit of love and concern, with the goal of restoring the individual to a right relationship with God and the church. This initial step provides an opportunity for the matter to be resolved privately, preserving the dignity of the individual and preventing unnecessary public scandal.

Involvement of Witnesses

If the person does not respond to the private confrontation, the next step is to involve one or two witnesses. This step ensures that the process is fair and impartial and that there is a record of the proceedings. The involvement of witnesses also serves as a protective measure for both the church and the person involved. It ensures that the process is conducted with due process and that the facts are documented and corroborated.

Church Involvement

If the person continues to be unrepentant, the next step is to involve the entire church. The involvement of the church serves as a final appeal to the person to repent and return to the faith. It also provides the church community with the opportunity to support and pray for the person. This step underscores the seriousness of the situation and the collective responsibility of the church to uphold biblical standards.

Excommunication

As a last resort, if the person remains unrepentant, the church must take the difficult step of excommunication. This involves treating the person as a Gentile and a tax collector, meaning that the person is no longer considered a member of the church community. The purpose of excommunication is not to punish but to protect the church community and to emphasize the seriousness of the person's actions. It also serves as a final call to repentance and a reminder of the consequences of unrepentant sin.

The Role of Humility and Gentleness

Humility and gentleness are essential qualities for those involved in the process of discipline. The Bible repeatedly emphasizes the importance of approaching others with a humble and gentle spirit.

Galatians 6:1

"Brothers, if anyone is caught in any transgression, you who are spiritual should restore him in a spirit of gentleness. Keep watch on yourself, lest you too be tempted."

The restoration process must be carried out with gentleness, recognizing that all believers are susceptible to sin. This approach fosters a spirit of humility and compassion, which is essential for effective restoration.

Ephesians 4:2

"With all humility and gentleness, with patience, bearing with one another in love."

Humility and gentleness go hand in hand with patience and forbearance. The process of restoration can be challenging and time-consuming, requiring a patient and loving attitude from those involved.

The Power of Forgiveness

Forgiveness is a central component of restoration and reconciliation. The Bible teaches that forgiveness is not optional but a command for all believers.

Colossians 3:13

"Bear with each other and forgive whatever grievances you may have against one another. Forgive as the Lord forgave you."

Forgiveness involves releasing the offender from the debt of their offense and choosing not to hold it against them. It is an act of grace that mirrors the forgiveness that believers have received from God through Christ.

Matthew 6:14-15

"For if you forgive men their trespasses, your heavenly Father will also forgive you. But if you do not forgive men their trespasses, neither will your Father forgive your trespasses."

The willingness to forgive is a reflection of one's own understanding and appreciation of God's forgiveness. It is a critical step in the restoration process, paving the way for reconciliation and healing.

Encouraging a Culture of Accountability

A healthy church culture promotes accountability among its members. Accountability involves being answerable to one another for one's actions and attitudes. It is a mutual commitment to support and encourage each other in living out the Christian faith.

Hebrews 10:24-25

"And let us consider how we may spur one another on toward love and good deeds, not giving up meeting together, as some are in the habit of doing, but encouraging one another—and all the more as you see the Day approaching."

Regular fellowship and mutual encouragement are vital for maintaining accountability within the church. By meeting together regularly and building strong relationships, members can support one another in their spiritual journeys and address issues before they escalate.

James 5:16

"Therefore confess your sins to each other and pray for each other so that you may be healed. The prayer of a righteous person is powerful and effective."

Confession and prayer are powerful tools for accountability and healing. When members confess their sins to one another and pray for each other, it fosters a sense of transparency and mutual support.

The Role of Church Leadership

Church leaders play a crucial role in the process of restoration and reconciliation. They are responsible for guiding the congregation in accordance with biblical principles and providing pastoral care to those involved in the discipline process.

1 Peter 5:2-3

"Be shepherds of God's flock that is under your care, watching over them—not because you must, but because you are willing, as God wants you to be; not pursuing dishonest gain, but eager to serve; not lording it over those entrusted to you, but being examples to the flock."

Church leaders are called to be shepherds, serving the congregation with humility and setting an example of godly living. Their role is to facilitate the restoration process with wisdom and compassion, ensuring that it is conducted in a manner that honors God and promotes healing.

Hebrews 13:17

"Obey your leaders and submit to them, for they are keeping watch over your souls, as those who will have to give an account. Let them do this with joy and not with groaning, for that would be of no advantage to you."

The congregation is encouraged to respect and support their leaders, recognizing their responsibility to watch over their souls. This mutual respect and cooperation are essential for the effective functioning of church discipline.

Restoration and reconciliation are integral to the process of church discipline. By following biblical principles and fostering a culture of love, humility, forgiveness, and accountability, the church can address disobedience and division in a way that promotes healing and unity. The ultimate goal is to restore individuals to a right relationship with God and the church, ensuring the spiritual health and integrity of the body of Christ.

Chapter 18: Skillful Counselors Are a Blessing to Their Churches

The Essence and Importance of Pastoral Counseling

Pastoral counseling is a vital aspect of church leadership, rooted deeply in biblical principles and practical applications. It serves as a bridge between spiritual guidance and emotional support, addressing a wide range of issues that individuals and families face. In today's world, where complexities and challenges are more pronounced than ever, the role of pastoral counseling has become increasingly essential. This section will explore the core elements of pastoral counseling and underscore its significance within the church.

Pastoral counseling is distinct from secular counseling in that it integrates scriptural wisdom with therapeutic practices. It is grounded in the belief that true healing and transformation come from aligning one's life with biblical teachings. This approach ensures that counseling is not merely about addressing symptoms but about fostering spiritual growth and a deeper relationship with Jehovah. Pastors are uniquely positioned to provide this form of counseling because of their understanding of scripture and their role as spiritual shepherds.

The Bible is replete with examples of counseling and guidance provided by spiritual leaders. For instance, Proverbs 11:14 states, "Where there is no guidance, a people falls, but in an abundance of counselors there is safety." This highlights the importance of wise counsel in maintaining the well-being of individuals and the community. Similarly, James 5:16 encourages believers to "confess your sins to one another and pray for one another, that you may be healed." This verse underscores the therapeutic value of confession and prayer in pastoral counseling.

One of the primary functions of pastoral counseling is to provide a safe space for individuals to share their struggles and receive compassionate guidance. This involves active listening, empathy, and a non-judgmental attitude. By creating an environment of trust, pastors can help individuals feel understood and supported. This is crucial for those dealing with sensitive issues such as marital conflicts, addiction, depression, and major life transitions. In such cases, pastoral counseling offers not only emotional support but also spiritual direction, helping individuals find hope and resilience through their faith.

Another critical aspect of pastoral counseling is its role in conflict resolution within the church. Disputes and misunderstandings are inevitable in any community, but unresolved conflicts can lead to division and discord. Pastors, equipped with counseling skills, can mediate conflicts and promote reconciliation. This aligns with Jesus' teaching in Matthew 18:15-17, where He outlines steps for resolving conflicts among believers. By addressing conflicts promptly and biblically, pastors can maintain unity and harmony within the congregation.

Moreover, pastoral counseling is essential in times of crisis and grief. Whether it is the loss of a loved one, a natural disaster, or a personal crisis, people turn to their spiritual leaders for comfort and guidance. The Bible offers profound insights into dealing with grief and suffering. For example, Psalm 34:18 assures us that "Jehovah is near to the brokenhearted and saves the crushed in spirit." Pastors can draw on such scriptures to provide solace and hope to those in distress, helping them navigate their pain and find strength in their faith.

In addition to addressing individual needs, pastoral counseling also plays a crucial role in fostering a supportive church community. A church that actively engages in pastoral counseling is likely to be more compassionate, understanding, and united. When members see their pastor actively involved in counseling and caring for their well-being, it sets a powerful example of Christ-like love and service. This, in turn, encourages congregants to support one another, creating a nurturing and spiritually enriching environment.

The importance of pastoral counseling is further highlighted by its preventive aspect. By providing regular counsel and guidance, pastors can help individuals address issues before they escalate into more significant problems. This proactive approach is akin to the shepherd's role in watching over the flock, ensuring that none stray or fall into harm. As Paul advises in 1 Thessalonians 5:14, "And we urge you, brothers, admonish the idle, encourage the fainthearted, help the weak, be patient with them all." Pastoral counseling embodies this holistic care for the spiritual, emotional, and relational health of the congregation.

To be effective in their counseling role, pastors must be well-equipped with both theological knowledge and practical counseling skills. This requires ongoing education and training in pastoral care. Resources such as "PASTORAL COUNSELING: Skillful Counselors Are a Blessing to Their Churches" provide valuable insights and strategies for pastors to enhance their counseling ministry. Such training helps pastors understand various counseling techniques, develop effective communication skills, and learn how to apply biblical principles to contemporary issues.

Pastoral counseling also involves addressing complex and sensitive topics such as addiction, mental health, sexuality, and ethical dilemmas. In these areas, pastors must navigate the fine line between upholding biblical truths and showing compassion and understanding. For instance, when counseling someone struggling with addiction, it is essential to offer both spiritual support and practical resources for recovery. The Bible provides a foundation for this approach, as seen in Galatians 6:1-2, "Brothers, if anyone is caught in any transgression, you who are spiritual should restore him in a spirit of gentleness. Keep watch on yourself, lest you too be tempted. Bear one another's burdens, and so fulfill the law of Christ."

Furthermore, pastoral counseling should be inclusive of all age groups within the church. This means providing age-appropriate counsel for children, teenagers, adults, and the elderly. Each group faces unique challenges and requires tailored guidance. For example, teenagers may struggle with identity and peer pressure, while the elderly may face issues related to aging and loss. By addressing these specific needs, pastors can ensure that everyone in the congregation feels valued and supported.

In conclusion, the essence and importance of pastoral counseling lie in its ability to integrate biblical wisdom with practical support, addressing the holistic needs of individuals and the church community. It is a ministry that requires compassion, patience, and a deep understanding of scripture. Pastors who embrace this role can significantly impact the lives of their congregants, helping them navigate life's challenges with faith and resilience. Through effective pastoral counseling, churches can become havens of healing, hope, and spiritual growth.

Scriptural Approaches to Common Counseling Issues

Pastoral counseling, deeply rooted in scriptural wisdom, offers a unique and powerful approach to addressing the myriad challenges faced by individuals and families within the church. By integrating biblical principles with practical counseling techniques, pastors can provide guidance that is both spiritually enriching and practically effective. This section will explore scriptural approaches to common counseling issues, offering insights into how pastors can leverage the Word of God to bring comfort, direction, and healing to their congregants.

Addressing Marital Conflicts

Marital conflicts are among the most common issues brought to pastoral counselors. The Bible offers extensive guidance on marriage, emphasizing the sanctity and commitment of the marital relationship. Ephesians 5:22-33 provides a foundational framework for understanding the roles and responsibilities within a marriage. Paul writes, "Wives, submit to your own husbands, as to the Lord. For the husband is the head of the wife even as Christ is the head of the church, his body, and is himself its Savior. Husbands, love your wives, as Christ loved the church and gave himself up for her." This passage underscores the need for mutual respect, love, and sacrificial leadership within marriage.

In counseling couples, it is essential to highlight these biblical principles and encourage open, honest communication. Pastors can guide couples to understand and appreciate their God-given roles, fostering a spirit of unity and cooperation. Additionally, 1 Corinthians 13:4-7, which describes the attributes of love, can be a powerful tool in helping couples cultivate patience, kindness, and forgiveness in their relationship.

Supporting Individuals with Addiction

Addiction, whether to substances or behaviors, is a pervasive issue that requires compassionate and comprehensive counseling. The Bible acknowledges the struggles with sin and the need for deliverance through God's power. Romans 7:15-25 captures Paul's internal battle with sin, highlighting the human struggle and the hope found in Jesus Christ. He writes, "For I do not understand my own actions. For I do not do what I want, but I do the very thing I hate... Wretched man that I am! Who will deliver me from this body of death? Thanks be to God through Jesus Christ our Lord!"

In addressing addiction, pastoral counselors can draw on the transformative power of the Holy Spirit and the support of the church community. James 5:16 encourages believers to "confess your sins to one another and pray for one another, that you may be healed." This verse underscores the importance of accountability and communal support in overcoming addiction. Counseling should also incorporate practical steps, such as creating a structured plan for recovery, identifying triggers, and fostering a supportive environment within the church.

Navigating Depression and Anxiety

Depression and anxiety are prevalent mental health issues that affect many individuals, including Christians. The Bible offers profound comfort and guidance for those struggling with these conditions. Psalm 34:18 reassures us that "Jehovah is near to the brokenhearted and saves the crushed in spirit." This promise of God's presence and comfort can be a source of hope for those experiencing deep emotional pain.

Pastoral counselors should emphasize the importance of seeking God's presence through prayer and meditation on scripture. Philippians 4:6-7 provides practical advice for dealing with anxiety: "Do not be anxious about anything, but in everything by prayer and supplication with thanksgiving let your requests be made known to God. And the peace of God, which surpasses all understanding, will guard your hearts and your minds in Christ Jesus." Encouraging individuals to cast their anxieties on God and to cultivate a thankful heart can help alleviate the burdens of depression and anxiety.

Providing Guidance During Major Life Transitions

Life transitions, such as the loss of a loved one, career changes, or relocation, can be particularly challenging. Ecclesiastes 3:1-8 acknowledges the different seasons of life, reminding us that "for everything there is a season, and a time for every matter under heaven." This perspective can help individuals see their transitions as part of God's greater plan.

In pastoral counseling, it is crucial to offer both emotional support and biblical perspective during these times. Isaiah 41:10 provides a powerful assurance: "Fear not, for I am with you; be not dismayed, for I am your God; I will strengthen you, I will help you, I will uphold you with my righteous right hand." This promise of God's strength and support can be a source of encouragement for those navigating significant changes. Counselors should also help individuals develop practical plans for managing these transitions, ensuring they feel supported and prepared.

Addressing Ethical and Moral Dilemmas

In today's world, ethical and moral dilemmas are increasingly complex and pervasive. Issues related to sexuality, gender identity, and bioethics challenge the church's adherence to biblical standards. Pastoral counselors must navigate these sensitive topics with grace and truth. 2 Timothy 3:16-17 affirms the sufficiency of scripture for moral guidance: "All Scripture is breathed out by God and profitable for teaching, for reproof, for correction, and for training in righteousness, that the man of God may be complete, equipped for every good work."

When addressing these issues, it is essential to remain firmly grounded in biblical teachings while showing compassion and understanding. Pastors should provide clear, scriptural answers to ethical questions, emphasizing God's design and purpose. For instance, Genesis 1:27 underscores the creation of humanity in God's image, "male and female he created them," providing a foundational understanding of gender. Ephesians 5:3-5 offers guidance on sexual morality, urging believers to avoid immorality and impurity.

Offering Premarital and Marital Counseling

Premarital and marital counseling are vital services that pastoral counselors provide to strengthen the foundation of marriages. Ephesians 5:22-33 and 1 Corinthians 7 offer comprehensive guidance on the roles and responsibilities within marriage. By exploring these passages with couples, pastors can help them build a marriage grounded in mutual respect, love, and commitment.

Premarital counseling should cover essential topics such as communication, conflict resolution, financial management, and family planning. Marital counseling, on the other hand, should address ongoing issues within the marriage, offering strategies for maintaining a healthy and fulfilling relationship. Hebrews 13:4 emphasizes the sanctity of marriage: "Let marriage be held in honor among all, and let the marriage bed be undefiled, for God will judge the sexually immoral and adulterous." This verse underscores the importance of fidelity and purity within marriage, guiding couples towards a God-honoring relationship.

Supporting Families in Crisis

Families often turn to pastoral counselors during times of crisis, whether due to illness, financial difficulties, or relational breakdowns. The Bible offers numerous examples of God's provision and support during such times. Psalm 46:1 reminds us, "God is our refuge and strength, a very present help in trouble." This assurance can be a source of comfort and strength for families facing crises.

Pastoral counseling should focus on providing practical support, spiritual encouragement, and community resources to help families navigate their challenges. Galatians 6:2 encourages believers to "bear one another's burdens, and so fulfill the law of Christ." By fostering a supportive church community, pastors can ensure that families in crisis receive the help they need. Additionally, developing a crisis response plan within the church can provide structured support for families dealing with emergencies.

Addressing Grief and Loss

Grief and loss are inevitable parts of life, and pastoral counselors play a crucial role in helping individuals and families cope with their sorrow. The Bible offers profound comfort for those grieving, with passages such as Matthew 5:4, "Blessed are those who mourn, for they shall be comforted," and Revelation 21:4, "He will wipe away every tear from their eyes, and death shall be no more, neither shall there be mourning, nor crying, nor pain anymore, for the former things have passed away."

In counseling those who are grieving, it is essential to provide a listening ear, emotional support, and spiritual encouragement. Pastors can guide individuals through the grieving process, helping them find hope and healing in God's promises. Encouraging participation in grief support groups within the church can also provide a sense of community and shared understanding.

Dealing with Confession and Repentance

Confession and repentance are critical components of the Christian faith, essential for spiritual growth and restoration. James 5:16 highlights the importance of confession: "Therefore, confess your sins to one another and pray for one another, that you may be healed. The prayer of a righteous person has great power as it is working."

Pastoral counselors must create a safe and supportive environment for individuals to confess their sins and seek forgiveness.

Counseling should emphasize the biblical process of repentance, as outlined in 1 John 1:9, "If we confess our sins, he is faithful and just to forgive us our sins and to cleanse us from all unrighteousness." By guiding individuals through this process, pastors can help them experience God's grace and restoration. Additionally, providing accountability and ongoing support can help individuals maintain their commitment to a transformed life.

Navigating Faith and Doubt

Doubt is a natural part of the faith journey, and pastoral counselors must address it with sensitivity and understanding. The Bible offers numerous examples of individuals who struggled with doubt, yet found reassurance in God's promises. Mark 9:24 records a father's plea to Jesus, "I believe; help my unbelief!" This verse encapsulates the tension between faith and doubt, offering a model for honest prayer and dependence on God.

In counseling those experiencing doubt, pastors should encourage open dialogue, provide scriptural reassurances, and offer practical steps for strengthening faith. Hebrews 11:1 defines faith as "the assurance of things hoped for, the conviction of things not seen." By helping individuals deepen their understanding of scripture and God's character, pastors can guide them through their doubts and towards a more robust faith.

Pastoral counseling, grounded in scriptural wisdom, provides a comprehensive and compassionate approach to addressing common counseling issues within the church. By integrating biblical principles with practical strategies, pastors can offer meaningful support and guidance to their congregants. This approach not only addresses immediate needs but also fosters long-term spiritual growth and resilience. Through effective pastoral counseling, churches can become communities of healing, hope, and transformation.

Implementing the Strategic Pastoral Counseling Model

Effective pastoral counseling requires more than just a compassionate heart; it necessitates a structured approach that integrates biblical wisdom with practical counseling techniques. The Strategic Pastoral Counseling Model provides a comprehensive framework for pastors to offer meaningful and effective support to their congregants. This model emphasizes a clear structure, scriptural foundation, and practical steps for addressing a wide range of pastoral challenges. By implementing this model, pastors can enhance their counseling ministry and better serve their church community.

Understanding the Strategic Pastoral Counseling Model

The Strategic Pastoral Counseling Model is designed to provide a structured approach to counseling that is both biblically grounded and practically effective. It involves several key components:

1. **Assessment:** The initial phase involves understanding the counselee's needs, background, and current challenges. This step is crucial for developing a personalized counseling plan.

2. **Biblical Integration:** Incorporating scriptural principles and teachings into the counseling process ensures that the guidance provided aligns with God's Word.

3. **Goal Setting:** Establishing clear, achievable goals helps counselees focus on specific areas of improvement and track their progress.

4. **Intervention:** Implementing appropriate counseling techniques and strategies to address the identified issues and help the counselee achieve their goals.

5. **Evaluation:** Regularly assessing the effectiveness of the counseling process and making necessary adjustments to ensure continued progress.

6. **Follow-Up**: Providing ongoing support and encouragement to help the counselee maintain their progress and continue growing spiritually and emotionally.

Assessment: Laying the Foundation

The assessment phase is critical in understanding the counselee's unique situation and needs. This involves gathering information about their personal history, current challenges, and spiritual condition. James 1:19 offers a valuable principle for this phase: "Know this, my beloved brothers: let every person be quick to hear, slow to speak, slow to anger." Active listening and empathetic understanding are essential components of a thorough assessment.

During this phase, pastors should use open-ended questions to encourage the counselee to share their thoughts and feelings. This not only helps build rapport but also provides valuable insights into the root causes of their struggles. Additionally, a spiritual assessment can help determine the counselee's relationship with God and their understanding of biblical principles.

Biblical Integration: Grounding in Scripture

Biblical integration involves incorporating scriptural teachings and principles into the counseling process. 2 Timothy 3:16-17 underscores the importance of scripture in counseling: "All Scripture is breathed out by God and profitable for teaching, for reproof, for correction, and for training in righteousness, that the man of God may be complete, equipped for every good work."

Pastors should use relevant Bible verses and stories to provide guidance and encouragement to the counselee. For example, when addressing anxiety, Philippians 4:6-7 offers reassurance: "Do not be anxious about anything, but in everything by prayer and supplication with thanksgiving let your requests be made known to God. And the peace of God, which surpasses all understanding, will guard your hearts and your minds in Christ Jesus." By grounding counseling in scripture, pastors can ensure that their guidance aligns with God's truth and provides a solid foundation for lasting change.

Goal Setting: Providing Direction and Purpose

Establishing clear and achievable goals is a vital component of the Strategic Pastoral Counseling Model. Proverbs 29:18 highlights the importance of vision and direction: "Where there is no prophetic vision the people cast off restraint, but blessed is he who keeps the law."

Goals should be specific, measurable, attainable, relevant, and time-bound (SMART). For instance, if a counselee is struggling with anger management, a goal might be to reduce angry outbursts by practicing self-control and implementing specific coping strategies over the next three months. By setting clear goals, pastors can help counselees stay focused and motivated throughout the counseling process.

Intervention: Implementing Effective Strategies

The intervention phase involves applying appropriate counseling techniques and strategies to address the counselee's issues and help them achieve their goals. This may include cognitive-behavioral techniques, prayer, scripture reading, and practical advice based on biblical principles.

For example, in dealing with marital conflicts, pastors can draw on Ephesians 4:31-32: "Let all bitterness and wrath and anger and clamor and slander be put away from you, along with all malice. Be kind to one another, tenderhearted, forgiving one another, as God in Christ forgave you." Encouraging couples to practice forgiveness and kindness can help resolve conflicts and strengthen their relationship.

Additionally, pastors can use practical tools such as communication exercises, conflict resolution strategies, and stress management techniques to support the counselee's progress. Regularly incorporating prayer and scripture reading into the counseling sessions can also provide spiritual strength and encouragement.

Evaluation: Monitoring Progress and Making Adjustments

Regular evaluation is essential to ensure the counseling process is effective and the counselee is making progress towards their goals. Philippians 3:12-14 emphasizes the importance of continual growth and striving towards spiritual maturity: "Not that I have already obtained this or am already perfect, but I press on to make it my own, because Christ Jesus has made me his own. Brothers, I do not consider that I have made it my own. But one thing I do: forgetting what lies behind and straining forward to what lies ahead, I press on toward the goal for the prize of the upward call of God in Christ Jesus."

Pastors should regularly assess the counselee's progress, celebrate successes, and address any challenges or setbacks. This may involve revisiting and adjusting goals, modifying intervention strategies, and providing additional support as needed.

Follow-Up: Providing Ongoing Support

Follow-up is a critical component of the Strategic Pastoral Counseling Model. It ensures that the counselee continues to receive support and encouragement even after the formal counseling sessions have ended. Galatians 6:2 highlights the importance of ongoing support within the Christian community: "Bear one another's burdens, and so fulfill the law of Christ."

Pastors should maintain regular contact with the counselee, offering encouragement, accountability, and prayer. This may involve periodic check-ins, participation in small groups or support groups, and continued engagement in church activities. By providing ongoing support, pastors can help counselees maintain their progress and continue growing spiritually and emotionally.

Practical Steps for Implementing the Model

Implementing the Strategic Pastoral Counseling Model requires careful planning and commitment. Here are some practical steps for pastors to effectively integrate this model into their counseling ministry:

1. **Training and Education**: Pastors should seek ongoing education and training in pastoral counseling to enhance their skills and knowledge. This may involve attending workshops, conferences, and seminars, as well as studying relevant books and resources.

2. **Developing a Counseling Framework**: Establish a structured framework for counseling that includes assessment forms, goal-setting templates, and evaluation tools. This framework will provide consistency and clarity in the counseling process.

3. **Creating a Supportive Environment**: Foster a supportive church community that encourages openness and vulnerability. This may involve establishing support groups, mentoring programs, and small groups focused on specific issues such as addiction recovery or grief support.

4. **Collaboration and Referral**: Recognize the limits of pastoral counseling and collaborate with professional counselors and therapists when necessary. Establish a network of trusted professionals to whom you can refer congregants for specialized care.

5. **Confidentiality and Ethics**: Uphold the highest standards of confidentiality and ethical practice in pastoral counseling. Ensure that counselees feel safe and respected throughout the counseling process.

6. **Regular Review and Improvement**: Continuously evaluate and improve the counseling ministry by seeking feedback from counselees, attending professional development opportunities, and staying informed about best practices in pastoral counseling.

Scriptural Case Studies and Applications

To further illustrate the implementation of the Strategic Pastoral Counseling Model, consider the following scriptural case studies:

1. **King David's Repentance (Psalm 51)**: David's heartfelt confession and repentance after his sin with Bathsheba serve as a powerful example of the importance of confession, repentance, and seeking God's forgiveness. Pastors can use Psalm 51 to guide counselees through the process of repentance and restoration.

2. **The Prodigal Son (Luke 15:11-32)**: The parable of the prodigal son illustrates the themes of forgiveness, reconciliation, and unconditional love. Pastors can use this story to encourage counselees to seek reconciliation with estranged family members and experience the transformative power of God's grace.

3. **Paul's Encouragement to the Philippians (Philippians 4:6-7)**: Paul's exhortation to the Philippians to bring their anxieties to God in prayer provides practical guidance for dealing with anxiety and finding peace in God's presence. Pastors can use this passage to help counselees develop a habit of prayer and trust in God's provision.

The Strategic Pastoral Counseling Model offers a comprehensive and biblically grounded approach to pastoral counseling. By following this structured framework, pastors can provide effective and meaningful support to their congregants, addressing a wide range of challenges with confidence and compassion. Through assessment, biblical integration, goal setting, intervention, evaluation, and follow-up, pastors can guide individuals and families towards healing, growth, and spiritual maturity. By implementing this model, churches can become communities of care and transformation, reflecting the love and grace of Jesus Christ.

THE CHURCH CURE

Edward D. Andrews

Appendix Recommended Reading List for Church Members and Church Leaders

Christian Publishing House Bookstore

https://www.christianpublishers.org/category/all-products

Bibliography

Andrews, E. (2019). *Misrepresenting Jesus: Debunking Bart D. Ehrman's Misquoting Jesus [Fourth Edition]*. Cambridge: Christian Publishing House.

Andrews, E. (2020). *FROM SPOKEN WORDS TO SACRED TEXTS: Introduction-Intermediate New Testament Textual Studies*. Cambridge: Christian Publishing House.

Andrews, E. D. (2015). *EVIDENCE THAT YOU ARE TRULY CHRISTIAN: Keep Testing Yourselves to See If You Are In the Faith - Keep Examining Yourselves*. Cambridge, OH: Christian Publishing House.

Andrews, E. D. (2016). *HOMOSEXUALITY - THE BIBLE AND THE CHRISTIAN: Basic Bible Doctrines of the Christian Faith*. Cambridge, OH: Christian Publishing House.

Andrews, E. D. (2016). *INTERPRETING THE BIBLE: Introduction to Biblical Hermeneutics*. Cambridge, OH: Christian Publishing House.

Andrews, E. D. (2016). *THE BATTLE FOR THE CHRISTIAN MIND: Be Transformed by the Renewal of Your Mind*. Cambridge, OH: Christian Publishing House.

Andrews, E. D. (2016). *THE CHRISTIAN APOLOGIST: Always Being Prepared to Make a Defense [Second Edition]*. Cambridge, OH: Christian Publishing House.

Andrews, E. D. (2016). *THE COMPLETE GUIDE to BIBLE TRANSLATION: Bible Translation Choices and Translation Principles [Second Edition]* . Cambridge: Christian Publishing House.

Andrews, E. D. (2016). *THE EVANGELISM HANDBOOK: How All Christians Can Effectively Share God's Word in Their Community, [SECOND EDITION]*. Cambridge, OH: Christian Publishing House.

Andrews, E. D. (2016). *YOUR GUIDE FOR DEFENDING THE BIBLE: Self-Education of the Bible Made Easy*. Cambridge, OH: Christian Publishing House.

Andrews, E. D. (2016). *YOUR WORD IS TRUTH: Being Sanctified In the Truth*. Cambridge, OH: Christian Publishing House.

Andrews, E. D. (2017). *CONVERSATIONAL EVANGELISM: Defending the Faith, Reasoning from the Scriptures, Explaining and Proving, Instructing in Sound Doctrine, and Overturning False Reasoning [Second Edition]*. Cambridge, OH: Christian Publishing House.

Andrews, E. D. (2017). *DEFENDING OLD TESTAMENT AUTHORSHIP: The Word of God Is Authentic and True*. Cambridge, OH: Christian Publishing House.

Andrews, E. D. (2017). *GOD WILL GET YOU THROUGH THIS: Hope and Help for Your Difficult Times*. Cambridge, OH: Christian Publishing House.

Andrews, E. D. (2017). *HOW TO STUDY YOUR BIBLE: Rightly Handling the Word of God*. Cambridge, OH: Christian Publishing House.

Andrews, E. D. (2017). *HUMAN IMPERFECTION: While We Were Sinners Christ Died For Us*. Cambridge, OH: Christian Ppublishing House.

Andrews, E. D. (2017). *HUSBANDS LOVE YOUR WIVES: How Should Husbands Treat Their Wives?* Cambridge, OH: Christian Publishing House.

Andrews, E. D. (2017). *IS THERE A REBEL IN THE HOUSE?: Youth Overcoming a Rebellious Heart*. Cambridge, OH: Christian Publishing House.

Andrews, E. D. (2017). *TURN OLD HABITS INTO NEW HABITS: Why and How the Bible Makes a Difference*. Cambridge, OH: Christian Publishing House.

Andrews, E. D. (2017). *WIVES BE SUBJECT TO YOUR HUSBANDS: How Should Wives Treat Their Husbands?* Cambridge, OH: Christian Publishing House.

Andrews, E. D. (2018). *LET GOD USE YOU TO SOLVE YOUR PROBLEMS: GOD Will Instruct You and Teach You In the Way You Should Go.* Cambridge, OH: Christian Publishing House.

Andrews, E. D. (2018). *REASONING WITH THE WORLD'S VARIOUS RELIGIONS: Examining and Evangelizing Other Faiths.* Cambridge, OH: Christian Publishing House.

Andrews, E. D. (2018). *THE POWER OF GOD: The Word That Will Change Your Life Today.* Cambridge, OH: Christian Publishing House.

Andrews, E. D. (2018). *WHY ME?: When Bad Things Happen to Good People.* Cambridge, OH: Christian Publishing House.

Andrews, E. D. (2019). *INTRODUCTION TO THE TEXT OF THE NEW TESTAMENT: From The Authors and Scribe to the Modern Critical Text.* Cambridge, Ohio: Christian Publishing House.

Andrews, E. D. (2019). *SATAN: Know Your Enemy.* Cambridge, OH: Christian Publishing House.

Andrews, E. D. (2019). *THE READING CULTURE OF EARLY CHRISTIANITY: The Production, Publication, Circulation, and Use of Books in the Early Christian Church.* Cambridge, OH: Christian Publishing House.

Andrews, E. D. (2020). *INERRANCY OF SCRIPTURE: How Can We Believe Inerrancy of Scripture In the Originals When We Don't Have the Originals?* Cambridge, OH: Christian Publishing House.

Andrews, E. D. (2020). *THE BIBLICAL MARRIAGE: Biblical Counsel that Will Strengthen a Strong Marriage and Save a Failing Marriage.* Cambridge, OH: Christian Publishing House.

Andrews, E. D. (2020). *THE NEW TESTAMENT DOCUMENTS: Can They Be Trusted?* Cambridge, OH: Christian Publishing House.

Andrews, E. D. (2020). *WALK HUMBLY WITH YOUR GOD: Putting God's Purpose First in Your Life.* Cambridge, OH: Christian Publishing House.

Andrews, E. D. (2023). *BIBLICAL EXEGESIS: Biblical Criticism on Trial.* Cambridge, OH: Christian Publishing House.

Andrews, E. D. (2023). *CHRISTIAN APOLOGETICS: Answering the Tough Questions: Evidence and Reason in Defense of the Faith.* Cambridge, Ohio: Christian Publishing House.

Andrews, E. D. (2023). *FAITHFUL MINDS: A Biblical and Cognitive Behavioral Therapy Approach to Mental Health and Wellness.* Cambridge, OH: Christian Publishing House.

Andrews, E. D. (2023). *HOW WE GOT THE BIBLE.* Cambridge, OH: Christian Publishing House.

Andrews, E. D. (2023). *INTRODUCTION TO OLD TESTAMENT TEXTUAL CRITICISM.* Cambridge, OH: Christian Publishing House.

Andrews, E. D. (2023). *INTRODUCTION TO THE TEXT OF THE OLD TESTAMENT: From the Authors and Scribes to the Modern Critical Text.* Cambridge, OH: Christian Publishing House.

Andrews, E. D. (2023). *LIFE DOES HAVE A PURPOSE: Discovering and Living Your Ultimate Purpose.* Cambridge, OH: Christian Publishing House.

Andrews, E. D. (2023). *MERE CHRISTIANITY REIMAGINED: Rediscovering the Faith for the 21st Century.* Cambridge, OH: Christian Publishing House.

Andrews, E. D. (2023). *THE BIBLE AS HISTORY: A Historical Journey Through the Bible.* Cambridge, Ohio: Christian Publishing House.

Andrews, E. D. (2023). *THE BIBLE ON TRIAL: Examining the Evidence for Being Inspired, Inerrant, Authentic, and True.* Cambridge, Ohio: Christian Publishing House.

Andrews, E. D. (2023). *THE OLD TESTAMENT: Commentary, Background, & Bible Difficulties (Introduction to the Old Testament).* Cambridge, OH: Christian Publishing House.

Andrews, E. D. (2023). *THE SCRIBE AND THE TEXT OF THE NEW TESTAMENT: Scribal Activities in the Transmission of the*

Text of the New Testament. Cambridge, Ohio: Christian Publishing House.

Andrews, E. D. (2023). *THE TEXT OF THE NEW TESTAMENT: A Beginners Handbook to New Testament Textual Studies.* Cambridge, OH: Christian Publishing House.

Andrews, E. D. (2023). *THE TEXTUS RECEPTUS: The "Received Text" of the New Testament.* Cambridge, OH: Christian Publishing House.

Andrews, E. D. (2023). *UNSHAKABLE BELIEFS: Strategies for Strengthening and Defending Your Faith.* Cambridge, OH: Christian Publishing House.

Andrews, E. D. (2023). *WOKEISM: The Predatory Grooming of Your Children.* Cambridge, OH: Christian Publishing House.

Andrews, E. D. (2024). *MISGUIDED THINKING: Correct and Guide Your Thoughts in a Healthier Direction.* Cambridge, OH: Christian Publishing House.

Andrews, E. D. (2024). *REASON MEETS FAITH: Addressing and Refuting Atheism's Challenges to Christianity.* Cambridge, OH: Christian Publishing House.

Andrews, E. D., & Farnell, F. D. (2017). *BIBLICAL CRITICISM: What are Some Outstanding Weaknesses of Modern Historical Criticism?* Cambridge, OH: Christian Publishing House.